Editor: Bernard-Henri Lévy

What Good Are Intellectuals?

44 writers share their thoughts . . .

Algora Publishing
New York

Algora Publishing, New York
© 2000 by Algora Publishing
All rights reserved. Published 2000.
Printed in the United States of America
ISBN: 1-892941-10-4
Editors@algora.com

Library of Congress Cataloging-in-Publication Data 00-010363

What good are intellectuals? : 44 writers share their thoughts /
  editorial director, Bernard-Henri Lévy.
    p. cm.
  Interviews with Paul Bowles, William Styron, Wietske Venema;
essays by Cécile Guilbert, Gilles Hertzog, Marc Lambron, Yann
Moix, Michel Onfray; and a survey of 36 writers from around the
world.
  Originally published in Paris as the 1998 edition of an annual
series entitled The Rules of the game [La Règle du jeu (Paris,
France); no 21 (c)]
  ISBN 1-892941-10-4 (alk. paper)
  1. Intellectuals—History—20th century. 2. Intellectual life—
History—20th century. I. Lévy, Bernard Henri. II. Règle du jeu
(Paris, France) III. Title.
HM728.W49 2000
305.5'52'0904—dc21
                    00-010363

New York
www.algora.com

What Good Are Intellectuals?

Originally published in Paris as the 1998 edition of an annual series entitled

The Rules of the Game
Literature, Philosophy, Art, and Politics

under the direction of Bernard Henri-Lévy.

Table of Contents

David Albahari, Tahar Ben Jelloun, Rachid Boudjedra, Breyten Breytenbach, André Brink, Hans Christoph Buch, Guillermo Cabrera Infante, Édouard El-Kharrât, Péter Esterházy, Nadine Gordimer, Juan Goytisolo, David Grossman, Yoram Kaniuk, Ivan Klíma, Aïcha Lemsine, Antonio Lobo Antunes, Claudio Magris, Naguib Mahfouz, Eduardo Manet, Pierre Mertens, Czeslaw Milosz, Arthur Miller, Joyce Carol Oates, Cynthia Ozick, Orhan Pamuk, Octavio Paz, Victor Pelevine, Salman Rushdie, Fernando Savater, Peter Schneider, Philippe Sollers, Susan Sontag, Henrick Stangerup, Mario Vargas Llosa, William Styron, A. B. Yehoshua.

Paul Bowles

Tangiers, For Example

Interview by Gilles Hertzog

*An interview with Paul Bowles – dozens of people have interviewed
you in the past several years...*

Yes, indeed they have.

*I came to see you ten years ago myself, with Bernard-Henri Lévy. Is
this a chore for you, or a pleasure? Is it always just the same old
song?*

Sometimes things turn out differently, and then it's a pleasure. But
frankly, I don't always get Bernard-Henri Lévy or you. And then it
might not be very much fun. It eats up my time. And there isn't
enough time in my day, there isn't enough time in life.

*Can you tell, more or less, what people are going to ask you, is it
always the same questions? Or do you sometimes get to discover
something new about your own life, or your work?*

No, not much. As you say, the questions are almost always the same.
"Why do you live in Tangiers? Do you like Tangiers better than other

cities in Morocco? Do you prefer Morocco to Europe?" I'm not even European! The questions don't vary much.

Well, I'll try to ask you some "new" questions.

What I really don't like are questions that start with the word "Why?" They're annoying, aren't they?

I'll try not to ask "Why"! Since I'm fundamentally not comfortable asking questions either, I've taken some of your phrases, either literary or philosophical, and I'll ask you about them in a moment.

Okay.

Everyone who loves literature considers your best book to be A Tea in the Sahara. Everyone asks you about A Tea in the Sahara. Aren't you tired of it? Isn't it a curse always to have to answer for a great work?

Yes, it is, especially since it was the first book. It's as though they were reproaching me for not repeating myself, for having written other books, for not perpetually re-writing *A Tea in the Sahara*. It's ridiculous.

You started out with a great book and that masterpiece, to some extent, has overshadowed all the books that followed. It diminished them in the eyes of the public.

Apparently. But what is public opinion? And which public? I don't know. I know that it exists, that it's the public that buys books, and reads reviews. I have only one thing to say: "I'd really like to forget *A Tea in the Sahara*."

Is it a curse to begin one's literary life with a masterpiece that is declared as such, decreed as such, by the public?

It is a curse, because, in my view, my other books are just as good and even better. I don't know. But part of this is due to Bernardo Bertolucci. He never should have made that film. I told myself that, beforehand, well beforehand, two years before. Of all my books, that one was the least suitable for being made into a movie. There's no action in it, right? Everything that happens is going on internally.

It's an internal voyage.

Yes. But Bertolucci didn't believe me. He said, "No, no, I want it." I think his movie was a flop.

Had he read your other books?

I don't think so. I don't think he reads much. I don't even think he read *A Tea in the Sahara*. He flipped through it, but he didn't read it. That's why he didn't understand. That's why he made a poor movie. Of course, authors always say that movies made from their books are poorly done. . .

. . . that the work was "betrayed."

Yes. But it's often true.

How do you feel about that book today, since it has in a way eclipsed the rest of your life as a writer? Do you still like A Tea in the Sahara? Or do you have mixed feelings about your own book, given the fallout that it's had?

It doesn't seem such a good book to me. If I wrote it today, it would be better. But all that happened in 1948. Long ago. But anyway, that's not important.

Not important?

No, not at all.

We can move on. I've selected a few quotes from your works. You once said, "For life to be tolerable, you have to make it absurd." You seem to be tolerating life very well indeed. Does that mean that your life is absurd? And how have you made it absurd?

Life is absurd. There is no need to make it absurd. I'm surprised to hear that I wrote such a thing.

You said, "It has to be made absurd."

Where did you find that?

In John Hopkins, Notes from Tangiers. *He reports a conversation he had with you.*

I don't know if he got it exactly right. I doubt it. I don't think I said, "It has to be made absurd." You can't make life absurd. Either it is absurd or it isn't. To me, it is absurd, yes, certainly.

But how does the fact that it is absurd render it tolerable?

If you are aware that life is absurd, you can tolerate it, because that which is absurd is tolerable. What you take very seriously is practically intolerable.

Okay. Another quote from you: "What is the writer's freedom, but that state of complete submission to the tyranny of chance?"

That, yes, I wrote. But the beginning isn't quite right.

"What is the writer's freedom..."

"The writer's," no, that's not what I said. No.

Just "Freedom," is that it?

Yes. I remember the passage very well. It's in a novel called *Tatiana*. Right?

Precisely. But, tell me again, in your existence, have you submitted yourself so completely to the tyranny of chance?

Aren't we always subject to the tyranny of chance?

Yes and no. One could maintain, just as well — this is Sartre's idea — that we construct our liberty, and that liberty is, in that sense, anti-chance?

I am not at all a devotee of Sartre.

In this arena.

He claimed that we have a choice. But there is no choice. As I've said, we are subject to chance. Being subject, we have all the liberty in the world, because no one is obliged to choose or to judge. One simply lives, that's all.

Do your characters adhere to that law?

I think so, yes. My impression — I don't know. I don't know my characters very well.

Really, you don't know your characters very well?

No.

But you created them, all the same.

Yes, but I created them without thinking, without a plan, without a design, blindly.

They came to life under your pen, by the law of writing, the law of the novel?

Yes, it happens all by itself. Whatever doesn't happen by itself is reprehensible: I don't like it. In other words, everything that I've written, I did it without thinking. And especially, the characters are secondary. The location is more important, the location is fundamental. And the location creates the characters and their actions. It's not me, no. I don't think I have created anything. Which means that one mustn't take literary life seriously.

And yet, we do nothing else.

We do nothing else?

Right. We ascribe to writers the creation of a universe, and in your case in particular, of a universe where all the characters are subject to a fate that gets the better of them. You seem to me to be a writer of destiny. Your characters are subject to . . .

They pursue their destiny, but I don't know what their destiny is. And I don't think they do, either.

Someone — a literary critic — once said that you aren't interested in fictional characters, in flesh and blood characters, but in characters that personify ideas. A bit like Camus. Do you agree with that?

I don't think so, because that would mean that I am an intellectual, which is very far from the truth. Of course I admire Camus greatly. But I am not Camus. Neither Camus nor Sartre.

Would it be fair to say, and I'm thinking of The Stranger, *that your characters seem to be more or less from the same family as those of Camus?*

But all of Camus' characters have that in common, don't they? And who are they, anyway? Can you characterize them? He wrote very little, actually too little.

Was Camus a significant author, for you?

At first, I preferred Sartre, because in those days, that is between the wars, he was the only one after Camus, for me. And I preferred Sartre, because he was more exact, more precise. But in the end, obviously, Camus was more human, and therefore more significant. But anyway. That was all long ago.

Did you meet him?

Never. Sartre, yes. But I never saw Camus. It seems to me that I would have admired him even if I had known him.

*Speaking of Camus, he said that American writers were "the only
writers in the world who don't feel the need to be intellectuals, as
well."*

That's funny.

Do you agree with that definition?

Yes, yes, I do, because the Americans aren't capable of becoming intellectuals.

What do you mean?

I mean that they aren't intellectuals, and if you aren't an intellectual,
you can't pretend to be one.

*Camus sees that almost as a freedom. Instead of the obligation that
some people feel, "I am a writer, I have to become an intellectual."
They don't have to justify themselves, they don't have to defend
themselves philosophically.*

Even if they wanted to be intellectuals, they couldn't be. That's all
I'm trying to say.

Why not?

Because they are far less cultivated. There is far less culture behind
the Americans than behind most Europeans. In Europe, there is a
continuous, flowing culture. In America, everything is fragmented.
That's how it is.

Let's go back to your books, to your universe.

If you insist.

> *In John Hopkins' book again, there is a scene with you. It's a lively scene, someone is dancing, goes into a trance — this is one of your friends — and he has a knife in his hand, very dangerous for himself. He might hurt himself, because he's lost his head. Hopkins describes you at that moment as being "like a scientist watching ants fight." Do you agree with that image of you? A "scientist-writer" watching ants fight?*

Ants?

> *People, ants, the world.*

Yes, yes, I think that's natural. Aren't you struck by the resemblance between people and ants?

> *In other words, you are fundamentally outside of the world whose history you spent your life writing. You are an observer, an entomologist.*

That's about right. But I don't know whether I'm a scientist. Whatever is going on, one should observe it, and reserve judgment.

> *The phrase could also suggest that a scientist is cold.*

I'm cold?

> *What's happening, the way people or ants fight, doesn't matter much.*

That's right.

Well, in my opinion you have more than a scientific regard for your characters, I think you have compassion or love for them.

Sometimes, I do. It would be abnormal if I hadn't any at all. But I don't have compassion for all of my characters, no. Sometimes, they deserve their suffering. The more time goes by, the more I think they deserve their suffering.

People often think of you as a user of kif.

That's such a cliché!

True. Except that you yourself have mentioned it, and the scenes you describe are famous.

True.

It's undeniable: kif plays a big role in your life and in your litera-ture. There are two types of writers: kif writers and hashish writ-ers. Is there a difference? They say that kif — I'm asking you — gives a high that is kind of immaterial and atemporal, more imma-terial, more abstract than that of hashish. In other words, it doesn't change one's personality, it allows you to look inside yourself, but without changing your personality. Would you agree with that dis-tinction between writers who use kif and writers who use hashish?

You think there are two categories of writers?

I'm asking you.

Writers who use hashish, I don't know. I have the impression that with hashish, you can't do anything. You can't write.

*Just the same, there are a few famous examples of writers who used
hashish.*

But it's important to know what they were using. Whom are you referring to, Baudelaire?

Baudelaire, Nerval.

But what were they using? I don't think they ever had hashish.

They smoked grass, almost hashish.

That was called "dowerness." But what is "dowerness"?

*It's true that hashish, as we know it, was invented recently; in the
1960's, I think.*

So, you see!

*Let's take some writers for whom the drug is an experience of deper-
sonalization or of modification of the personality. That's never
been your experience with kif.*

Kif isn't strong enough for that. I can't do hashish. I've tried it, but
with disastrous results.

*Can you clarify the relationship between kif and your writing? Do
you write after smoking?*

Sometimes I do. But *kif* doesn't bring any new ideas. You either have
an idea, or you don't. *Kif* has no effect on that. It gives you a kind of
tenacity, it enables you to write for a long time. I am very impatient, I

can only sit still for ten minutes, and then I absolutely have to get up and walk around the room. That is why I am still a composer, at the same time. I can literally go to the other room, write some music, and come back to my prose. But with *kif*, I can stay at it for half an hour without getting up, without getting too impatient. It extends my attention span.

> *So fundamentally, it is a purely literary tool, it doesn't enhance your vision, your psychological acuity or creativity?*

No. I think you either have that, or you don't. But when you say "purely literary," do you mean "purely practical"?

> *Purely practical.*

I prefer to call it "purely technical."

> *Let's talk about your friends, all those writers and artists, first of all, of course, Tennessee Williams, Burroughs, Gysin and all those folks who came to join you in Tangiers. You were here before them. The rest are either no longer in Tangiers, or they've died. You are the only one from that legendary period who is still here.*

I don't know. I was here before, and I am here still. That's all. I have nothing more to say about it. Although I do feel, from time to time, very lonely. . .

> *Do you feel like the last of the Mohicans, like a figure from the legends?*

No, I don't see it that way. First of all, I don't have a clear sense of self; I can't say whether I feel like the first or the last, a writer or not a writer. I've never had a career. I accepted destiny and that's all. One has to accept what comes along.

You don't feel like a survivor, a last witness?

No. That's a romantic notion, but it's not mine, no. I'm not a romantic. Fortunately.

Some writers have made it to an advanced age — Ernst Jünger, for example.

He was over 100, wasn't he?

Yes. You, you're still a young man.

I'm only 86.

There's Julien Green, in France, and there's you. Still, you've attained a respectable age. . . I allude to these great elderly writers in order to ask you an obvious question: do you think about death?

Death! Ha! What can you think about death!

How do you see your years, the rest of your life?

I have no idea. You can't think about death, because death doesn't exist. You can think about dying, and that's unpleasant because it can entail suffering and all sorts of unpleasant things. But death, in itself, is absolutely nothing. I know there are people who are religious and who think of death as though it were a sort of continuation of life. It's not like that, in my case. When I was little, no one ever talked with me about religion or God, because my parents didn't believe that all that existed, and they thought that one should not pervert a child's mind. They only said to me, "You must never make fun of those people, the Christians, Jews or Moslems. Let people believe what they believe, and don't point out their false ideas. You mustn't say that they are false."

Is that the time, the period that you live in now? How do you relate to time, these days, do you think more about the past, about your past? You once said, "That is how we advance, a boat battling a current that constantly pushes us towards the past." Are you, to-day, a boat that is being driven relentlessly back to the past, or, on the contrary, does the present count more for you than the past?

Oh, no! I think that at my age, the past becomes more and more im-portant and the present, less and less important. If you can't think about the present or the future, you have to think about the past. I remember all sorts of things. I remember a scene that I haven't thought about in 70 or 80 years, since childhood. I am in closer con-tact with my childhood now than I have been any time in the past 70 years. I think that's normal. And I don't have Alzheimer's.

Are you in literary contact with the past?

Literary, no.

Do you write about your past, your childhood?

A little, sometimes.

In writing, do you rediscover things from your past?

Yes, but I don't write anymore, not really. Do you know Cherry? She absolutely wants me to write a book that she can sign, her book. I'm doing it to please her, but you can't do it for months and years, I don't have the energy anymore. That's what I'm writing.

Ah, you're writing Cherry's book, with the photos of her?

Yes. It's ridiculous.

That's the best Italian photographer.

Italian?

Is this the book you offered to Bernard-Henri Lévy?

Yes, Vittorio Santoro.

You once said of Jane Bowles, your wife, in defining her work: "She was primarily a humorist." And you? Are you a jokester? You seem like an actor playing the role of a writer.

I don't think so, no. It's more serious than that, being a writer. More essential.

So then, you are not an actor?

You shouldn't ask what I am. I have no idea. No idea at all! I know that I'm still breathing, therefore I'm still alive. What I am, I have no idea.

You knew that Jane was a humorist, but you don't know what you are, yourself?

It is always easier to talk about others than about oneself, that's natural, isn't it? I can't talk about myself.

Can we talk about Tangiers, then?

We can talk about Tangiers.

Of course, it's Tangiers-Bowles, like Dublin-Joyce, Florence-Henry James, etc.. In the end, you are the literary symbol of Tangiers. And how is this marriage between city and writer getting along? Is it like a woman or a being whom you love? Are there moments when you love it less, or do not love it, or want to separate, or make up with it? You seem to have been extraordinarily faithful to Tangiers.

No, that's not true. I am here because I don't want to go anywhere else. That's the only reason. I am in my prison, here. I always say that. But people don't understand it. Or they pretend not to understand.

And you never feel like changing prisons?

I don't want to. I'd like to, but I'll never be able to. I don't have the energy, and I don't know where to go. Where? I had my island: Sri Lanka. I've lost it. There is no more island like that. So, here I am and here I stay. But I didn't choose it. I came here by accident.

An accident that has lasted a long time.

Yes, a long time, indeed. I came here in 1931, 66 years ago. But it was an accident; and I liked it. And that too, was an accident. I came back every year. That was no accident; I came voluntarily. But finally, my wife became ill, and I had to be near Malaga, where she was in the hospital. I'd go there every three weeks, every month. And finally, she died, and I stayed here. I felt like going someplace else, but I didn't do it. And not now, either, because I don't know where to go. Never to America, nor Europe, I don't like the climate. So then in Africa, the only country where I could live is Morocco. And that may not last forever, either. I hope no one slits my throat before I die.

That's a funny thing to say. Why would anyone slit your throat?

It's very simple. Because I'm not a Moslem. That's what's happening to whites in Algeria, isn't it? They not only kill them, they cut off their heads.

That's not a risk in Morocco, however.

Not yet; that's what I'm saying. But you never know. It's possible. I think, yes, I think it's quite possible. Islamism is always ready to boil over. I hope it doesn't, not only for my own good, but for the Moroccans. No people can withstand such bloody experiences. Anyhow, I never think about these things, but you asked me why I am here. . .

It's not a marriage for love, then, with Tangiers?

A marriage, maybe, but the wedding took place long ago. And like all marriages, things have changed. You might be very much in love at the age of 25, or 20 — I came here at the age of 20 — but you don't stay in love forever. Devoted, yes. But that's not the same thing. Devoted is not the same as "in love."

Have there been moments when you detested Tangiers?

I detest it more now than I used to. There's too much crime in the street. So many knifings, every day. At the hospital, the other day, they told me the statistic: some fifty or sixty attacks every day.

I've never heard these statistics! Where do they get this information?

This is direct from the nurses at the hospital.

Knives? Stabbings?

Yes. But these aren't murders.

Then what, robberies, muggings?

These are fights between men, because the men don't have guns. But wait until they start to get them, and you'll see! Tangiers has become an unlivable city...

Aside from the fights, one last question about Tangiers: what makes a city a literary city?

Nothing. To me, that is an expression that makes no sense.

Let's give it a try, anyway. Is a city literary on its own, because of its charm, its perfume? Is it a place where the spirit expands? Or are literary cities basically cities that writers have put in their writings? Are they literary on their own, by vocation, or is it just that writers have said so much about them that has made them so?

I wonder. When I hear the word "literary," I have nothing to say. What does it mean?

A literary city?

Yes. What does that mean? Isn't Paris a literary city? I think it is.

*It's a city where there are writers, and about which writers have
spoken, that they have used as a subject or a character, or the basis
of their work. Dublin is a literary city because Joyce wrote* The
Dubliners *and* Ulysses.

That's what they say, yes. Is it true? Joyce never spoke about Dublin
that way. He wrote Ulysses, and that was the end of it.

Let me ask again, is Tangiers a literary city?

Not for me. It depends what you mean. Because the "Beat" generation
came here, and all that? Because Burroughs was here? And Allen Gins-
berg? But does that make a literary city?

*Then why did they come? They came because the city had something
that they found helpful, that helped them be writers, or become writers. Why Tangiers rather than some other city? It can't be entirely
chance. You said that you, yourself, came here by chance.*

Yes.

Nothing but chance?

No. I know you don't agree.

Oh no, no, no!

I think that everything in life is chance.

*Could you have established yourself in an extremely boring city like
Casablanca?*

No. Certainly, there are differences between cities. Every city is distinct from all the others, as every person is unique. But I wouldn't agree that Tangiers is a literary city. Nobody knew that those people were here. People were completely unaware of the presence of those writers.

> *Yes but they, they knew that they were writers and that they were going to talk about this city. They were clearly thinking of their posterity, they were thinking about creating works that, indeed, became important. And I'm not even talking about the painters! Delacroix... the 19th century painters.*

Because in your view, Delacroix was the first writer who...

> *A writer in paint, if you will.*

Okay... Tell me again... When you say "literary," are you referring to a legend?

> *Yes, but one made by writers, artists, musicians. Wagner, for example, took up residence above Positano, at Ravello, up the hill from Amalfi. Well, and Ravello became a little literary city where today, in the wake of Wagner, many musicians and writers go.*

Ravello. . . . To me, that's where Corvida lived. That's the only one I know. And what did Wagner do, at Ravello?

> *I think he was finishing Parsifal.*

At Ravello?

> *Yes.*

I never heard that.

> *Recently, you told Bernard-Henri that you stopped reading the news, long ago.*

Yes, quite a while ago.

> *The world doesn't affect you anymore, doesn't interest you anymore — or you get your news by other means?*

No, no, no. I'm interested in the world, but it seems to me that you don't have to read the papers to know what's going on. Once you start to read the paper, you're hooked, because if you read it today, you might read it tomorrow and so forth. And I don't want that.

> *It's like a drug?*

More or less, yes. We could get along very nicely with a paper that would come out once a month, and we would have a very good idea of what was going on in the world, without following all the details.

> *What's your goal? To save time? Not to waste it?*

Yes.

> *And to maintain your freedom?*

That too, yes. To stay free. It gives you more time. I see how the Americans are, they read a newspaper at breakfast. In the cafés here, they are looking at the paper. There's nothing in these newspapers, but they follow them everyday as if it were a question of life and death.

You find all these newspapers are useless?

Yes, believe me: think about my idea of a monthly newspaper.

This monthly, that would spare us all the details, what would it be?
A summary of major events? What would be the ideal newspaper?

You read the newspaper to find out who is winning the war. There's always a war going on, and you have to keep track of it. In 1937, I was in the state of Chiapas in Mexico, and I noticed that in every pension and every hotel, there was a fairly detailed map with pushpins that were moved every day. And always with the legend, "Our campaign against Communism," because the hosts were Germans. Chiapas was practically all German. I don't think it is now (*laugh*). They were thrown out. They didn't win. But I saw how they followed the details of the war with great attention. I am not German, and there is no war now with Germany nor against the Communists, nothing. Where is the war, these days? I don't know. So I don't read the paper.

That's the main thing in the world, the wars?

The world is always a question of wars.

Not the new technologies, the Internet, the global economy? War?

It's war that decides everything, isn't it? I think it is.

But isn't war conducted by non-military means? Wars be-
tween civilizations, Islam against the West? Hasn't the na-
ture of war changed?

I don't think so, no, because it's still force that determine the outcome. It always boils down to killing the others, or being killed, yourself. Such is the history of the world. And I am not Ernst Jünger. I know he adored that, and of course he adored militarism. From this stand-point, I think he was right.

Did you know Ernst Jünger?

No, I never met him. I never knew whether he was a Hitlerian or not. Nobody bothered him during the war. He's like Leni Riefensthal. Was she a Hitlerian, or not? She called herself a "sympathizer," that's all. What does that mean? How can you be a Nazi sympathizer with-out being a Nazi yourself?

Do you ever feel tempted to get involved in the world's war-related issues these days?

Me?

Do you ever feel like giving your opinion, like saying what you think about the state of the war? For example, during the Iraq war, or the war in Yugoslavia, did you have an opinion? Did you feel like ex-pressing it? And if a newspaper had come to talk with you, would you have done it?

No. I would have shown the journalist the door.

Why?

Because I have never wished to judge — neither people nor things — openly.

You were anti-Fascist. You did take positions that were anti-Fascist.

Yes, I was a member of the Communist Party; but that doesn't mean anything.

But if Fascism is coming back, today, don't you feel like expressing your viewpoint and your revulsion against Fascism? Against Islamist fundamentalism, for example?

Feel like, yes. But one hardly does everything that one feels like doing. At least, I don't. No. I keep it all inside, without expressing myself overtly.

Why?

The surest way to win is through conspiracy: not by expressing oneself openly. Sometimes, you win at a decisive moment, by doing everything by surprise.

Conspiracy?

Conspiracy, yes, that's what counts.

Are you, for example, conspiring today?

Always, always. But I am very weak and too old to do anything.

Can you give an example of a subterranean, discreet plot?

No.

In your work...

It's a concept, it's more figurative than literary — literal.

That is why you've never been an intellectual, because you are a conspira-tor? They are opposites, in the end: an intellectual and a conspirator, they are opposites.

Remarks recorded by Gilles Hertzog

Marc Lambron

In Passing

Marc Lambron kept a journal throughout 1997. Here, he offers some excerpts from January, little things seen around Paris.

Thursday, January 2

A wave of Egyptomania in France: after Christian Jacq's cycle of five volumes was published, we had a surge of publications over Christmas 1996: special editions of *L'Express, Science et Vie, Historia,* and others. Yesterday evening we saw "The Course of the Century," about Egypt — from which I am just returning. Madame Desroches-Noblecourt, who published her *Tutankhamon* in 1967 and had General de Gaulle visit the exhibition at the Grand Palais, repeated the performance with Ramses II, thirty years later. Malraux, Aragon and de Gaulle are gone, but *Tutankhamon* and Mrs. Desroches-Noblecourt are still with us.

And Malraux, flanked by four Egyptian cats, has just been ensconced in the mastaba at the Pantheon. For the ceremony, rectangular cases were arranged around the bier (next to the Egyptian cats), for school-children to fill with photographs. Jeanne Moreau was on a dais during the ceremony, and she supposedly looked at those cases and said, "Isn't that nice, they've even prepared litter boxes for the cats."

I wonder whether this focus on Egypt around Christmas 1996 was intended to commemorate, more or less consciously, the anniversary (one year afterwards) of François Mitterrand's flight to Egypt in his final days, followed by the great funerary ceremonial in the mastaba of Jarnac (*Old Cataract*, the photograph of the recumbent figure, veiled women, teary-eyed Esmeralda at Notre-Dame, posthumous manuscripts, the enigma of the Sphinx, the romance of the mummy). He who gave us the pyramid at the Louvre looked to Egypt before dying: the great pagan gods with head of animals, the embalmed bodies, Pierre Mauroy and Sérapis.

Doesn't the phantom of Mitterrandian socialism (soon to have an Alexandria-like library at the edge of the Seine) echo with a nostalgia for Egypt?

Last week an Egyptian guide said that Mitterrand sometimes used to go to the Saint-Catherine monastery, in the Sinai, where there is a relic, one of the saint's fingers, that oozes a miraculous liquid once a year. Mitterrand is supposed to have been there during the critical moments. A tall story? But it would square with the rest (rumors of witch doctors, pilgrimages to Mont Beuvray, alternative medicine, the healer Georgina Dufoix, holistic cures, Doctor Tarot, etc.).

If you like to play with strange coincidences, you can amuse yourself with the streets of Paris. Behind the lycée Carnot is a tiny street where, in the course of time, Daubigny, Marie Laurencin, Paul Morand, Joseph Kessel and Patrick Modiano all lived. But Paul Morand rented from Marie Laurencin, and Modiano must have been aware of the street's history when he moved in, which makes it less a coincidence.

Rue Saint-Ferdinand is not bad, either. Aragon, as a child, lived right around the corner on avenue Carnot; he mentions it in *Le Paysan de Paris*. Drieu committed suicide at number 25, in 1945. And the school on the street has been renamed Andre-Malraux.

That places the Aragon-Drieu-Malraux triad in the same street, which starts at a statue of Tristan Bernard; Truffaut lived there as a newly-wed. Let us add that in Clouzot's *Les Diaboliques*, the laundry where Paul Meurisse would drop off his clothes is at 29 rue Saint-Ferdinand. And now, Philippe Bouvard's residence is there, too. Although I see less significance in that.

What a lot of baggage an address can acquire. Especially in Europe. The Arts channel showed a documentary on the rich history of the Adlon Hotel, Berlin. The producer Percy Adlon (*Baghdad Café*) is a member of the family. There were images of the tenor Richard Tauber, Marlene Dietrich and Thomas Mann. Then a shot of the first Madam von Karajan, during the war, hiding her furs in the wine cellar during air raids.

Tuesday, January 7

The emotional distress of certain forty-somethings who have experienced everything — including children, and romantic fantasies — increasingly leaves them prey to two forms of religion without a god: astrology and lesbianism.

François Taillandier's essay on Louis (Andrieux) Aragon (whose centenary is coming up) has been serialized in *Le Point*. A book on old Louis the Red, written by someone from the "decontaminated" generation, with a good grasp of the texts and with less politics in his head, should be interesting. What's left when you take away the paeans in "*Huma*" [the newspaper *L'Humanité*], Jean Marcenac, and Elsa's monocle? Obviously, a very great writer, with some signs of 1900 na-

tionalism: the pages where Taillandier copies some of Edmond Ro-
stand's verses, without the punctuation. That sounds like the Aragon
of *La Diane Française*.

A member of the Conseil d'Etat was talking to me about Andrieux,
Aragon's half-brother, a legitimate son of the prefect Andrieux. In the
1950's, he used to pick up young graduates; he would take the Conseil
d'Etat jubilee medallion out of his pocket and say, "Keep this on you;
it's always handy if they catch you in the john." A Voltairian profile, a
great Aztec of the Council, he was particularly smitten with a jockey,
whom he fixed up after the war with the RATP [the public transpor-
tation authority]. The lad followed him to Royat, where the Conseil
d'Etat had holed up in 1940. The married members had their wives,
Andrieux had his jockey. He is said to have run into his half-brother
for the first time during an intermission at the Comédie-Française, in
the 1950's. "Aragon," said one. "Andrieux," said the other. They had
the same father, and the same taste in men.

Andrieux apparently used to tell a story about Aragon, which I have
never seen in print — it's oral history, as they say. Around 1895, the
senior Andrieux was a prefect in Paris. He had authority over certain
public buildings, an authority that he sometimes transformed into a
right of use. And so the police prefect would use the old Ledoux rotunda that marks the entrance to Monceau Park, with its domed cupola, as a bachelor's pad. He would invite his mistresses there, including the girl who became mother of the bastard Aragon. So most
likely, Aragon was conceived under the cupola of a rotunda designed
by Claude-Nicolas Ledoux, in 1896. In the rich neighborhood, the
17th arrondissement, a fantastic and facetious bourgeoisie.
That explains why Aragon did not want to enter the French Academy: he was born under a cupola.
Another story about the Conseil d'Etat: a few years ago, an old coun-
cilor died. One of his colleagues went to pay his respects at the home

of the widow. She took him aside and said, "The Council killed my husband, with all those late night meetings." The colleague didn't say anything — and for good reason. The Conseil d'Etat never meets at night.

Wednesday, January 8

I found a note in the *Official Tax Bulletin* on the VAT rate applicable to "authors and composers considered to be classics." It's worth reading. Here you may learn that Francis Blanche, Raymond Legrand and Jean Nohain are classics; John Lennon, yes; but not Jimi Hendrix. Joaquin Nin, but not Déodat de Séverac. George Gershwin, but not Irving Berlin. Nino Rota, but not Érik Satie. Etc.

Thursday, January 9

A preview of *Evita* at the Kinopanorama, hosted by *Le Figaro*. Yves de Chaisemartin greets his guests rather provocatively, laughing into the microphone: "If the film is as bad as the critics say it is, I wish you a pleasant nap." All the barons of *Le Figaro* were there, with Marie-Claire Pauwels, Giesbert, and Guilbert with Raphaële Billetdoux, Christine Goguet (of *Figaroscope*), and plenty of publishers, Ducousset and Isabelle Laffont, the Frémy's, Mrs. Yves Berger, Olivier Nora, Nourissier (he says to me, "Hello, Mr. Marc," — and I say, "Everything OK?" — "Everything sucks," he answers). Claire Chazal is there, and she's appealing because she says she is unhappy, and looks it.

The film is one gigantic video, a story that is somewhere between *The Cardboard Suitcase* and *The Lady of the Camellias*; with Busby Berkeley attributes re-visited by Mussolini. Madonna indeed — she is the Evita of the Internet era, the whore who regains her virginity before the eyes of the movie audience. *Like a Virgin*: a real Peronista.

Enormous budget. Teary eyes. The musical parts are pleasant, but nothing more than pleasant, and sometimes long. If only we could have a film with the same budget, the same set designer and the same crowds, but presenting an epic story without the song: this has all the makings of a David Lean film, except that Alan Parker thinks he is in Pink Floyd's *The Wall*, a maracas and daiquiri version.

The real spectacle was Mayor Tiberi and his wife Xavière, in the audience. Madame Tiberi may be Corsican, but she still has a way to go to achieve real Latin caesarism. When she steps out onto her balcony, looking out on the Pantheon, she doesn't see a crowd of *descamisados* come to cheer her, but the tonsure of Judge Halphen as he disappears under the portico.

In 1983, I lived just a stone's throw from the building in Madrid where Isabelita Perón lived. *Moreto* Street. No one ever saw her, but two guards patrolled in front of the door night and day. The house was built in the Sixties, and it was not a particularly attractive block. From her window, she must have had a view of the Spanish Academy, the Prado and the military Museum.

At least Xavière Tiberi, the Isabelita of the 5th Republic, has the Pantheon, the Sorbonne and the Henri-IV college.

A friend was telling me about a dinner party he attended in the 1970's, at the home of a leading medical professor in the 17th arrondissement, with a movie producer and his current wife, an actress. At the end of dinner, the conversation got out of hand and the producer started telling the company at large how his wife had just made a double skin flick, to make some extra money. "But I didn't recognize her voice," said the producer. His wife snapped back, "You'd have to have made me come." The guests were shocked. The producer, enraged, threw himself on his wife and ripped open her fine blouse, exposing her bosom. "I need breasts!" he shouted, pointing at his wife's flat chest. The guests were shocked again. . . I guess the producer must be a difficult husband.

Friday, January 10

Suzanna Lea and Antoine Audouard (from the publishing house Editions Laffont) hosted a dinner for the Argentine writer Toma Eloy Martinez, whose novel *Santa Evita* had just been translated into French. It's a mystery-comedy that is both macabre and amusing, on the postmortem adventures of the body of Eva Perón, embalmed, buried, exhumed, abducted, lost, hidden in an Italian cemetery, returned to Perón where he was exiled in Madrid, etc.. Eloy Martinez is a kind of elegant *porteño* with a *quechua* profile; he's friendly with García Márquez, Luis Sepulveda and several others, the gang of Latinos courted by the American universities — he teaches near New York and has taken up the good practices of North American writers, notably, keeping the copyright on his books for himself.

On the pretext of writing a book of interviews, he became a part of Perón's entourage in 1971, when Perón was living in exile in a villa at Puerta de Hierro, in Madrid. Perón lived there with Isabelita, flanked by the magus López Rega, the Rasputin of the second pressing of Peronism. Perón was still rewriting history, including other people's. One day he was telling Eloy Martinez his memories of an Argentine general's funeral, in 1913 (Perón was born in 1895). Then Perón added, "López Rega was with me."

"Are you sure?" asked Eloy Martinez. He knew that López Rega was born in 1916, and thus could not have been attending funerals in 1913. "Certain," said Perón. "Write that, López Rega was with me at the general's funeral in 1913."

It was less a matter of senility than a bit of window-dressing: in the Perón legend, it was important that López Rega had been there since 1913, like a kind of Count de Saint-Germain* of *justicialismo* (Peron's "Third Way," between communism and capitalism).

---

* Saint-Germain, an adventurer, musician, chemist and historian, was close to Louis XV in the late 1740's and, for a time, carried out secret missions on behalf of the French court.

Eloy Martinez recorded the interviews, then stuck them in a bank vault: a dictator's read-write memory, the CD-ROM of the Peronist psyché.

After awhile, he was told that he was going to be granted a favor: he would be taken in to see Evita's mummy. Eloy Martinez presented himself at the villa of Puerta de Hierro. He was escorted to the main kitchen. There, on the table, in the presence of Isabelita and Perón, he saw Evita, removed from the box in which she was kept. The body was naked, but covered with a kind of towel that hid the breasts, the belly and the pubis. Due to some fluke in the process of embalming, the body had shrunk: Eva Perón was about 5' 2"; mummified, she measured more like 3' 9". A knee had gone dark brown: it had been rubbed against the wood of the coffin while being moved. The tip of an ear was missing. And, during an act of profanation by the anti-Peronists, the corpse had been subjected to a ritual and vengeful ablation: a postmortem attempt to exorcise Evita.

Isabelita Perón looked after the mummy; frequently, she would comb the cadaver's hair, a Barbie doll in formaldehyde. Eloy Martinez confirms the rumor that Isabelita would sometimes lie down next to the mummified Eva; and the magus López Rega would seek by magic to perform the transmigration of Eva's soul into Isabelita's pea-brain.

Martinez thinks that Perón rarely touched Isabelita. But he says that the dictator's predilection for very young girls, thirteen- or fourteen-year-olds, was indisputable. He was the Humbert Humbert of Buenos Aires, whose Lolita became a Madonna — Santa Evita. Martinez also interviewed several women who had enjoyed Perón's favors; apparently, he was always a little too fast.

Sunday, January 12

Jean-Édern Hallier died this morning in Deauville. The news hits hard. I just saw Jean-Édern last Wednesday at the screening of Evita; and I thought he looked fine. Sophie says that she'd had the impression that he was staring at her. For a blind man, that was strange. But this blind man combed his own hair, went to the movies, and died riding his bike.

I thought back on some dinners with Jean-Édern, in 1989 or 1990, at rue de Birague. The *Idiot internationale* was launching its incendiary campaigns against Mitterrand, Tapie, and Françoise Giroud; Hallier was holding an open house in his apartment. The Wall had just fallen, and he was planning to go back to Hungary, where his father had been military attaché in 1944-1945; he lived through the bombings as the Soviet troops invaded the city, then tracked down the elite Nazis in the cellars under the fortress of Buda.

He implied that it was there that he had lost an eye, and he maintained that his father, like a French Wallenberg, had saved dozens of Jews. Others described General Hallier to me as a Vichyist. Okay. Jean-Édern dreamed of a triumphal welcome in Hungary, with girls throwing of rose petals at his feet: the liberated East would be the way to his Roman triumph. He talked about Ezra Pound in Venice, then about his taste for young men — a confidence that was blandly reiterated on Channel One, five years later. He was immature and hotheaded, always ready to bite the hand that he had recently flattered, hitting everyone with libel and demands, and then sending vicious faxes.

He was enthralled by literature, it made him dart his head like a fascinated cobra. A dervish of the great years — he had associated with Sollers and Dominique de Roux, Huguenin and Nimier, in the shadow of Gracq — I feel that he accepted the histrionism that the new era expected from him with the smile of the Buddhist monk who burns himself with kerosene for the movies. We went for a drink at a café on the Place des Vosges. Somebody dared to say, right in front of him, that Sollers was a nothing; and he smashed his glass on the floor with all the theatricality of a jealous twin. Nonetheless those two met again, played table tennis with some girls, and hung around with Léotard, then Minister for Culture.

During a roundtable where Léotard, Hallier and Sollers were all participants, he declared: "You have before you a liberal, a libertarian and a libertine." I also remember the dedication printed on the proofs of *Tonton and Mazarine*, in 1984, the first version of his lampoon against Mitterrand: "For Michel Rocard, of course."

I met him again a few months ago. After the martyrdom of the Mitterrand era, Jean-Édern was back on his feet like some Terminator whose recomposed molecules dauntlessly repair all circuits to an operational state. Under his cormorant wings, he hid the fur of the Duracell bunny. He had a weekly program on Paris TV-1 and a monthly on M6, dedicated a painting exhibition at the Louvre and a new company headquarters at Ledoyen, and young people like Beigbeder and Yann Moix would come to listen to the tiger in his tank; support from Chirac, and a print run of over 300,000 copies for his lampoon on Mitterrand. He had his heyday at around fifty. He had invited me to a dinner for Douste-Blazy, attended by Yasmina Reza, Karl Zéro, Frédérique Pons, an assistant to François Pinault, and several others. He launched several missiles against Balladur, who was on the ground at that time. Douste-Blazy, who had been his minister and had survived him, didn't say a word. Hallier had given up the post-Mao black tunic that he'd worn five years earlier for a wool jacket, vest and cigar. I had a few moments with Jean-Édern apart from the crowd. Sitting opposite him, speaking to this blind man, I had the impression that he could see me. He was a ghost who made me think of a ghost story, a novel by Balzac. I said to him, "The son of General Hallier has become colonel Chabert." He had a strange smile, like a child who has always been gnawed by the internal night, and who was seeking the light of things before the night caught him again. He had an innocent venom. I think people liked him.

One day Sollers said, "I armed Hallier as a fragmentation bomb, set to blow up in the hands of the Left."

Monday, January 13

The same Sollers declared, in this morning's *Libération*, "I think he will be remembered more as a polemicist than as a writer." Hallier had told me the same thing: "Sollers is a great literary critic, but he's not a writer."

They spent their youth fighting for the title of *Heavy Weight Champion of French Literature*. They shared a bewildered reverence for "The Writer," that each one refused to grant the other. They could share women, yes. But give each other that professional recognition, never.

I read this in the paper: "The Garden Dwarfs Liberation Front (FLNJ) acted Saturday to release dwarves in the forest of Écouves, near Alençon. Ten figurines taken from their owners' gardens thus found freedom. 'We do it for their well-being,' explained the commando members. The FLNJ, which was founded in the Orne last summer, claims to have conducted some two dozen rescue operations."

Tuesday, January 14

Lunch at Récamier with Manuel Carcassonne of Editions Grasset. He's got the flu, and had to leave the table in the course of lunch, but he came back, courageously, for coffee. The vocation of editor calls for such self-abnegation, and Carcassonne does it better than anybody else.

Récamier is a very good lookout post for anyone interested in watching the comings and goings of the Paris scene. Every day at lunch, you can take a picture of the waltz danced by the elites, as they say. This is a restaurant where the menu is bourgeois and the guests are ostentatious, and tend to come from the publishing-political-media arenas. The sampling on this Tuesday in January is not lacking in picturesque details. At the secluded table tucked in a corner close to the entrance, a kind of private room whose windows look out on the street as they do in the chic parts of Hanseatic towns, today we have Jacques Derrida sitting with a sad-faced beauty. It is interesting to see how the deconstruction of Western metaphysics can lead to one's eating mushrooms in cream sauce by a window with a woman with dreamy eyes. Not far away, Jean-Denis Bredin is having lunch with Maurice Druon's administrative assistant at the French Academy; he goes by the name of Mr. Personne ["Nobody"] — and I'm not making that up. So Bredin is thus talking to Nobody, and Nobody answers. After the treaties of Brussels, of Kanakie* and of the Arab world, we see none other than Mr. Edgard Pisani himself just two tables away, unsinkable and ready to serve again. The politician of the day has met his match: seated next to Jacques Pilhan (the trans-presidential guru) are Alain Duhamel, Jean-Marie Colombani and Jerome Jaffré. I saw Duhamel on television just yesterday evening; he and Arlette Chabot were questioning Jacques Delors. A great moment, at the end of the program: pianist Michel Petrucciani and violonist Didier Lockwood appeared, to give a jazz serenade. Delors was filmed from the side, and the Christian-Democrat figurehead wasn't sure how to act, on a live broadcast. He marked the tempo by blinking his eyelids, and sometimes by a slight movement of the chin. What is called a liberated body.

Grasset has its own table at Récamier. Yves Shepherd and Françoise Verny are having lunch with Laurence Cossé, a writer from Gallimard. Looks like a player is going to be traded to another team. Grasset, which had its Marie Cardinal era, is short of ladies just now, whereas Gallimard is overflowing with them (Pierrette Fleutiaux, Anne Wiazemsky, Paule Constant, Marie Nimier, Annie Ernaux, Emmanuelle Bernheim, etc.). The balance needs to be adjusted. They are working on it.

Sooner or later, everyone surreptitiously turns his eyes toward Daniel Toscan du Plantier, who is back in town. He has the creased face and the desperately fragile black eyes that show the passage of death. He

* A step in New Caledonia's de-colonization process

still wears his *chatouch*, the Indian scarf that is so soft and fine that you can pull the whole thing through a wedding ring. He's eating lunch with a bald man. His face displays real sadness. The woman with Derrida just looks bored, by comparison.

Manuel Carcassonne takes a swipe at the novelist Éric Neuhoff who, since he has become a father, has gone from the tones of a Hun to tender pro-family proselytism. "You think you've got a Bernard Frank, and he turns into a Michel Debré."

Heard and reported by Érik Orsenna: "Jean-Édern Hallier dying by falling off his bicycle is like Jeannie Longo dying of apoplexy upon opening a book by Marcel Proust."

Like anyone who spent the first nineteen years of his life in Lyon, I had a thirst for Paris. In Lyon, there was nothing much to see. You had to go look for it. Now, I watch the spectacle of Paris without always understanding it, but I note that it is still expanding. It has a grandeur. Writing here, I am part of it.

I spoke with Érik Orsenna about my plan to keep a journal every day for a year. He thinks it's a good idea, photographic, a way to force myself to see and to synthesize what I see. But the principle point he makes is this: not to stop at the description of events, not to leave the televisual worldview with a monopoly. Writers see from a different angle, another truth. It is already worth something if they simply try to stick to that. Then the day-to-day world does not yet completely belong to the filmed media.

Orsenna is always like that: he accentuates the positive, and you only feel the sting the next day. In his own, very diplomatic way, he too is at war.

Thursday, January 16

It's jury day. Why would anyone agree to be a part of a jury for a literary, or para-literary, prize? Primarily, because to they ask you. It can be tedious, it's unpleasant for the authors who are not selected, and it engenders false relations with everyone if the prize is important — with the result that it's only an acceptable task when it comes to minor prizes.

At nine o'clock this morning, the Grand Prize for fashion books is going to be awarded. It was created three years ago by some academics from Lyon II, specialists in the history of clothing and fashion. There isn't really anything at stake, and I am very much afraid that the cost of the review copies (these are art books) sent by the editors to the members of the jury may be greater than the amount of the prize, if there even is any money involved, which I don't know.

But it was pleasant to talk with Maïmé Arnodin, Jean Lebrun, Olivier Lapidus, the Spaniard Evelin Mesquida and Decitre, the bookseller. The final vote is between a book on the artisan trades related to the fashion industry (very nostalgic about the exquisite small trades) and the Christian Lacroix-Patrick Mauriès album on the making of a collection.

I hold out for Lacroix; the book is immediate, coded, subjective, useless, pure fluff — and beautiful. Its disadvantage: it came out last fall, it is already sold out, and will not be reprinted.

The book on the artisan trades beats Lacroix by seven votes to five. A real social rift.

This evening, at 6:00 PM is the final selection for the Deux-Magots prize. Here's a funny little café story: in 1989, I was given this prize for my first novel, which was very kind of them. Time went by. In 1994, the Café Flora created its own prize, and I joined the jury with young journalists from all sides (*Le Figaro*, *Le Nouvel Observateur*, *Actuel*, *Elle*, etc.); that year Vincent Ravalec won.

The owner of Les Deux-Magots was furious to see that Café Flora had created its own prize and that a former Deux-Magots laureat was a member of the jury; he asked the jury of his award to co-opt me. After some gnashing of teeth, this was done, and I received news of this wondrous election in the mail. So here I was, a member of the juries of the Flora and the Deux-Magots prizes, at the same time. The owner of the Flora, Miroslav Siljegovic, was outraged. I was kicked off the Flora jury. Café wars! And neither Finkielkraut nor Professor Jacquard intervened in my favor.

So that is how, without having understood much of what was going on, I found myself sitting this evening at Les Deux-Magots with Éric Deschodt, Jean-Paul Caracalla, Anne Pons, Éric Ollivier, Jean-Marie Rouart, and Jacques Brenner; Paul Guilbert and Catherine Nay couldn't make it. For the Flora prize, Jim Harrison and Virginia Despentes (the author of *Kiss Me*) were on everyone's minds; here, they are thinking about André Bay and Jacques Brosse. An uproar versus urbanity: both have their charm.

The final selection: Denis Tillinac, Eve de Castro, Jean-Luc Coatalem, François Cérésa.

Rouart, whose latest novel I just received this morning, talks to me so enthusiastically about Aragon's *La Semaine Sainte* (which he has just read and which I have not read), that we go out to La Hune to buy a copy. However, it's not out in paperback.

Rouart, a little depressed, tells me that he is afraid that the French novel will soon suffer the same status as poetry: private clubs, clandestine aficionados, and catacombs.

He talks to me with good grace about the Jean-Édern Hallier's criticism of him, remarks like: "Rouart must have worn out his pants, kneeling before so many different French scholars." They had had a falling out, had just been reconciled, and had planned to have lunch together tomorrow.

Around noon, a meeting in a photography studio with the model Stella Tennant, newly promoted by Lagerfeld as the image of the House of Chanel. A portrait for the paper, *Madame Figaro*. It's always useful to keep a finger on the pulse of the female species. Five years ago, we had the Schiffer-Campbell assault. Campbell had met me once beside the swimming pool at the Ritz, half an hour late, dressed in a mauve dress and cap, with a Chanel bag, and high boots which she unzipped, revealing naked skin, while she talked. She was very much a courtesan for rock'n'roll stars, talking about Eric Clapton and Marvin Gaye; a black Venus, an Isis for the tabloids.

Times change. With Tennant, we have a return of the aristocracy, on the defensive. A hint of the Thirties, the Beaton-camellias line. She is surprisingly fresh, quick and easy, without being aware of the genetic-cultural code that makes her so British.

In the afternoon, I take the portrait: there are undoubtedly many definitions of Stella Tennant. The young woman (some twenty years old) who walked into this photo studio in the 5th arrondissement of Paris on a winter's day has a certain appeal. She's very tall, and she's pulled her hair back under a pirate's bandana, wearing a jean-jacket over a skin-tight top and a knit miniskirt, with socks and clogs. Just as she is, she looks like a London girl caught by Morand in 1919: "Aurora isn't wearing any blouse, and thus deprives us of the hidden pleasures, but only of those."
At an age where others are baby-sitting, this elf from Titania's entourage now embodies the image of the House of Chanel. She hasn't yet had time to be spoiled by yachtsmen and weekly suicide attempts, and probably never will. Stella Tennant does not say, "men." She says, "my boyfriend." In the Victorian era, even the legs of a piano had to be covered; Miss Tennant, all freshness and sex appeal, is pure, bare charm: neither debauched nor sanctimonious, she represents life as a dance.

The Little Lady of the House of the great Miss Chanel — this is a return of history. Before the war, Gabrielle Chanel lived with the Duke of Westminster for several years. "I loved him, or thought that I loved him, which amounts to the same thing," she would say. Today, here is

Stella Tennant, a very small sailor from *Britannia*, storming Rue Cam-
bon using Kaiser Lagerfeld as a bridge. It is true that she swings between two family trees: she is a granddaughter of the Duke of Devon-
shire, and the daughter of Lady Emma Cavendish (a renowned
painter) and the Honourable Tobias Tennant, who we all know, of
course, is the half-brother of Lord Glenconner. So that you have the
fox hunt and a dubious baronetcy bringing forth one of those British
nymphs who is part fairy and partly of the triangle. At the risk of
overloading the boat, we might add that the maternal grandmother
was the fifth Mitford sister, Deborah, which brings us back to the
Paris of Duff Cooper and Louise de Vilmorin, whom Nancy Mitford
portrayed in *Not a Word to the Ambassador*. Also lurking among these
branches is a certain Stephen Tennant, a well-known eccentric of the
1930's, who designed little tights and corsets in the style of Beardsley,
Cocteau nicknamed him "the Carnival of Venice." Stephen Tennant
was famous for his greeting to GI's arriving in Europe during the last
war, "My loves, coming all this way to save us!" A background like
that is more than a family, it is a memorial. The interested party says,
"People think that my grandparents' titles are all there is to me." In
other words, that is not all there is. Is Stella Tennant British right up
to the point of wishing to escape Britain? Years ago, Nancy Cunard
came to parade with her bracelets on the Île Saint-Louis, the prince of
Wales could be found at Le Chabanais and Violet Trefusis in her
French preserve. Then came the 1960's, when you could find the
Drugstore bustling with Julie Christie doubles, wearing their geomet-
rical dresses and pop art earrings. The English and the Continent: an
ongoing affair.
Stella Tennant, who says she likes "the milky light of Paris in spring,"
was not immune to the little impulsive actions that mark an insular
youth. When she was eighteen — so long ago, yet almost yesterday — she tended a little toward the punk. As a student at Winches-
ter College of Art, she had her nose and navel pierced. It wasn't long
before she came to the notice of a modeling agency. The photogra-

pher Steven Meisel tried her out for the English *Vogue*, then propelled her to the cover of the Italian *Vogue*. And suddenly a turbo-charged ascent, at the same time as the new wave of super models Amber Valleta and Shalom Harlow, toward the catwalks where the acknowledged princesses stroll, Linda and Cindy, Claudia and Naomi. At first they tried to say that Stella T was just another of the neo-anorexics; but the eye of an honest man contradicts such a classification. Quite simply, vis à vis some of her elders, Tennant stands out. Are the superstars going to be de-throned? Time will tell.

In conversation, Tennant has the allure of those beings who are unaware of their own poetry. You can imagine her in a palanquin in Srinagar, as a nurse during the Blitz, or munching an apple in a James Ivory film. After all, what is a man? A sahib? A lord? A Spitfire pilot, the Honourable Tobias or Rudyard Kipling? She simply says, "My boy-friend," with (as George Bernard Shaw would have written) that pious English way of looking at the world as a moral grade-school expressly built to firm up the character. My boy-friend? It turns out that the boy is kind of French, kind of a photographer, and that they share an apartment in New York City. She comes up with innocent sentences that cut to the heart of the matter, sentences that bring to mind what Louis XIV said when he first saw the new gardens of Versailles: "It rather takes you back to childhood." She says, for example, "I haven't had a broken heart in a long time, but I remember that it hurts." You can ponder that for a long time. Then, "I don't like my knees." One doesn't dare to look at them, for fear of not sharing her severity. Or indeed, the fluid elegance with which she ties things together: "Impatience is not a quality. Patience is a virtue. I'll have time for regrets."

Miss Tennant confesses that she likes the wrong kind of music (Gary Numan), and Mozart. She reads Dostoyevsky and Graham Greene, likes Charlotte Gainsbourg, declares that on the whole she is not particularly obsessed with clothing, but far more with happiness — "being happy with another person." Not far away, the make-up girls and the dressers are waiting. The sound system is broadcasting rhythm'n'blues. Stella has that sparkle in her eyes that make-up will turn fatal. For now, she is merely beautiful, which is much more. As for the nasal piercing, she says, "The rings have disappeared, but that doesn't mean that they're gone." And when one asks her what is the strongest feature of her personality, she answers, "I don't know. I can't be cut into pieces." Thus Stella Tennant, the New Divinity. She pierces her nose. She cannot be cut into pieces.

Friday, January 17

Dinner at Caroline and Gilles de Margeries'. Extraordinary presentation by Alexandre Adler, who has launched himself into the Hernu affair. He held forth for half an hour, giving us a dazzling view of the post-war world of espionage, unraveling each strand, untying it knot by knot, ferreting out the details: this one went here, Andropov went there, and to handle Philby in Beirut, Caraman, the Romanian; the Farewell episode, the history of the DST, the very John Le Carré account of his visit with Markus Wolff in 1990 (Adler says that in his youth, Wolff's father had posed as the discus thrower for a chocolate company), etc.. He knows the names of the contact officers, the betrayals, the parenthetical stories, and he speaks in precise sentences, interrupting himself with sidebars and incidental anecdotes, then picking up the main thread again; a little bit like listening to a spy story being recited live, a little bit like the ballad of a dynastic history, a little bit like a Russian novel — one can imagine Proust, perhaps, giving a monologue on the aristocracy the way Adler speaks about spies.
You could have heard a pin drop. Even with Nathalie Duhamel and François Stasse present, and Érik Orsenna, Sophie Moati, Agnès and Joel Touraine, Jean Kaspar and his wife, and Caroline's sister, Anniella.

Around 1:30 in the morning, I found myself in the street with Adler. He lives near the Town Hall, and I live in Maubert. We decided to walk home, past the quays. We walked until a quarter to three, passing back and forth between the Île de la Cité and Île Saint-Louis, saying good-bye and then talking some more. These things that one does at the age of fifteen — walking all night, chatting with a buddy, going back and forth with him: the old peripatetic disease of schoolmates. Adler thinks that many things might happen before the next legislative elections, and that we will see calls for action, sooner than we think: the need to go on the attack, new civic organizations, new men. Like everyone, he sees that the old boys from the ENA [the École National d'administration] are fatally exhausted, and he is looking forward to the advent of another approach, something that would not be so diametrically opposite to the political view of those from the École Normale Supérieure. Philippe Séguin worries him, he thinks (at least, lately) that he may be a particularly dark Bonapartist, reading Leon Daudet and perhaps planning parliamentary alliances, not far from a kind of democratic Péronism, if that means anything; he tells me about his lunch, four or five years ago, with François Sureau. At the time, Adler had been thinking that Séguin was a died-in-the-wool republican, son of a teacher, his father dead on the field of honor, etc.. Sureau thought otherwise, and called Séguin "the man with the stinking armpits;" he suggested that Séguin was looking to come up with an acceptable form of Doriotism. Adler gave it some thought; by now, he was not far from thinking that there was some truth in it.

He had just broken off with his paper, *Le Point* — squabbling, and a protest by some of the editorial staff when he defended Artur London in *Le Monde*, etc. He's going to join *L'Express.*

We finally parted on the Île de la Cité, at the corner of rue de la Colombe. Trucks, projectors, lights and microphones were lined up in front of Notre-Dame; at 3:00 AM, someone was making a movie.

Monday, January 20

Thinking back on my conversation with Alexandre Adler, and our night on the quays. It's one thing to condemn the coterie of ENA alumni, but he should be looking at it differently. We constantly forget that ENA alumni are, like those of the École Normale Supérieure or the agrégés [the most highly qualified pedagogues], the offspring of competition: the written exams are anonymous, the oral examinations assessed by committee, the classification has to be earned. Logic is republican, at its source. And I have been quite surprised to see how many "sons of the people" there are at the ENA. I believe, in fact, that that was one of the keys to Juppé: armored in his myth of omnicompetence, and having erased in himself all signs of his origin. That is, he reinvented himself through learning, through effort, so that he was no longer the son of anything but his own intelligence: he had a class complex. And this was, oddly enough, at the heart of a party — the RPR — which is not afraid of its popular roots. But he was made to feel ashamed of his background, in the finance administration. Which gave rise to a funny evolution: in constructing a new identity to set himself apart from his own people, he invented a mechanical identity, a new body, a "novalanguage" purged of any telltale signs. They called him "Amstrad."

He had to forget all sentiment, to prevail against the sons of Parisian archbishops. He fell hostage to this hardening of the heart, for the softies of populism, on the dole, require heart.

I think that his unpopularity is to some extent a revenge on the part of those whom he left behind. He doesn't want to know them anymore? Then they no longer recognize him. It would be easier for a true patrician to become a demagogue: just look at Giscard, who was peerless in this respect.

In short, the ENA can hardly be criticized for how it recruits people, for it is the republican melting pot in a pure state: the title is not granted, inherited or bought, it is won through merit.

It is only afterwards that everything is spoiled: by the ever-increasing power given to minds that are only moderately guarded against their own defects; by the schizophrenic schedule of lectures and seminars from which one inherits various technostructures that one reproduces without understanding them; by the lack of gurus in recent generations: by the uncultivated — ahistoric — vision of a world seen only through the lens of the immediate future, seldom placed in perspective. These are not defects based on one's origin. They are shortcomings that are accepted out of interest, fatigue or cowardice.

Tuesday, January 21

Deliberation over the Deux-Magots prize: Ève de Castro wins in the second round, with eight out of thirteen votes. She comes to pick up her prize with Sylvie Genevoix, Richard Ducousset and Francis Esménard, the editors from Albin Michel, whose every project turns into a success.

The most notable patrons in the café are Juliette Gréco and Slavik, the man who adorned the Drugstore in the 1960's. Saint-Germain-des-Prés convenes its icons when the corpse stirs, between a Vuitton shop and a discount bookshop, Belphégor and op art.

At the luncheon which follows, I am at table with a few members of the jury, Catherine Nay, Paul Guilbert, Jean-Marie Rouart. At another table sit the former prize winners, Neuhoff and Frébourg. Helene Schoumann, of *Joyce*, has found a nickname for Rouart: "The Chevalier des Touches."

Somebody says:

"What's good about Jean-Marie, is that he's succeeded in cohabiting with his former mistresses, and they all still get along with each other very well, too."

Paul Guilbert:
"We should rather say that they were all friends beforehand, and that he has not succeeded in making trouble between them."
Ève de Castro's book is mostly set in the Palais Royal. In other times. Today, the great staircase built under Louis XVI has taken the place of the old theater where Molière played, and the Regent's apartments are occupied by Mr. Douste-Blazy. Douste-Blazy thus finds himself at the heart of two great French incests: Molière and Armande Béjart, the Regent and the duchess of Berry. The Palais Royal — the house of incest, more than the mayoralty of Lourdes.

A little anecdote: when Voltaire's tragedy Œdipe was first being staged, the actor playing Œdipe had made himself up to look like the Regent, who was in the audience. The public recognized the allusion immediately. What did the Regent do? One week later, he granted Voltaire a stipend.

Helene Schoumann says that she was in Deauville before Christmas; Jean-Édern Hallier was there and spent a good part of the day playing chess. Helene says that the playing pieces were marked with different pieces of tape so that Hallier could recognize them.

Some tricks to make you a real writer for today:
1. Move to the countryside and learn to walk like a goatherd.
2. Take a sabbatical, and give yourself up to complete indolence, so that when your book finally comes out, you can say: "After four years of silence, X comes out of his shell with a major book," consisting of 134 pages in large type.
3. Don't force your talent; avoid the hatred that your style inspires.
4. If you are an alcoholic, pass off the fact that you cannot finish your books as a sublime abruption. Talk about white writing, minimalism.
5. Read Thomas Bernhard and Fioretti to make everyone forget that

you never read Chamfort and Crébillon (son).

6. Use the notes you took in prep school on de Dumarsais' *Tropes* to give your work a smart and antiquated tone, reminiscent of *La Nouvelle Revue Française* under Paulhan.

7. Display an air of vernal melancholy.

8. Never laugh.

9. Remember the inspired Scandinavian airs of the priests of your childhood: that is what you want to emulate.

10. If you didn't have a childhood, invent one. There are still priests around, you can always observe them.

11. Hate life: she won't return the sentiment.

Wednesday, January 22

Strange dream last night: women with long curled lashes, like Cleopatra. But these lashes were coming out of their noses.

There is a lot that could be discussed about Alain Juppé's little book, *Between Us*, starting with the name of his ghost-writer. But this morning, *Libération* was interviewing the novelist Annie Ernaux, a specialist in sad revelations ("my defloration," "my Mitteleuropa lover," "when dad died," "when mom died," etc.).
Ernaux makes an acid comment on Juppé's book: "An exhibition of sentiment." Oh no, not that! This is like the hospital spitting on Charity. Or, in fact, Charity spitting on the hospital.

Overheard from the mouth of a lady: "To annoy my psychoanalyst, I made my transfer directly on Sigmund Freud."

Here is a story, probably made up. In America, a guy on death row requests his last cigarette before being executed. Refused. Why? It could be bad for the executioner's health.

Thursday, January 23

The grinding intermissions that interrupt the show. Actually, a writer between two books, is that an intermission in a show?

Stopped in at the reception given by Hector Bianciotti, who was received this afternoon into the French Academy. It was 7:00 PM. At that hour, the ambulances had already come to take away the hoariest members of the Institute. No one was left but Pierre Rosenberg (red scarf), Jacques Laurent (whisky); Jacqueline de Romilly and Bertrand Poirot-Delpech (green clothes). This was at the School of Fine Arts, in a room with dim lights, Gothic and spectral, with rose windows and replicas of some of Michelangelo's great sculptures. Also present were the House of Grasset, a few Argentines and one of the Aga Khan's brothers. One could feel around Bianciotti that thing that cannot be neglected: friendship. No crowds of fake acquaintances, no bankers, just a kind of soft fluctuation in the half-light. Perhaps we were in a scene from one of his novels. Living characters saved by literature, or unredeemed, burning with a despair that keeps life warm.

Bianciotti seemed to be miles away, very far away, perhaps in that Italian Argentina whose words alone remind him that it no longer exists; or in the hungry Rome of the 1950's, or even Madrid, when Antonio Machin's *boleros* were being played on Bakelite radios. The young sexagenarian with the flowing beard, in his green outfit like a *gaucho* about to enter the corral, what was he seeing, what was he thinking of? Did this day of triumph appear to him like one more shroud to be torn up, the way he'd torn up so many? It's easy to step out before the public under a vaulted roof, like a scene from an opera, to play the celebrity who speaks and is about to sing; no one will leave. Perhaps the measure of Hector's triumph was the moment when he left his mother, to become this thing that cannot be presumed, that was not in the cards for him: a French writer.

I haven't seen his sword. They say that on the pommel, designed by François-Marie Banier, is the letter "A." As in Argentina, amity, or a friend's name?

At a certain moment, a photographer comes to look for Bianciotti, to take a picture in the room with the Michelangelo reproductions. The author of *Sans la miséricorde du Christ* walks past the *Piéta*, ignores *Moses* and leans on the cold, muscular thigh of a *Slave*. And there he stands, in his casual posture, leaning, linked to that stone flesh, under the light that could be that of some back street in Buenos Aires, on the swirled and somber background of a Caravaggio. The truth of this coronation is that is shows that he is liked, and perhaps he alone.

I go to congratulate him.

"Now, I suppose, we can call you 'Master'?"

Bianciotti pouts. "That's not a good word, it's too abrupt, too short. And 'Monsieur the French Academician' is too long, I don't like that either."

"So, then?" I ask him.

"All in all, I would prefer 'mistress.'"

Friday, January 24

A great scandal these days over Calixthe Beyala's plagiarisms. People keep finding fragments from other authors in her books. After her, men! This virtue is quite strange. When one reads Perec's *Les Choses*, for example, it's clear that twenty percent of the sentences have been lifted from *Flaubert*.

Perec did it knowingly, technically, as if to indicate that the universe which Flaubert entered with *L'Education sentimentale* had, in 1960, become the rule.

I am surprised that Beyala, who loves to claim that she is the voice of the African shantytown, does not plead the Texaco technique: that she is building a book the way a cabin is built, from rubble and recycled material. She comes from a generation where the dressmakers are still copying Schiaparelli and Madame Grès, where the rappers are constantly re-using a bass sequence, a guitar riff, a line of melody, and integrating them into their patchwork of sound. That is called *sampling*. Beyala is a sampler, unrepentant in her literary kleptomania, although it only gets her into trouble. An amusing protest from Paule Constant, one of those who were robbed: "That really takes the cake, when an African woman borrows descriptions of Africa from a White." An indirect and unconscious way, I imagine, of underscoring the homage Africa renders to Paule Constant by holding her to be the author of its best descriptions.

Beyala is, however, a crafty devil; her mistake is in playing Voice of Africa. Inoculated in spite of everything against the politically correct, part of the press prides itself on not having fallen into the trap. But I always feel queasy when one attacks a pretty woman whom one avoids kissing only in order to get her entire hide (cf. Barzach). At least Beyala reads other people's books — we have the proof. These days, that is already pretty good.

Perhaps I am indulgent because this lively lass is an amusing scamp. Two years ago, she and a hundred other writers got together for a photo shoot on the terrace of *L'Express* during the 20th anniversary of *Lire*. In a conversation during the cocktail party that followed, I said something, not especially sexual, to her, which made her laugh. But she wasn't satisfied with laughing. She very quickly touched her hand to my fly. A gesture of affection, I imagine. *Sticky Fingers*. But it was so unexpected, comical, and burlesque that I wanted to say of Beyala what a 17-year-old says of a girl who blows him: "Damn, she's good!"

A hand on your fly is enough to make you forgive quite a few plagiarisms.

Rue Chabanais. Viollet-le-Duc was born at house No. 1. Around 1900, the big deluxe brothel was there, where the Prince of Wales used to spend his time. Today, the neighborhood is under dispute. On one side is the Caesar, an establishment with "topless waitresses." But on the other side is the Family Association headquarters. Who will win?

Saturday, January 25

This morning is an Open House at Pauline's school. All the loving self-abnegation, so poorly rewarded, of the nursery school teachers. Circles, squares, triangles, and tubes of construction paper: it is always striking to see that the contemporary nursery school is modeled on the Russian constructivist workshop of 1919. The victory of the modern: Tatlin and Rodchenko have won.

Nassim came to spend the weekend at our house. He is fifteen years old, the son of an architect and a diplomat at the Algerian Ministry for Foreign Affairs. His parents live in Algiers, and Nassim is a second year boarder in a school near Paris. He went to see his parents at Christmas; he tells of the cautious traffic in the street, the paranoia throughout the region, the spontaneous militia that keep out any foreign cars. A law on linguistic Islamization is creating enormous problems at the moment: university classes and diplomatic correspondence, which used to be conducted in French, from now on must be conducted in traditional Arabic. Which obliges diplomats, doctors, and professors to take courses in Arabic, with all the difficulties of technical transcription, in particular for the exact sciences, medical programs, etc..
On the other hand, the night clubs are all playing Anglo-Saxon hits.

Jean-Paul Gaultier's "Men's" show. Like Bianciotti, he chose the School of Fine Arts as his venue, but you won't find any member of the French Academy there today. The real show is the audience. The dominant trend: a cross between Mahatma Gandhi and the Austrian Jäger (by the front door, they are giving out Bavarian beer), with all the usual quota of Captain Fracasses, Nosferatus with earphones, and Sardinian widows. A little poster hanging on a column announces a conference at the school, "Intricacies of the Intimate in Deleuze and Foucault," by the editor of the review *Vacarme*. Gasp. The public awaits, like the Japanese poised for the tea ceremony, gays exchanging propitiatory remarks (in English): "Come on, darling, I won't bite you unless I get excited," journalists, François Baudot, Mariella Righini, Marie-Christiane Marek (known as "Proud Marek") and Gerard Lefort, the star of *Libération* — about whom they were saying, last year, "Straight, and ashamed of it."

Catherine Deneuve, perfection, in the first row. She's over fifty, but she always turns up for certain shows, like the little girl in *La Ronde de nuit*. When I interviewed her last July she was wearing a strawberry-red wig for a film by Raul Ruiz. Breezy blonde hair suits her much better.

The fashion show is choreographed to music from 1979 (Madness, The Specials), with the usual silhouettes that we have come to see as cartoon figures: skinheads carrying signs that say "Love and Peace," prisoners escaped from Alcatraz who look as though they've raided a sale at the Salvation Army, mad hatters disguised as silk moths in a mulberry tree, Sicilians in their wedding costumes, Mormons fallen into a pot of phosphorescent paint, nephews of the Ras d'Amharas running the Tour de France. There were a lot of smiles in the audience. Gaultier even managed to cheer up some empty-eyed sylphids — or maybe they were on Ecstasy.

Overhead, the following inscription is engraved in the stone: "*Incoeptum a Ludovico XVIII Ludovicus – Philippus peregit monumentum anno*

MDCCCXXXVII." No doubt JPG's fans will have immediately decoded that and learned that this monument, begun under Louis XVIII, was completed in 1837 by Louis-Philippe.

Sunday, January 26

Five hours of Frank Sinatra on the Arts program. Some beautiful recordings from the archives, including a 1965 recital and *The Autumn of My Years.* Tracing his career, you can really get a sense of that exposed feeling, between the ages of 40 and 50, when Sinatra was no longer young but not yet a legend. You have to paddle hard, to hold your own against the rise of Elvis and rock'n'roll; you have to get a lot of TV time to keep from being forgotten. It was a human moment, too human, in the history of the vulnerable crooner. In fact, Sinatra made the best of it: this is the period in which he recorded his most beautiful albums.

What happiness to hear, behind him, the dream-like orchestras that existed in the United States at that time: Gordon Jenkins and Nelson Riddle for melancholy, Count Basie for swing.

Why is it that certain of Sinatra's devastating songs, such as *The World We Knew* (a little bit like the Doors' *End of the Night*) seem to evoke the infinite?

Monday, January 27

In Switzerland, they have a flippant expression to indicate the tabloid press, the scandal sheets: "boulevard journalism."

I was surprised, in Egypt, by Mathieu's and Juliette's inability to dial a telephone. Then I realized that they had never seen one; that, born in 1985 and 1988, they had never known anything but push-button phones.

A headline in *Le Monde*: "National Museums Hold 1,955 Artworks Stolen from Jews during War."
One of the two members of the Consistory who took us to visit the synagogue in Manhattan's Lower East Side, during a study trip in 1987, said, "There are two of us. So, for every question you ask, you'll get at least three answers."

11:00 PM. Beethoven's 14ᵗʰ quartet. Night has fallen on the Seine, and Notre-Dame stands between the leafless trees. Music, like the truth.

Tuesday, January 28

The *Crédit foncier* scandal is still unfolding. *Libération* points out that executives have been sequestering their director for six days. Comment: "A blow to the image of the executive as the transmission belt of the employers' goodwill. . . Tired of playing along with the corporate culture only to wind up in the street like the others, the executives more and more are joining in the fray."
It's an irony of history, just the same, that the white collars are finally discovering the culture of Petrograd. Should they be looked upon with charity? They have been conned, but they did it to themselves. Will they remember the 1980's? Pushed into business schools by parents who (having come from the land and having worked in the shop) believed in progress, the young future-executives were ready to trample everything in their paths. Egotistical, looking to make a quick buck, with kicks in the shins and knives in the back, Nipponization of attitudes, and mouths full of a marketing new-speak in which the most beautiful pearl was the phrase, "Director of Human Resources" — like mineral or halieutics resources. They did not encumber themselves with solicitude, then: the grandsons of the wartime black-marketeers had discovered salvation through the big enter-

prise. The women also joined in: squeezed into their triangular and turbo suits, claws open on the vacuum, running toward Wall Street. Virtue is slow, and speed always despises it. They had found contempt in the cradle of their haste. Civilities were soon curtailed to a recitation of paychecks and bonuses over dessert. Their grandfathers had signed up at the construction sites in their youth; they ran to get a job as marketing managers. Capital, here we come!

Ah! It was a rude Flaubertian disillusionment, *L'Education sentimentale* in sitcom version, the moment when they understood that the company is not a religion — does a religion fire its faithful? They had stunk up the atmosphere with their arrogance, and now they would weight it down with their sadness: harming civilization twice over. After the strass, stress. Bitterness, divorce, the returns of gurus, sophrology, numerology, astrology, channelers and prophets! In their euphoria, they saw trade unions as the height of tackiness. And so they reinvented the strike, and they were astonished, after imagining themselves to be the aces of reorganization — of technical purification — to be thrown out, themselves, like used Kleenex . . .

I'm waiting for the new revolution and the world that is to come.

Wednesday, January 29

Last night I saw Paul Amar interview Maurice Papon on Channel One. It was rather painful. Amar was waving photocopies of documents from the file, but he was not prepared, historically. Papon was wearing one of those dark blue pinstriped suits that still seem to me, even on the big figures of the 1960's, to be a sign of Vichy. The arrogance is still there. You can guess that this is the profile of someone from the administration of this country: a servant of the State, burning to hold the reins — to become minister — which makes career men alternately cold and flexible at the same time.

Papon, fired up to defend himself, didn't give an inch; he set on the table the photographs of two little deportees that Amar, very theatrical, had waved under his nose. He laid the blame on foreigners, New York, Chirac — as always, a plot.

I'd like to know what the 90 prefecture secretaries-general were doing at that time. A new book is supposed to come out in the next few weeks: the history thesis of a certain Baruch, an ENA alumnus at the Ministry of Culture. It's supposed to be a shocker involving several senior civil servants.

There was a rather outrageous series on *Arte*, on Wednesday evenings, in November and December: portraits of dignitaries from the Nazi regime, Goebbels, Himmler, Hess, etc.. On each program, several witnesses, people who had known them, were called to testify. There were aides-de-camp, former secretaries, administrative assistants, members of the NSDAP. All these people told their stories calmly, although at the time they had been auxiliaries to these big bosses and were undoubtedly wheels in the Nazi machine, and close to the top, at that. They were all still free.

I have trouble understanding the conduct — or misconduct — of Germany today, where there must still be hundreds of Papons who will die in their beds.

Thursday, January 30

Frank Sinatra's *Witchcraft* keeps running through my head, over and over. The elegance of attack, the accuracy of that plain voice, beautiful as the phrasing of Davis Miles. Crossing the Seine this morning, life danced.

A press screening of *Lucie Aubrac*, by Claude Berri. A predictable success. All the detractors of the new French quality certainly will shoot on sight. One can imagine *Libé*: "A double of Regis Débray and a James Bond girl in a Lyon remake of *Casablanca*." For me, there was the special emotion of seeing my birthplace, which in certain respects remains to me as mysterious as a Lhassa on the Rhone, under the rec-reated colors of a time that I did not know. Carole Bouquet, whom the press this morning called the best-paid French actress (13 million francs in 1996 — they give the statistics, now, as in Hollywood), finds a degree of maturity, beyond that which she must have attained, herself, at a certain time. When I had lunch with her last September, she was dreamily serene, as if the roles that she couldn't keep herself from anticipating had finally arrived. Lucie Aubrac, Mme. de Rênal.

Sometimes a film makes a difference, whatever reproaches it may incur, by touching on an aspect of things that one had previously misunderstood. Here, the loneliness of the resistance fighters in a France of 40 million inhabitants. Max, the legendary Jean Moulin, was a solitary man in a white scarf who would make his rendez-vous in the park of Tête-d'Or. What a strange feeling to be, by date of birth, so close to that world, and yet so far. The Tête-d'Or park is where I took my first steps, in about 1958. The same trees, the same alleys, the mystery of these places where, for me, in childhood, nothing happened except for the soft succession of the seasons — and yet, all that did happen, those men, alone in their contingent, legends of heroism and loneliness.

Friday, January 31

Interview with Jean-Paul Gaultier. He receives me in his offices, near the Bastille. Exhausted from the fashion shows that have just ended, including his first haute couture show, and already concerned about the upcoming deadlines for the next one. Few institutions rest on the shoulders of just one man as much as a house of couture; the founder's work being to secure the future, so that the name will survive under another hand: Dior without Dior and Chanel after Chanel.

With an accessible urbanity, Gaultier talks for an hour and a half. He talks about his childhood bear, Nana, that he dyed blonde, that he subjected to a heart transplant in homage to Doctor Barnard and on which he would try, at the age of ten, the first conical breasts that became the emblem of Madonna's *Blonde Ambition* tour, in 1990. Anything in common between Madonna and the bear, Nana? Yes, he says: the blonde dye. He acknowledges being exhausted after working on the film that Luc Besson has just finished at the Pinewood Studios, in England. Then he tells me about his beginnings in costume design: one day he was drawing a dancer from the Folies-Bergère, in class; the teacher caught him and, with no mercy, made him walk through all the classes with the drawing pinned on his back. However, his young comrades enjoyed it and even looked on the revolutionary with a certain respect. In a way, this was the first Gaultier show. He says, "The fun that the others had that day, that was a passport to being accepted." I ask what, for him, ugliness is. He answers: "The stuff I don't keep."

Obviously, he is endowed with immense, protean energy: his collections, perfumes, film and ballet costumes (for Régine Chopinot), new looks for musicians (Yvette Horner, Rita Mitsouko), two years of success with the "Eurotrash" program on British television, advertising appearances for M&M's, etc.. He lives on Avenue Frochot, where Jean Renoir lived in 1950: one part *La Vie est à nous*, crossed with Panama and an aristocrat of the boulevard.

It's strange to find two sides to him that should be contradictory, and yet are not completely. On the one hand, the irreversible rise of the audio-visual culture — he thinks in terms of MTV, of 1960's TV series, and certain bits of pictorial culture (De Chirico, constructivism), confesses having read Süsskind's *Perfume* in the course of several months, and having opened Petronius's *Satiricon* because he saw Fellini's version (although he wasn't able to finish the book). He says of a common friend of ours, an English designer who is his assistant: "She talks like Pollux." He's not referring to the mythological hero, but the dog from *Manège enchanté*, a children's series with voice-overs by Jacques Bodouin in 1966. Professor Allan Bloom would have had an apoplectic fit at this bird, this woodpecker with the apache wit. Good. On the other hand, there is a legacy that I cannot help but perceive, adulterated no doubt by industry, exempted by birth from having rubbed elbows in school with the Faubourg mindset, re-fashioned by both the streets and the world, a legacy to which he is, however, heir, due to his talent as an Indian goddess with a thousand arms: like Cocteau the juggler, a way of going in Médrano to see erudite geese walking with a Spanish gait, to toss onto the stage a parade of idiotic horses and lady tennis players — images from the nursery — and to hear a furious woman declare, "If I had known that it was going to be so dumb, I would have brought the children," which to Cocteau would have been like receiving a personal Legion of Honor. To be everywhere, in the worlds of movies and painting, with the Six and with Picasso, at the Noailles' and with the sailors of Toulon, this is a 20th century lineage that was still putting out new shoots in this Paris of 1997, including Gaultier's big game. I would not go so far as to say that he is a new Cocteau — that mask would not fit his features. But a vein of energy runs through him that, Paris being Paris, does no dishonor to what this city used to be. Gaultier plays on a global keyboard, in Tokyo and New York, between London and Italy: those are the wavelengths on which he plays. How many French writers, how many French painters can say as much today?

I ask him what kind of new look he'd like to give to some well-known contemporaries, starting with Jacques Chirac.

"I wouldn't suggest a skirt or kilt," says Gaultier, "although I'm dying to know whether he has nice legs. But when one is Head of State, one must dress in beautiful classics."

— Jacques Delors?

"I would put him in gold, to play on his name. Gold lamé, gold spangles, and everything shining!"

— Anne Sinclair?

"Anything but those mohair sweaters that she used to wear ten years ago. It was terrifying! She is fairly pretty, isn't she? So I could see her in something sexy, rather light and open, slightly transparent, with ostrich feathers and fur trim at the feet, like in the 1950's. . . But the one I would really like to dress is Arlette Laguiller. A big evening gown with fifty yards of taffeta, split sleeves, make-up and stiletto heels. A glamorous Arlette, and Bardot, . . .

— Bardot?

"All in fur! I know very well that there are massacres of baby seals. But to be against mink in couture is snobbish and grotesque. If you take Bardot's position, you have to go all the way, no more leather shoes because that's leather. And the poor little crayfish that cry when you throw them into boiling water? You'd also have to found a group against the assassination of vegetables, the horrible murder of carrots under the knife! As for the feathers, I have just the thing. A turkey sleeping bag used by the *plumassiers* who make toiletries and accessories! But also a short fringe on a very full skirt, or a little braid on a slightly convex surface, pleated or cut." Gaultier doesn't read much. But he can teach you new words.

Marc Lambron

Michel Onfray

Preaching
the Decline of the West

The end of a century, and the end of a millennium when they
coincide, always gives rise to a Decadentist trend that echoes the
sempiternal conservative and reactionary refrains — hatred of one's
century, contempt for one's own time, despise for the environment of
the moment, all accompanied by praise for the virtues of yesteryear,
that delightful era adorned with every virtue. This simple formula is
easily detected in all the theorists of decline: earlier, with Joseph de
Maistre and Donoso Cortès; more recently, with Maurras and Dru-
mont, Spengler and Rosenberg; today, with the smaller fry who spe-
cialize in the great virtues, the requiem for the avant-gardes, the wisdom of the moderns, the era of the void, the comedy of culture, the
defeat of thought and other variations on the well-worn topic of the
decline of the West.

Pure products of millenarian anguish, ignorant of the causes that
shape them, these symptoms disguise themselves with the most beautiful plumage and wrap themselves in alleged virtues: as heralds and

heroes of their time, they supposedly display courage, audacity, non-conformity, honesty, frankness, perspicacity and all that constitutes the great man in a time when he is so much needed. Where others supposedly practice only subservience, conformity, and platitudes, they are daring. Daring what? To think the way people speak, people who do not think? In this sense they have succeeded, perhaps beyond all their hopes.

In a strange paradox, by promoting the banalities of all their chattering, the philosophers of the Sorbonne, government bureaucrats, cultural officials, the auxiliaries of the triumphant neoliberalism and producers of intellectual programs, become (small comfort) monumental best-sellers and get all the media coverage that goes with it. Kantian or Spinozist spangles, paroxystic rhetoric, play-acting and other scholastic tools are not enough; offering thoughts that flatter the spinelessness of the majority, dressed up with grad-school philosophy citations, only amounts to a form of active support for those who plow this fertile soil, that is, the Gramscists of the Right who are patiently and confidently awaiting converts. They have already recruited, on a regional level, those who espouse the basest of policies, and they won't have long to wait before the ones who insidiously cluck against modernity and disparage the work of artists here and now (the way they used to organize noisy exhibitions of degenerate art), to be eating out of their hands.

This is intellectual war, unquestionably. It has its various camps, with partisans and enemies, networks and defectors, press organs, forums, magazines, editors and journalists, henchmen, troops, and cannon fodder. The much-ballyhoo'd Decadentism on the aesthetic and intellectual terrain corresponds very explicitly to the terrain favored by the political forces of the Right, federated around Bruno Mégret. Every salvo lobbed against the paragons of cultural modernity (Pierre Boulez springs to mind) has actually produced, on the pure and hard political ground, an effect of cohesion, complicity, association, and allies. The catastrophe theory applies to geographical continents, but also, unfortunately, to intellectual continents.

In this war heralding the promises and the dangers of the next millennium, I am somewhat astonished to see the partisans of reaction and conservatism appealing to the concept of pleasure. For ten years I have been traveling a hedonistic course, and trying not to leave any sector untouched (especially contemporary art in all its forms). I have met with nothing but disdain from the opponents of pleasure, about whom so much has been written and who, under no circumstances, could be considered a sufficient basis for a philosophy. Okay. But why, then, do they criticize modernity only in the name of pleasure, which supposedly needs to be retrieved and which the moderns have been challenging for a century? How can we denigrate all the cultural product of this era simply by deploring their cardinal sin: having turned their backs on pleasure?

I am delighted to see hedonism finally recognized for its qualities as a subversive and alternative course, but I am afraid the decadentists will attempt to praise it in its vulgar formula, the nature of which I would like to try to spell out. For the notion of pleasure that these people complain about, when it suits them, and praise whenever they find it may support their feeble theses, seems to suggest the same notion of pleasure for pigs and for people, for primitive beasts and for higher mammals. This is a strange indistinctness that allows one to believe that pleasure is simply a matter of the immediate and summary satisfaction of an elementary need, as though hunger, thirst, sexuality and culture were concerned with the same logic, as though the orangutan of the savanna and the man of the megalopolis experienced the same desires and enjoyed satisfying them in an identical way.

Admittedly, the more highly evolved mammals and those which are less so do seem to share the same desires. But let us admit that how they experience them, differentiate between them, circumscribe them, isolate them, defer them, modulate them, and erect the screen of conscience and culture between their empire and their satisfaction, all that makes a difference. The animal submits to its desires, man can choose to respond via culture. And the difference is fundamental. *Homo sapiens* does not have a blind desire for indistinct objects. A culture that determines which desires are thinkable leads to a philosophy of the possible pleasures.

The pleasure to which I am referring is a construct, not a given. For one never wishes for anything by chance nor freely, but always in relation to a civilization, an era, a culture, a milieu. Our desires, our wishes and our pleasures signal our membership and we only accept them insofar as they also satisfy social, tribal requirements. If you consider the planet as a whole, the tropism that naturally leads insectivores to satisfy their desire of hunger by the pleasure of food, expressed through predation, leaves the protagonists no mental latitude. On the other hand, on the same score, hunger, mankind has a multitude of options for addressing this need in a cultural context.

A priori, and in a hypothetical natural state, humans do not strive for any aesthetic satisfaction. There is no sign of the beginnings of art, religion, metaphysics and philosophy. And if nobody educated human offspring as to these needs, they would never feel any simple, immediate need in that regard. The desires of the senses derive exclusively from that which is transmitted intellectually, surely not from an inborn inclination. This graduated scale of aspirations ranges from the simplest to the more complex, to the most elaborate. Anyone who is not educated, who is not initiated, will be either unaware of this type of desire or will be content with a superficial demand, which can be satisfied with a product that is equally poor. Wanting a simplistic pleasure, unworthy of the philosopher, seems entirely justifiable to those victims who have never had access to the pedagogy of pleasure.

· I blame this on those who propose to respond to the desire for culture with insipid mush. Is philosophy needed? The decadentists rush to offer a pitiful response gauged to please the greatest number. The pleasure designated by their wishes coincides with quantitative flattery. For it is easier to lower the philosophical proposition (whatever is left of it, anyway) to the level of the demand, rather than to require those who are waiting for an answer to their questions to strive and to elevate themselves. Satisfying the masses with rudimentary and simple pleasures is a long way from behaving in a liberal and democratic way; it is dangerously demagogic. Calling for the massive and immediate pleasure of a public that allegedly has been neglected for too long is a way of maintaining the fallacious idea that effort is useless when it comes to the experience of culture.

When it comes to learning a language, we accept the investment of time, effort, will power, patience, humility, and slow progress; why do we reject all that when it comes to being initiated into those languages which are the fine arts and philosophy? Demagoguery aside, who can believe that it is possible to learn a complex language without making an effort? I see it as a demagogic perversion, this false idea that it is better to lower the aesthetic or philosophical standard to the level of the majority, rather than to elevate them sufficiently to enable them to appreciate and know a true pleasure. Quality of pleasure must precede quantity. The first option, wrongly seen as democratic, is really demagogic; the second, which may appear aristocratic, is really democratic. Flattering the people is certainly one of the worst ways of showing that you despise them.

Pleasure supposes at the very least a knowledge of what one wants to transmit. I am surprised to find two viewpoints co-existing in the decadentists' arguments: one, the statement that they do not like contemporary art; and, two, that they do not engage in it in any manner. If you have no contact with contemporary art, then you are not in a position to consider whether it is deteriorating and bankrupt. Who would accept any assessment of a language, its nature, syntax, grammar, precision, rigor, and evolution, from somebody who did not practice it? Only familiarity with the auditoriums where today's musical creations are brought forth, proximity to the galleries, familiarity with the exhibition halls and contact with artists make it possible to form a judgment, and not the vague impression left by hearing a few

CD's or casually flipping through a magazine or an encyclopedia.

Any condemnation of contemporary art is unthinkable, intolerable, coming from those who neither know it nor practice it. Competence of judgment supposes something more than the vague opinions of falsely enlightened amateurs. The philodox turns his back on the philosopher. And the bourgeois experience of Schubert's chamber music, on disc, does not help to form a competent judgment of contemporary works. Those who give lessons are not learning their own, and they join the uncultivated in calling for the demolition of a continent of which they are ignorant, which they have not visited, but which they hate without batting an eye. They add their own incompetence to the incompetent public, in the hope that it will bring them a better-founded appreciation and legitimate understanding.

Judgment, which is to say the capacity to experience pleasure, supposes real competence. Admirers of Plato (which the decadentists often are) should know that when it comes to piloting a ship the philosopher prefers sailors over shoe-makers, and that you don't consult a chef when your shoes need mending. Who has competence, in matters of aesthetic judgment, of taste? Surely not the true incompetents, who say they don't understand it at all. This seems all the more problematic when the moralizer hides behind a pretence of knowledge and testifies to an apparent competence. Such as?

Such as those who claim that, since Platonic esthetics opened the way, then that of Christianity, and finally that of German idealism, there are certain legitimate and exclusive approaches to the question of beauty; that all we have to do is to consult Plato and the Platonics, Kant and the Kantians, Hegel and the Hegelians. Those who would carve up esthetics into three separate compartments, the term-paper approach; but this does not deserve the epithet *Beautiful*. As if we would have to follow up the end of philosophy, announced by Hegel, by announcing the death of art, as well. Thus, philosophy would come to an end with the man from Jena, as if Nietzsche and Marcel Duchamp had never existed. Trying to understand today's art using yesterday's esthetics is like trying to conquer outer space with the mathematics of Descartes as one's only tool. Or trying to appreciate Joyce's *Ulysses* within Boileau's constructs.

The decadentists are not Nietzscheans. However, when it comes to fine art, the 20th century was. And rather than agree with it, they prefer to fire off an auto-da-fé, to throw the art of the last hundred years into the flames and to call for a return to the esthetics that were current before *La Volonté de puissance*. Ah, what a lovely era it was, when one could speak of the Beautiful in and of itself, of the sensitive realization of an understandable idea, of the spiritual incarnate in matter, even of what is universally pleasing, or of disinterested satisfaction! Lord, how sweet were the times when one could recycle the old Platonic concepts and those of the *Critique of the Faculty of Judgment*! But there you have it: Duchamp showed up, and he was to fine art what Nietzsche was to philosophy: a blast of dynamite that blew up all the old categories. God is dead, along with the father of Zarathustra; and beauty, with the father of the ready-made. *Like it or not*. The fact is proven. Thus the problem of the decadentists: they do not like it, they do not accept the idea, they reject it with every fiber of their beings, as Joseph de Maistre rejected the accomplishment of the French Revolution, as he vowed to strive for a return to the monarchist spiritual order.

The old pleasure in beauty, elegance, balance, harmony, symmetry, and consonance has rendered up its soul, in the same way that the Christian after-world, religious security and eschatology have expired, with the biblical visions of the world, catholic Soteriological constructs. *Like it or not*. The incompetence of the public goes hand in hand with that of the philosophers who try to conceptualize their century using out-of-date instruments. They cannot comprehend interplanetary flight, which they deny because their calculations are no more advanced than Huygens'. But if we don't understand a thing about conceptual art, if we think according to the principles of Kant's third *Critique*, that does not mean that the work of art should be dismissed — it means that the dog-eared philosophical Fodor's Guide is out of date — by about a hundred years. It has been replaced by Duchamp's manifestos. Judgment, taste and pleasure do not exist in themselves, but in the context of a specific time. However, times have changed: Poussin's esthetics will never give us any handle on contemporary installations. By perpetually refusing to use the appropriate methods, the decadentists condemn themselves irredeemably to the past, and more and more so.

After the death of the Beautiful, Meaning took its place. Beauty, that non-existent virtue that used to be adored, and that always hid other interests — God, the Church, the King, and then the Capital — vacated its niche in favor of Meaning alone. Art works make sense and it has fallen to the philosophers, in tandem with the artists, to decipher it and to explain it. In the same way, a Poussin canvas makes as much sense as work of land art: the people and the power, from time immemorial, need explanations. Simple pleasure is denied to them. Anybody who knows nothing about Virgil, Diogenes Laertius, stoicism and the classical humanities, cannot appreciate these paintings; and anybody who is still ignorant about these subjects nowadays is condemned to enjoy only the surface of Poussin, his reputation and his work as a skilful and talented craftsman, and to miss his message as an artist. The 17th century peasant did not find pleasure in this painting, any more than today's urban worker can grasp the nature of a minimalist or conceptual work by Carl André, Richard Long or Walter De Maria.

The decadentist uses the wrong handbook to decipher these works. I reject the demagogic approach of saying that yesterday the average Joe was comfortable with art, that he liked it and understood it, whereas today the creative sector has divorced itself from the general populace: the breach is wide, but it can still be remedied. Decadent thinkers give up this position, and teach that it is not those people who refuse to learn and understand who are in the wrong, but those who produce and create this art. They have inverted everything. Conceited, sure of themselves, arrogant, pretentious, and unaware of their own lack of culture — oh! remote Socratic nonscience!, the philosophers put themselves at the service of the uncultivated, whom they flatter and seduce. . .

Superficial and simple pleasures give superficial and simple joys. Similarly, subtle and refined pleasures beget commensurate satisfactions. Seeking only immediate pleasure is not enough: *quid* our pleasure in Mozart's *Requiem*? Was Picasso focusing on the pleasure of museum-goers when he was painting *Guernica*? Was Michelangelo thinking of the tourists when he was decorating the ceiling of the Sistine Chapel? Was Schubert pandering to middle-class women when he composed his *Opus 100*? How about Bosch, and the Flemish peasants, when he gave birth to the monsters in *The Temptation of Saint Anthony*? Or were they obeying other requirements, which it would be useful, essential, to know in order to understand, to grasp, to enjoy and appreciate the works in question? Historical and cultural requirements, in fact.

How can one enjoy an object if one knows nothing about it? About its meaning, its raison d'être, what it says or could say, the materials that are used, the techniques, methods, forms? Parking yourself in front of a work of art and expecting it to give you pleasure is like watching for a comet to go by in broad daylight. You are likely to wait a long time, and in vain. Aesthetic pleasure is accompanied by all that allows it and supports it: as much information as possible about everything that has gone into it, an intellectual jubilation, a rich context of references, a puzzle of quotations, knowledge, competence and an educated eye, ideas, opinions, experiences, and patience in looking, patience overall, a permanent counterpoint between the object and what reveals it, of the texts, the readings, the comparisons, all that sets it into perspective. Acquiring a new language requires a grammar, a syntax, an orthography. The decadentists do not even recognize the existence of the language, and they refuse to make any effort to learn the rudimentary elements. Pleasure that has been re-lieved of conditions, doing away with all conditions, makes it abso-lutely impossible to "get" it.

Isn't Pleasure more of a pure idea than "the Beautiful," "the Truth" or "the Good"? For we define all these entities in relation to one epoch, one time, one society. Any attempt to understand the Nu-bian music of the Nile, the rhythms of the Tigara cult in Ghana, the *sertão* of the Brazilian favelas, the harmonies of Central Europe's gypsy music, the tantric statuary of an Asian temple, the Zen garden and the tea ceremony, Japanese origami and ikebana, Mayan solar architec-ture, or symbolic Roman town planning, immediately and without any related concepts, references, or culture, without any information, would be an impossible project, hopeless, if not imbecilic. Every work of art, to give pleasure, requires something more than itself. And this other thing is composed with input from history, sociology, geography, ethnology, religion and many other activities. Philosophy serves as a connection, it synthesizes and conditions the possibility of this hedonism.

Lastly, conservative thinkers are mistaken as much on the na-ture of pleasure as on its origin. Far from being a simple and immedi-ate response to true, sincere and authentic artworks (I'm using their vocabulary), it comes from mediation. Sociologically speaking, pleas-ure is definitely impure, as a historical product. It would be banal to say that the same artwork produces different, even contradictory, ef-fects according to the moments and the conditions under which it is examined. The history of the mediation of the object contributes to its hedonistic appreciation. The pleasure appears all the greater for being complete, profound, fine, delicate and subtle. So that it devel-ops density in proportion and resonance to the period of domestica-tion that one is willing to accord it.

Duchamp wrote about the importance of the one who is look-ing, of the subject whom he elevated to the dignified station of crea-tor, affirming that a work is not created by the craftsman who puts it together so much as by the spectator who gives it its form, its power, its consistency. An age can be measured by the quality of its public, more than by the mediocrity of its artists. We must take care lest the decadentists invite today's public to persist in its idiotic thick-headedness, trusting that they can rely on philosophers to reproach the language for its inanity rather than questioning their own lack of culture and refusal to try to appreciate the work on its on terms. The origin of pleasure rests in the intelligence of the person seeking it. But wanting it isn't enough. You have to have something to work with.

Never is pleasure a summary satisfaction, the simple satisfaction of an immediate desire. Desire in the realm of art must be maintained, in order to make possible a higher pleasure. The heart's effusions are taught, and they go beyond primitive urges to the extent that they are fostered through talent, even genius. When it comes to the natural needs to drink, to eat and to copulate, when it comes to these necessary desires, vulgar hedonism does answer simply and invites us to a summary satisfaction; but in regard to the same obligations, one can also act as a transformer, a sculptor of need, inventing oenology, gastronomy and eroticism. From one world to another, from one man to another, the distance may appear to be more vast than between the highest of the animals and the lowest of men.

Between the animal pleasures of the former and the human pleasures of the latter, the thick layer of culture is interposed, and with it all that we are taught about pleasure, the distinction between vulgar pleasures and philosophical pleasures, the virtues of conceptual artifice, intellectual mediation, the plastic formation of judgment, and beyond demagogic and populist prejudices, the patience of initiation. Hedonism builds the soul, with art contributing to the process, in a perpetual motion of ebb and flow. The bonfires lit by the decadentists represent a real danger because they encourage other incendiaries, hiding in the bushes, looking for the right moment to unleash their dogs.

They too speak of a decline and degeneration, of the values of the lower classes and the arrogance of the elites, of the defection of the general public and of prohibitive costs; they, too, rail against subsidies for contemporary art, the experimental novel, atonal and serial music, abstract painting, all the aesthetic currents of the avant-garde. They like to see the figure, the face, and something spiritual in art, they like to see the people flattered and celebrated by the artists. That's how they start. Then they wind up preferring above all the Nation, the State, the Fatherland, they want to see race and other trinkets associated with the national identity. At one time, they organized exhibitions of Negro, Masonic, Judeo-Bolshevik art. Today, the butchers are administrative; impersonal municipal offices are populated by political clones of these decadentist prophets, and other priorities rule the day.

That is one of the surest means of destroying the art of an era, not so much by prohibiting it as by making it impossible, in practical terms. For the moment, the philosophers who build their careers on the notion of the decline of the West consciously or unconsciously make contemporary art impossible in spirit. Like Gramsci, they prepare the ingredients that herald catastrophe. First, political rallies, then those intellectual fellow travelers: conservatives, reactionaries and neofascists cannot hope for a better way to conquer the power. And, who knows? far from Schubert and Boulez, far from the more or less scripted debates or the choreographed skirmishes written for the moment, it may be that what this blindness presages is only the noise of boots and military bands. And then it will be too late to put out the blazing infernos.

Michel Onfray

Gilles Hertzog

Farewell, Captain

You've had a long life.

It started in another time, another world, in 1913, in German Alsace.

I know almost nothing of that life, of your childhood, of your adolescence. To us, your children, you spoke very little about yourself (I think you may have said more, to others). Your generation, your culture, held the "me" in contempt. And you spoke still less about your past, only in bits and pieces — suddenly evoking the precise taste of a tart made of quetsch plums; the first airplane seen in the sky over Colmar in 1922; your complicated relationship with Uncle Edmond, the Jesuit; grandmother Madeleine welcoming your orphan cousin, Germaine; the cherry trees that lined the roads of Alsace, offering fruit to anyone who wanted to pick them; your grandfather's trellised vineyard, which produced its hundred kilos of grapes; and the trams that were introduced, if I am not mistaken, during the inter-war period by your father, then mayor of Colmar; or, more recently, me telling you how, while driving through a forest on my way to Brittany, I came across a herd of deer, and you telling me the story about your father running into a cow with his car and killing it. Your father, about whom you never spoke to us, with these two exceptions; your father, whose first name I hardly know: Eugene — I had to ask my sister, Sylvie, again yesterday — and whose image I had never seen until your brother Étienne showed us a picture, a little while ago. As if there were a black hole, a painful taboo.

And so, Alsace. And then, after a none too productive year in philosophy at Strasbourg, your medicine degree in Paris, when the great adventure of your life began.

I won't go over the story of your life; I've already recounted a part of it — and what a part! — in a book. I will tell you in four brief characters who you were, in my eyes: doctor, Communist, sailor and, finally, as you expect, of course (and, I imagine, with the perplexity of a father under the gaze of a son) the most important — father.

Every now and then, in the most unlikely of places, it has happened that when I introduce myself to someone new, when I give my name, he grips me by the arm, looks me right in the eyes and says, "Hertzog? Any relation to Paul Hertzog, the surgeon?" "Yes, he is my father." "Oh, he saved my life!"

You were a great surgeon, in those times not long past, when chemo and radiation therapy were still in development and surgery was the only option, and removal of the affected parts was the only hope. In addition to cancer, hundreds of people suffering from serious pulmonary diseases owe you their lives, in Foch, the Val-d'Or, and the Sanatorium Hubert, at Villers-le-Lac, where they treated tuberculosis patients. You, who contracted it during the war and lost a good bit of lung to it (which fifty years later would have fatal consequences). According to the unanimous testimony of your patients, you were a perfect man, and if I were not jealous, I would say you were a father to your patients. While we would often face your imperious side, they would have the right, for decades, to your continuous gentleness, your humanity, your anxious compassion. Today or tomorrow, when they hear that you are gone, hundreds of people will pay you homage for that — which is not the least of your paradoxes. As for the operating teams with which you worked, your peers among doctors, the attending nurses, all of them, I believe, respected you for the high degree of commitment that you demanded of yourself as of others, plus your saintly character and the sharpness of your command. But it appears that, soon, everything would go so smoothly, so right, in a team spirit so tightly knit, that you were all sugar, and even as you left the operating room you would occasionally gave rein to your famous good humor and the cheery familiarities that are born between those whose vocation is to be on close terms with death.

Some even loved you. You were a true, a great, leader.

Jean-Lou Accard (to name just one), had worked at your side through the almost filial care that he lavished upon you all through your final days, in the company of Étienne, your brother in blood and in medicine, he was proof of the bonds that tied you to those who were, a thousand times over, for half a century, day after day, your real family.

At the same time that you, rebellious son of a fervent and militant Alsatian Catholic, married the daughter of one Marcel Cachin, you married Brittany and Communism, with all its battles, its bright spots and its shadows. Of which there would be no shortage.

It started with the incredible voyage from Bordeaux to Chile, on board the *Winnipeg* in July 1939, by way of a honeymoon: a couple of doctor-newlyweds escorting three thousand Spanish republicans, with your friend Seillon and the housemaid Philomène. The episode, however, cost you dearly: you left behind your son Daniel, born just a few months before. When the Communist Party of France approved the Germano-Soviet pact, the police repatriated you from Chile to war-time France, and you were tried in Bordeaux — that city, already! — for mutiny. You were released shortly before the defeat of France. Then came your arrest with Marcel Cachin in Brittany, upon the arrival of the Germans; your incarceration in Rennes, your liberation in Paris and, a little later, that controversial letter from Cachin repudiating individual attacks against the Germans. And then you disappeared in Savoy; and then came your tuberculosis. After the war was the apogee of French Communism, under the Stalinist baton, and young doctors from socialist countries came to be trained under you; but there was also, during the disastrous episode of the White Shirts (either duped or blind), and your signature, among others, on the wrong side of the truth. There was your trip to North Vietnam, with the anti-imperialist war in full swing at the instigation of General de Gaulle, where you equipped the embattled Vietnamese with a French hospital. And then would come your gradual disillusionment (though you always remained loyal to Cachin's party), your growing skepticism, your incredulity in the face of the Soviet rout, and finally the war in Bosnia against the Serbs (who in your eyes were crowned with the haloes of anti-Nazi resistance and Yugoslav Communism) in which you eventually came around to join our battle, with Bernard-Henri (Lévy) and me, in favor of the Bosnians. I thought of you then, fifty years earlier, in connection with Spain. In this, I was walking in your footsteps. You soon understood. Anti-fascists, father & son.

Your captain's hat is still there. Brittany — Lancerf, where Cachin (a native of Paimpol, the city of the Newfoundland fishing boats), and Uncle Marcel and Mathilde would welcome you and later us, every summer — would be your chosen land, and doubled as your home port. With three pennies in your pocket, you rented a house with Mom, then a different house, at the end of a dirt track that was soon paved. Kermouster, today, is in its third, should I say, its fourth generation! A terrestrial anchorage. I say anchorage, not root. As for the neighboring sea and its phenomenal tides, there was not a stone, not a rock, not a current that you (duly instructed beforehand by old Pipi), did not flirt with on board your *Winnipeg*, named in remembrance of the other one. This boat was not great, and you were no Magellan, but I have beautiful childhood memories of azure dawns far from the island at Bois, of pink rocks and a perfect sea which opened the beauty of the world to me. On board, oddly, you would drop your mask — you smiled, you were afraid of an unknown current, you worried about possible rocks that I thought were imaginary, you studied the wind to see whether it was a friend or foe? In short, you became human. Happiness, far from other people, I suppose.

It is there, at the mouth of the Trieux, which Signac painted in the many watercolors that you and Mom so enjoyed, and where you sailed, too, it is there that your ashes — according to your wishes — will be cast upon the waves. We'll be heading out soon on the *Dragon*, crossing your old wakes, to throw the dust of your being into the wind. May your grandson Tancrède, your great-grandsons Charlie, OJ, George, and all the others, sail in your paternal waters as long as the wind blows.

And then you were a father. That was more complicated; the passage was rough, tempestuous, before it came to calmer waters.

Your three children, Daniel, Sylvie and me, we loved you and each other, despite the conflicts, the rifts, the merciless confrontations and interminable silences. You were a difficult father, evolved from I am not really sure what kind of tormented, incomplete son, still reacting to his own father, who I understand was rather intransigent himself. I do not know how many scars you bore from our wars. We, ourselves, got quite a few. Each of us, on our own and in defiance of both the others, has sent letters to a father, letters that would only suffer, compared to Kafka's, for poverty of style, and that are, like his, completely useless since you don't read them anymore. It took my marriage with Anna to reconcile us. A little bit stunned, she headed out, the day before the ceremony, on an urgent mission to Croissy, where I had not set foot for ages. It took nothing less than an Italian and her disarming charm to win over such a character. Tancrède's birth transformed the armistice into a lasting peace. Paola, who bears your first name, and the frailty of your old age made it final. But the eternal question that haunts every son who becomes a fathers remains: how much of the father do we carry within us, what part of that which we suffered will, without our knowledge, resurface for our own children to face? To be worthy is to reproduce, to continue, to transmit, and it is also to mellow.

As a grandfather, you were perfect: Careen, Claire, Abel, Pauline, plus both of mine every Saturday at Croissy, know something about that. And as for your great-grandchildren who knew you, Alice, Phébée, Charlie, OJ, Chouncey and, still more recent, George, born just five days before your death, the only reproach they would make is that you abandoned them too soon. Must we add to your many defects the fact that you were insanely generous and, considering the aforementioned, a loyal friend in any difficulty for your buddies, starting with Daniel Wallard. Three women, Mom's friends, embellished your life: Monique Bongrand, Consuelo Garrido, and Madeleine, who closed your eyes this Tuesday. And Sylvie, your daughter, whom you used to abuse so much, and who took such good care of you in your old age, until your last poor breath.

And Mom, whom you called Kath because, like so many others, she was named Marcelle; you know all about her, and more.

You died of tiredness with life, of concern for your dignity given that your body was weakening, that it was on its way to condemning you to a living death. But yesterday, more than ever, in your open coffin, you were, as you had been all your life, the most wonderful man I have ever known.

And now it remains to me, now that you are no longer here, to discover you, to resolve one or two persistent enigmas, to probe the impenetrable. You won't be there anymore to prevent us from loving you.

Hello, Captain.

Gilles Hertzog

Wietske Venema

Chronicle of a Publicized Suicide

Remarks recorded by Rosalie van Breemen

This is the strangest suicide by a writer in recent decades. Adriaan Venema was fifty years old. He was one of the most prominent novelists in Amsterdam. He was also a historian, a specialist in the Second World War and the Collaboration. He enjoyed debating ideas. He could take it as well as give it. And, it should be noted, he seemed to be in good physical and mental health. And then one day in 1993, he declared, urbi et orbi, *that his life was "80% successful" and that "Nobody achieves 100%;" that he was "one year older than Maria Callas and nineteen older than Christ when they died." In short, he announced to the intellectual community and to his readers the date and the hour of his suicide.*

Final gestures. Final writings. Last-minute touch-ups. Leave-taking ceremonies. And, at the appointed hour, as they say, a cocktail of barbiturates washed down with good champagne.

These are his final moments, and this is the countdown, related to us by his widow. Death in the media age. Suicide in the era of the all-powerful visible.

‹ 87 ›

I didn't believe it, at first. I thought that I could keep him from doing it. I thought that it was going to change, just a bad spell, that he would come out of this slump; that I was wrong...

We don't have any right to force somebody to live, and neither do we have the right to prevent him from dying.

I was so afraid that he would do it in some horrible way... I thought that by keeping him company throughout his course, I could help him complete it in serenity.

The task that he had taken on in life, he had achieved by then. He had set the bar very high. He was very demanding of himself. A "loser." A recluse. And, at the same time, he had a terrible need for human contact. A need to maintain friendships. He had achieved his mission thus far. But he was afraid that he was no longer up to the task. He did not want to witness his own decline. Quite simply, he wanted to quit at the top.

He wrote forty books, most of them on the Second World War and, in particular, the collaboration with the Germans. Who did it? And especially, *why* did they make that choice? And then, after the war, how did people accept the choices they had made? These questions haunted him.

Documented works. Accumulations of details. Whole years of his life spent in the middle of the war, documenting the war. To expose the truth.

Contrary to what one might think, he was someone who hated violence. Even on television; he never watched violent films. Sometimes I would try not to turn on the television news. He suffered from the evil in the world and, at the same time, he sought it out. Very ambiguous.

On vacation in France, we would go by the many war cemeteries. He always stopped to read the names, the ages. He cried. And I cried with him. "A little pathos never did any harm," he would say. The melancholy of the world. Sad. And, at the same time, pleasant.

Simon Wiesenthal is one of the people whom he greatly admired. And Simone Weil. Persecution "produces" very strong men, who are able to accept their past and, at the same time, their future.

He worried about the rise of hard Right. Some time before his death, he was attacked by neo-Nazis, just across from a television studio. He formally identified his attackers, but the police and the justice system preferred not to take any action. He was shocked.

Searching for the truth. Tirelessly. To expose *das zweite Verbrechen*, the second crime: who collaborated with the Germans? and especially, how did those involved live with their behavior, after the war?

It was important for him to find out whether "the collaborators" took full responsibility for their acts, after the war, or whether they lied? Sometimes I would ask him, "Why don't you write a book on the heroes of the war?" He answered me that he would never write that kind of book. Men are capable of heroic acts. But they can also exaggerate, lie. Whom should we believe? And are the reasons they give each other then, their noble motives, real reasons or retrospective justifications?

Why the Second World War? Why this strange passion? We are all, more or less, influenced by our past, the life we have lived. For him, it was hatred of his parents; a hatred that is reciprocated, even today. Is it true that his grandmother was involved with the Germans? I don't know. I know that he had an early childhood without love. He was born in 1941. He lived in the Anne Frank district, immediately after the war. This young boy going around, visiting local shops, asking what kind of person she was, what she did, where he could hope to find traces of her.

Nothing fired him up so much as the war. But he had written everything. There wasn't anything left to write. He had "lived" that war. And he did not come out of it unscathed.

He couldn't bear to see people who committed crimes during the war and who are respected by our society today.

He said it. Wrote it. He had accomplished his mission. He was so afraid that he would not be able to keep it up. He had no more vitality. He felt that something was about to happen to him: disease, heart attack, the wheelchair. He wanted to decide, before life decided for him. And then, especially, he was running out of strength.
He didn't advertise his decision as a provocation. Nor a media act. Just this: he did not want to witness the decline of his life. He was neither disappointed nor bitter. He simply wanted to leave with his head held high. A question of honor.

He announced his departure long in advance. It was well-pondered, reflected, weighed. He wanted to lift suicide out of obscurity. To de-dramatize it. To make it acceptable as one way of dying, like the others. So that it would no longer be taboo. With that intention, he taped a one-hour interview for television, five days before his death. To explain his act. So that nobody would feel guilty. To explain that a suicide is something that one prepares, reflects upon, far in advance.

He said, "I am not committing suicide because of a woman, a piece of writing, or a bad review the press." He even envisioned that, in the future, there would be an institution that could assist people in this situation. So that they would not be obliged, like him, to hunt around feverishly to get enough pills.

He did everything to get those pills. He would say anything, to any doctor, to get a prescription. It took him months to collect them. And he succeeded.

One evening, he came home and said to me, "Look, five more." He had met a doctor in a café. They played poker for a prescription. He won. A bit of Russian roulette. And there was a doctor who was dying of AIDS, in the final phases, who gave him several prescriptions right before his death. On the fringes of medicine.

When his plans started to take shape, he got rid of a lot of things. He threw it all away: his books, his correspondence. He even got rid of his collection of paintings. He really ceased to exist. I don't have anything personal, anymore; just his clothes, that's it. He's disappeared.

I was very upset when he publicized his decision. The fact that it wasn't a secret anymore, that it had become public, that was horrible. I didn't like that at all. There were even critiques in the newspapers, critiques of his suicide announcement, as if it were just a piece of theater!

I wanted to avoid polemics around his death. Even today, I have not taken advantage of the right of reply in the newspapers. I have not given any interviews. Perhaps, one day, I will. For example, a television show, to speak about the need for an institution that can help people wishing to commit suicide, to make suicide acceptable as a distinct way of dying.

From the interview that was taped five days before his death, you might think that he was taking the matter calmly, that he was serene. But he also had moments of panic. I was so afraid that I might not be at his side in one of those moments, afraid that he would be hit with it sometime while he was in town. What would he do?

It was an incredible period. He was overflowing with energy. On every side, seeing friends, a very active social life; every evening at a bar, dinner downtown, every night at a casino. Full of energy, and so tired at the same time. . .

The last week, he said "good-bye" to his friends. He's have lunch with this one, supper with that one, up to about ten days before his death. After that, we were alone together, or with our children.
I tried not to be away from the one I loved, not for a second, to stay next to him at all costs, until the last moment. He insisted that I continue to work, the last week. I worked for two more days. Then I stopped; but he wasn't happy about that.

There was so much to do! The interview with I. for the newspaper. The TV interview.

Did he, at any moment, feel trapped by his word, by the commitment he had made? I told him that many people would be happy to release him from his promise. But he answered me that that was not in the cards.

At the beginning, I even tried to get him to go to the hospital. He thought about it. But he didn't want to go. For fear of being talked out of it. And he made a point of excluding that possibility.

I even wrote to a psychiatrist. I asked him to speak to Adriaan, to offer him another perspective. He was supposed to go four times. The last time, he came home late. And he told me, by way of explanation, that he had sent a letter to a friend in which he explained to him why he would not go to see him anymore. The psychiatrist, of course. He had organized everything. His funeral, for example. He bought the plot, chose the music; he even made up a guest list, a list of those who absolutely had to be invited.

He experienced the mourning before his death, he orchestrated everything, organized everything, even that last interview where he was already managing his legacy after he was gone.

They announced his demise on the television news, on the radio; it was the top headline in the news. I was shocked; I didn't expect that. Saturday evening, we went to a restaurant where we used to go so often. It was very hard. Afterwards, we came home, tired, and he wanted to see the movie that I had rented: *Beauty and the Beast*. After that, we went out again, for a drink. You are there; you know something that nobody knows; but people just look at you as if you were the same person as before. . . It's horrible! (Almost nobody knew when D-day was to be, they only knew that it would be in the autumn.) We went to see friends who didn't know about it yet. There were even friends who did not want to know: and especially, not to know when they would be seeing him for the last time!

Monday, at eight o'clock in the morning, I called all our friends. He was still there, with me, in the house. The coffin was there. I wanted to keep him close to me.

I told him about my day, who had sent flowers, who had called, the letters that I had received.
He had relied on me absolutely. To the last moment. I would not call the ambulance, he was sure of that; me too. It had would have been a total betrayal . . .

There will still be a few more publications, but not before the year 2000, out of respect for his parents. I still have responsibilities, texts to publish when his parents are gone. I'll start writing them, soon, with a friend who is a writer. A lot of me will go into the work.

Everything is clear in this story, except my special role. I was a kind of heroine, for him. But, for my own children? They have suffered too much from all this. That weighs upon me very heavily, today.

I am happy to have counted for so much to him. But in the end that has cost me so dearly!

I should have felt that before now. But I did not want to see. I chose my love for him. I chose to stay with him as long as possible. I was selfish. Sometimes, I was upset with him. I did not think that he would have been able to make this gesture all alone, nor even to pre-meditate it. He needed my strength to make it to the end. It takes so much strength to succeed with such an act, one cannot do it all alone. I was with him to the last moment. It wasn't horrible while he was still conscious. . .

His act was also a question of pride: he wanted to leave with his head held high. It was his choice. Did I believe for one second that, at the last moment, he was not going to do it? No. And I didn't hope for that, either.

Remarks recorded by Rosalie van Breemen

Cécile Guilbert

Appreciating Godard

And what if Jean-Luc Godard, contrary to the image that has been so thoroughly disseminated by certain humorists, were not at all a has-been? What if he were one of the rare people, today, who have obstinately, lucidly resisted the wholesale standardization of cinema? What if his recent work, ignored or scorned by the general public, turned out to be one of the most inventive of our time — both a bitter recapitulation of a cinematographic ethics that is fast disappearing and a will to reinvent cinema with every new film?

What if a film like JLG/JLG, in particular, were an authentic masterpiece? These questions are not being raised by a few surviving cinephiles from the "olden days," in protest against contemporary prejudices, but by a young writer, Cécile Guilbert, author of two remarkable books on Saint-Simon and Guy Debord* — and who, let us emphasize, was not yet born at the time when Godard was filming Contempt...

* Saint-Simon ou l'Encre de la subversion and Pour Guy Debord, Gallimard, coll. "L'Infini."

To tell the truth, I don't know Godard. And when I say that, I obviously am not talking about the individual, although the foolishness of our times obliges me to spell it out. Why the hell would I know Jean-Luc Godard? I don't even know his films.

I can already hear the caustic laughter of the nonbelievers. . . Yes, "I don't know Godard" is a statement whose truth, honesty and probity are so obviously incredible that it seems to me that it deserves to be said. To be written there, black on white.

I have vague memories of *Breathless* and *Pierrot Le Fou*, seen over fifteen years ago and ever re-visited.

One + One is a little less fuzzy, probably because of the unforgettable jangling of the nerves from listening to the Rolling Stones constantly playing the first measures of *Sympathy for the Devil* and not going any further.

I haven't seen any else except for *Prénom Carmen* and nothing since then, except this admirable *JLG/JLG*.

I could try to clarify the reasons — I'm not that much of a movie-goer, I lack curiosity, I prefer reading, I'm fascinated by my studies, I have other things to do, the idleness of youth, I don't know what all — but I don't feel any shame or guilt about it. I'm used to gibes. Just think, I saw *Citizen Kane* for the first time last year!

Some of these late discoveries are interesting. You think you are going to verify megatons of superlatives, commentaries, interpretations, and nothing comes out quite the way you expected, that is, the way the cultural propaganda has conditioned you to expect. It wouldn't take much for us to be almost sorry to be disappointed, if a certain moral strength, a salutary impulse, did not keep us from these abysses.

Oh yes, I've had my doubts about the value of "cinema" for a long time. . .

On the other hand — and this is more or less true of everyone — I think I know a lot about Godard. Through hearsay. Through reading. Through seeing. Through the vulgate and the rumor mill. So-and-so knows So-and-so. His ex-assistant told me. . . Articles and synopses. Anecdotes and gossip. The media circus, TV, magazines, interviews, shows. . .

In short, I think I know a multitude of representations (which the principal party, it should be said in passing, manipulates with the hand of a master).

Why not? In titling his last opus *JLG/JLG* and maliciously piquing those two-initialed beings who might be jealous, he proves once again that if you are not to be the butt of the game, you'd better play. And play all-out.

For he says "JLG" the way they used to say "JFK" or "VGE," or "PPDA" or "BHL" today: acronyms that mimic the names of companies and institutions with all their notoriety, indices of personal quotes on the Stock Exchange of Spectacles, "singles," "hits," "products."

Suddenly, the acronym of his own name, here, seems like a trick. While meddling in the underwriters' game during the centenary of film ("Successors to Louis Gaumont)," he actually exposes what this ingenuous commemoration masks so well.

After all, wasn't he the only one to hammer home the fact that all this pomp was not to celebrate the anniversary of the invention of the camera, but the anniversary of the first paying projection?

So much for the state of the world.

And then we come to the bar between the two acronyms, "Jean-Luc Godard by Jean-Luc Godard," with a subtitle that is so immediately pictorial that it is already cinematic: *December Self-Portrait*. A whole program. And, consequently, the occasion of a very simple pleasure, a pleasure so singularly unlikely today that it would be a shame to deprive oneself of it.

Push open the door of a movie theater. Allow the darkness and silence slowly to erase the habits and Pavlovian apparatus — psychology, pathos, moralism, over-simplification, pseudo-adventures, sexual credulity, family neurosis, social neurosis, and so on. Observe the body of a man reflecting aloud. Listen to the meditative inflections of his so particular voice, nasal and metallic. Feel the living palpitations of a soul trapped inside its body — the soul tripping over its body, he says — his thoughts, his recollections, his hopes, his spiritual concerns. And see that, in the end, JLG definitely is not the same as Jean-Luc Godard.

Good news, all things considered.

Portrait of the Artist as a Screenwriter

JLG/JLG is short and dense. It's a film of mourning, loneliness, exile. A disillusioned film in which the poet *distills life in his heart*, and where Dostoyevsky, *who was born in autumn and died in winter*, passes through and passes through again to say that Europe is condemned to death, while an off-stage voice calls out, *Shut up, Cassandra...*

However, while it does not really amount to an assessment of a man or of an era, and relates the former's pessimism to the cruel sallies of the other, it does cast some light on the nature and the mortal future of the "seventh art," it raises questions as to whether a film can constitute a work of art, it responds to the challenges raised by literature, painting and music — those other arts which are neither numbered nor commemorated. ("You don't say, 'an old book,' when you are referring to Shakespeare or Virgil, do you? So why does one say, "an old movie'?" He bristled at this later, in an artificially candid moment, in another film entitled *Twice Fifty Years*).

So, here is a portrait of the artist as a screenwriter, of the man as an artist, and the screenwriter as a man, nothing but a man, struck one *fin de siècle* evening in his life by one burning question that he seems to be quite alone in wanting to face, to wit: Given that cinema is the quintessential art of the 20th century, what happened during that century that has inescapably affected us all?

Godard gives us his own voice offstage, uninterrupted, sometimes artificially reproduced by computer, intersected with scraps of dialogue and expanses of silence, spliced with other monologues, readings, aphorisms, and the titles of books, and punctuated from time to time by the dark tones of a quartet; he interweaves this with images on the screen, with a handwritten message scrawled on the pages of a grade-school notebook, with titles that are short, enigmatic and — let's not shy away from bad words — *metaphysical*, little scenes that are by turn facetious, serious, light, profound, humorous, emotional, worried, sly and nostalgic, questioning the writing of cinema in an orgy of words, where objectivity meets subjectivity, where poetry meets narrative. The soundtrack is polyphonic and *fugato*. Because it is important to support the notion that a truth expressed in cinema can by no means be proven by images alone. Because when the image and the sound coincide, the mental distancing is abolished that would permit one's own thoughts to take wing.
Because *things are not what they are said to be*. In other words, what you see is not what you are seeing.

But even though Godard gives us the history, the memory and the essence of thought, what passes for art in culture and merchandise, even though he mocks his own nihilistic questions about a Europe at the end of its rope by summarizing the painters' merry sensuality and the writers' stylized prophecies, let's not be misled; to him, in the great century-long trial, cinema has failed overall.

I wear mourning in anticipation of death, but death has not come, he says at the very beginning of the film, with a shot of his own photographic portrait from childhood, "little Jeannot," whose *catastrophic air* he emphasizes.

According to him, it was cinema's mission to analyze the 20th century, a century that preferred to confine it to other roles. "The art of our time," it should have spearheaded the historical investigation that time. For, like Debord in his excellent *Im girum imus nocte et consumimur igni* wrote, "It is a society, and not a technique, that made cinema the way it is. It could have been historical examination, theory, essay, memoirs. It could have been the film that I am making." And which Godard made, too, in *JLG/JLG*.

Montages

You want to see an example of how this works?
A page from the book, *Donner à voir*. Then the fluid pours out of Lake Geneva, its banks padded with snow. On location, the scenario writer is polishing up a few final phrases.
Culture is the rule. Exceptions are art. Everything emphasizes the rule, nobody mentions the exception. Then an interruption by another frame, *Ventôse* [the sixth month in the French Revolutionary calendar, February 20-March 21], followed by a still: a forest misted over with white frost, with the words: *The exception is never stated.*
Finally Godard, sitting in his office, pen in hand, buffing and polishing the final notes, sounding out the phrases, allowing the writing to be seen and heard as though he were scanning a verse, the flux and reflux of the body, pulsating immobility.

There is culture, which follows the rule, and there is the exception, which is art. Everything repeats the rule: computers, T-shirts, television. Nobody mentions the exception. It is not spoken. It is written (Flaubert, Dostoyevsky), or composed (Gershwin, Mozart); it is painted (Cézanne, Vermeer), or recorded (Antonioni, Vigo). Or it is seen, and then it is the art of living (Srebrenica, Mostar, Sarajevo). The rule inherently seeks to kill the exception.

(It's not out of the question, here, to think of Sollers' *Theory of Exceptions*, in which this can be read through the examples of Proust and Faulkner, and heard in Webern and Bach, and seen in Watteau and Rothko, but in which it does not, itself, have a place.)

A few minutes earlier, another frame had shown an empty room furnished only with a framed poster of *L'Avventura*, propped up on the floor in the dim light. A sober illustration of the theory that is stated much later on: *The image cannot be born from a comparison but only by bringing together two more or less distant realities. The more remote and the more right the relationship is between the two realities you are bringing together, the more powerful the image will be. Two realities which have no relation cannot usefully be brought together. No image is created and two contrary realities cannot be brought together; they oppose each other.*

Thus *JLG/JLG* is itself just an immense image, a *pure creation of the spirit.* Thanks to the great care taken with the montage. . . Which makes one sequence in the film particularly cruel: it shows Godard hiring a film editor who turns out to be blind!

Europe has memories, America has T-shirts, he jokes, not without a touch of seriousness.
The aphorism is not very good, but what follows is more edifying. "Those who run the movie world" disembark at Rolle and take an in-

ventory of the director's video cassettes. Sixteen racks of American films, two racks for the Germans, one for the Russians, another for the Italians, and a whole rack for Jean Renoir alone. Godard tries to highlight a few outstanding events of the century: the burglary of Mé-liès's New York offices during the Verdun offensive, the extermina-tion of Jews, Kristallnacht, the smoke and fog, the dark years of the 1930's when, across the Atlantic, the machine took over.

Trade follows films, the U.S. Congress declared in 1934. . .

Art ithout Innocence

There is no point in trying to systematize all the possible interpreta-tions that flow out of these continual juxtapositions of frames, texts, dialogues, sketches, and even paintings. For, in this self-portrait (which is not an autobiography and expressly says so), painting plays a central role. Painting, the crucial link in the history of viewing. Painting, at the origin of the image. Painting as anti-spectacle and anti-merchandise, in spite of its being culturally compromised, in spite of its fetishization in the new religion of art, in spite of its ersatz imagery. Painting discovered in the age of technology, not as it was primarily and originally intended, but in its replicas, its copies, its reproductions. Such as, for example, the *Portrait of Helene Fourment* by Rubens, posed on an easel, an instantaneous shortcut for something that would take us many sentences to express.

Slow scroll over a series of prints replicating mythical canvases, im-ages of female nudes, joyful flesh. The merry freedom of the bodies, the fundamental lightness of the paintings which are not images but mental constructs, emanations of thought, *cosi mentale*.

Courbet's *Woman in White Stockings*, Fragonard's *The Lock*, Manet, Re-noir, *Venus in the Mirror* by Velasquez, Boucher and Schiele, who are finally dismissed from the screen with a powerful sentence in which Godard gives vent to his Protestant Puritanism, after all: *"Tragedy in sexual relations is the truth of mankind."*

Can you make movies the same way you make a painting? He picks up that gauntlet, too. So he films empty spaces, the lake and its shores under every condition, the solitary footpaths, the landscape, the storm, white blankets of snow, *vistas of childhood and days gone by, with no one there.*

He is not filming nature as it is, but nature in its states of grace, states that he has patiently awaited in order to reconstruct it.

The pebbles and the dead leaves call to mind other pebbles, other leaves; thoughts turn toward Courbet, exiled to the banks of Lake Geneva after the Commune, and who, in the splendid excess of a sovereign vigor, as though his brushes had been plunged into the sap of life, painted everything: women's bodies, stones, harts in rut, mountains and waves, all part of a gigantic coitus involving nature in its entirety.

Then our thoughts turn again to the ingenious self-portraitist, for as this film plunges into the fluid layers of time, it constantly sparks correspondences, resonances, reminiscences. And then the mind oscillates between following the lesson and playing hooky, grasping and letting go, fixing and fleeting. It is as though the film represented the scenario writer himself, whom a voice is asking, Where do you live? and who answers: *in language.*

Want another example of a magnificent sequence of polysemous density?
The camera shows him dressed all in black, standing ankle-deep in

the lake. Back on shore, he takes a notebook out of his pocket and writes a few words, which we do not see. Voice off: "The spirit is strong only insofar as it squarely faces up to the negative, and stays with it." At this moment, Godard points his finger at the opposite side of the lake, and exclaims successively: "The Kingdom of France!," then "Beloved land, where are you, then?" The art of counterpoint. Verbal punctuation of images. Continuous recomposition of meanings. Pan to the books on a library shelf, where one sees Dante's *Hell* and *Purgatory*, but not *Paradise*.

(One may think of Joyce comparing *Ulysses* and *Finnegan's Wake* to the first two volumes of the *Divine Comedy*, the transposition of *Paradise* having become, according to him, impossible in the 20th century. And it is not out of the question, either, to think of Sollers' *Paradise*.)

Toward the end of the film, a message board is inserted that reads, "*The blank page is the true mirror of man,*" (in other words, cinema is not — it is not the reflection of a reality or an original truth but an art of pretence that lacks innocence). Then we hear, "*There is a land in the landscape, we are given a fatherland and we attain a fatherland, the positive was given to us at birth.*"

Here. Flashback to the nature scenes, subjective, emotional spaces. All is revealed about the problematic identity of the most French of Swiss screenwriters, the freedom achieved by successfully traversing the negative.

The Resurrection of Cinema

Is that the heart of the matter, as one frame suggests?

The art of our century, whose foundations were laid in the 19th, a child of technical and industrial development, cinema has gradually deteriorated, devolving more and more into nothing but spectacle, where the old distinction art/industry no longer obtains — part of the same trend that made technology's global domination the unreachable objective of our era.

"Modern science and the totalitarian state, while they are necessary consequences of the fundamental application of technology, also coincidentally constitute its continuation. And the same holds true for the management of worldwide public opinion and the day-to-day representations of men." Heidegger, "Why Poets," in *Roads That Lead Nowhere.*

Sein und Zeit, Roads That Lead Nowhere, all these frames sprinkled throughout *JLG/JLG* are like fleas in the ear. It takes a certain courage.

In another essay from *Roads*, "The Origin of the Work of Art," we read, "When the work of art itself stands up, then a whole world opens, where the work reigns forever." And also, "The question remains whether art still exists, or whether it is no longer an essential and necessary means of approaching the truth that decides our historial *Dasein*."

Having taken up the challenge of telling the story cinematographically, without any regard for chronology, of showing elements of his life that are actually un-showable and in-visible, by interweaving art and time (symbolized by a very beautiful sequence where, during a game of tennis, during a volley, he gets hit by the ball and declares, off screen: I get the same satisfaction from doing as from being done to), Godard does not lay down his weapons, he is buoyed by a hope which is also that of the resurrection of cinema.

As if the cinema only existed to invent its own death, for *art is like fire, it is born out of that which it burns.*

Isn't there anything up there?, a voice off asks, in the final sequences. As-sertions rather than questions, and yet . . . *If there is any truth in the mouth of the poets, I will live. I have said that I love; there is the promise.*

A still shot of round trees in the deep grass of a meadow, the sounds of an organ playing. . .

Death isn't what they say it is.

Cécile Guilbert

Yann Moix

Personal Messages

Coleman, Steve

Maurice Papon is a nice guy; Che Guevara isn't dead; Joan of Arc was a guy; Steve Coleman is not a genius: can writing, like mathematics, be absurd? Who cares; Coleman disproves every theorem. With him, in his music as in his conversation, everything comes straight from the source, from his mouth or his sax. The words that they fling at you are only a prelude to the notes; sentences, to the chorus. Baseball cap on backwards, he answers idiotic questions with diversions that are like the bridges that he delivers right in the middle of his solos, punctuated by "*man. . . .*" This is live, and his sweat *swings*. He perforates the waves with his alto, tracing rivers where Coleman swims the backstroke, and, in the hotel where the dead greats hang out, Parker is applauding. Steve Coleman, who is not impressed by any specter, improvises himself, changes the tempo when it becomes annoying, invents styles in midstream. He sketches everything out in real time, erases space itself, experiments, exploits a sound, tosses it away, brings it back and demolishes it. Coleman isn't just playing when he interprets. This is not jazz, it's not rap. It's not music. It's Steve Coleman. His signature is on every sound he makes. And when a comfortable melody settles in, he smashes it to pieces. This is a music of hematomas and traumas, that gets restless when it lasts too long, that trips itself up all by itself by being so aggravated, by anticipating too much. It's a music that catches itself by surprise. Jazz with pseudopods, taking over the ambiance and rewriting it in arpeggios. Once the concert or the disc is over, you always have the impression that Coleman's playing will go on all alone, without you. The Coleman sound barrier does not exist. Of course, one invents points of reference, for reassurance: we think of Zappa and the "Big Wazoo" era, or Éric Dolphy's great moments, at Pastorius. Coleman accepts these comparisons, without getting a swelled head: what he wants is to seek the truth. Like a physicist, he intends to utilize his art to re-transcribe reality. Blowing like a sick man into his instrument, that is the truth that he seeks, the truth as a revelation, the *alētheia*. All is fair in the attempt to achieve this impossible goal: exorcism through Afro-Cuban rhythms, Eastern philosophy, perfection, redemptive improvisation, reading the classics. And dance, which brings together all these impulses. On the stage, among the musicians, a dancer gyrates in a trance, giving body to sound. But what is incredible, with Coleman, it is that you always get the impression, with every piece, that he is telling us a story. All his compositions have a beginning, a middle and an end that feels like a denouement, a moral or a punch-line. And that is his genius: rather than giving us free-jazz or machine-rap or hysterico-blues, he narrates. Sometimes it's tales, sometimes it's news, or even jokes, fables; different things, casual anecdotes, musical criticism, film scenarios, poems in verse (free or not), prose. He is closer to Borges than to Miles Davis. He has a talent for using the right word, but musically. That is why we are never bored: we want to know what's going to happen. Are Steve Coleman's discs autobiographical? "I just play what I am," he says. For example, "I don't see myself anymore in my earlier recordings. . . I've moved on. I'm interested in the moment. Now." Coleman finds his inspiration in the vibrations of his body: his music is only the echo of his internal palpitations. All his albums are a snapshot of his life at one precise instant. The next to last one, *The Sign and the Seal*, is a masterpiece recorded in Havana with the percussionists from the group AfroCuba de Matanzas: jazz returning to its roots. Far from the asinine category of "world music," Coleman, with complete liberty, shows that musical genres do not meet but have always been interdependent, have always grown out of each other. "That is why I love to improvise; it's the only way to forget the categories and leave room only for the music in itself and for itself." For those who want to take Coleman at his word, they can now refer to the legendary triple album recorded at Hot Brass in 1995, by three different groups: Mystic Rhythm Society, the Metrics and Five Elements. Because of his continuous serendipity, his poetic power and his always unexpected rhythmic variations, this album is without any doubt one of ten greatest live jazz recordings of all time. But the year 1997 will also stand out in the Coleman annals, with the simultaneous release of *Genesis* — his first big band recording (25 musicians), with a new ensemble dubbed The Council of Balance (of which the pieces "Day Four" and "Day Seven" were hits) — and *The Opening of the Way*, the tenth album by his original group, Five Elements; the tracks "Law of Balance," "Wheel of Nature" and "Fortitude & Chaos" had a major impact. In just a few months, these opuses revitalized jazz like nothing else in the last thirty years. Not by falsifying it, commercializing it, or electrifying it, but, on the contrary, by stripping it bare, with all its eccentricities and its excesses, its arabesques and its brutalities, its variations and its memory, Coleman sets jazz free. Others, before him, tried to do it by wearing their jackets inside out. Steve Coleman just left his cap the way it landed, backwards. It was as simple as that.

Faulkner, William

With a coat of dried mud, some horse droppings, two pitchforks resting against the wall of a barn and a little straw, Faulkner succeeded in building a planet. It is full of silences, sun, criminals, idiots and incest. No one (except perhaps Gombrowicz) is his equal in weaving out of two uninteresting situations the questions that concern the entire universe. William Faulkner has a genius, that of the magnifying effect. Like ours, his world tends toward increasing entropy. Two stones in the road leading to the church, that's all it takes to set off riots, then chaos, then the Apocalypse.

Gide, Andre

Old Gide dusted off his felt hat, worn by the years, grumbled a few words that the Little Lady did not hear, carefully folded the letter into the inside pocket of his jacket, then slammed the door. The Vaneau neighborhood weighed on him, this Wednesday in November, where a cloudless sky met him at the foot of the stairs. On the sidewalk, greeting with a weary gesture the occasional passersby, neighbors or tradesmen who acknowledged him with a pleasant smile or some respectful courtesy, he made his way along, taking small steps, with the prudence of a cat on a high rooftop. No one thought to wish him a happy birthday. Probably because the man had, long since, ceased aging. Indeed, time no longer seemed to have the least influence on that immortal face, solidified by legend, engraved by now in the marble of posterity. Alone, all alone in an already extended old age, isolated from the world by an enormous stone wall built of reminiscences and the yellowed images that one calls "memory," the writer thus lived outside of time. To tell the truth, it's been said that he existed in relation to a frame of reference suited solely to him, measured by his *Journal*. Indeed, he seemed to be living out his œuvre, more than his life, as he made his way gingerly along that afternoon. The walk would surely appear one day, in all its most irritating details, on the smooth and glossy page of a volume published by Pleiades. Sometimes, he stopped for a few seconds, halted his laborious walking in order to appreciate the sounds of the street. Then he would drink in the noises and odors like a child discovering the forest. On Rue du Bac, he pulled out of his sleeve, like a magician, a little book with a frayed blue cover that accompanied him at every moment, and read a few excerpts out loud. He never went out anymore without Hugo, whose stature had always impressed him and who now seemed closer than ever, as the weight of age bore down. Oh! he could have declaimed these lines by heart, these verses so often sung and which had already delighted the heart of André Walter, in the shadows of his youth. But visual contact with the flesh of the written object, printed, still moved him and brought a spark to his weary old eyes that used to blaze like the thousand flames of hell. But what remained of the demon in this old gentleman with the mannerisms of a dandy, pitiful and maniacal, making his litigious way toward nowhere? What? A firebrand, this old man wrapped like a mummy in miles of wool and flannel, protecting himself from every draft the way one wards off death? Let's be serious. In Saint-Germain-des-Prés, he pretended to hunt for a few minutes for one specific work in the many piles of old books. But the wisdom of great age bade him make haste, for who knows whether he might not still have a chance, while skirting the quays of the Seine, to enjoy the spectacle of the sun setting over Notre-Dame. . . At rue Saint-André-des-Arts, two medical students recognized him and ventured, intimidated, practically on their knees, to praise the imperishable genius of this master of thought, whose most enthusiastic disciples they claimed to be. The scowl, somewhere between indifference and contempt, sketched by the author of their bedside reading marked the end of their puerile audacity and the beginning of a painful disappointment. Upset, the two fans went off to seek other topics for exegeses in the hustle and bustle of a nearby crowd.

"How strange is this world," thought the astonished writer, whom this bout of flattery (metamorphosed into irritation) had driven to observe something other than the slowness of his own footsteps on the pavement.

Strange? If the crumpled old Corydon had been in the habit of venturing more often into the mob of the Parisian streets, no doubt he would have foreseen how hopelessly banal it all was. The astonishment faded, and the old man continued to amble carefully down to the quays, panting as he trailed his weak shadow behind him, the way one drags along a burden.

The burden of writing. With a dense black ink, in a wandering, spidery scrawl, the writer still wrote every day. He'd get up early, and with the odors of night still covering his body with a dirty tar, he would grind out his prose; he wanted to force himself to come up with a few good morning thoughts, that he would painfully distill with his pen. He persuaded himself to produce something, in spite of everything, while he watched the falling rain. To be as relentless as the rain: that was the secret. The phrases, unfortunately quarantined in a grave and inescapable disease, remained frozen. He had no appetite for it anymore. He didn't feel like doing anything anymore, not reading, and still less writing: even Virgil had become an effort. The incomprehensible chasm of old age, this lassitude. The least comma exhausted him, as he snuggled in a small bedroom in deepest winter, searching for ideas. Grace, exhausted, was slipping away toward other, younger tumults. Only a useless and illusory past glory remained, faded and mildewed like an old sepia print, to legitimate in some vague way the foolish act of insisting on still writing.

Glory. He had known glory. These scenes that were coming out so poorly on the scrap paper thus would never be completely common, *Nobel oblige.*

Dead was the thirst to innovate. Broken, the creative force. Extinct, the magic. The words wouldn't turn into anything anymore but words. How sad were these inanimate sentences, inert as statues, without love, without hatred, without fruit. Doubt itself had been drowned, in the lugubrious gurgling of the shipwreck. Literature had sanctified him, and now it wanted his death. No sparks were firing anymore under the felt hat. His body of work seemed to be refusing with all its strength any late and futile addenda, any superfluous en-gagements with Words, pathetic and desperate fights, empty, vain, long since lost. Silence was winning. There was nothing left to do. The old man was witnessing, slowly, in the impotence of belated con-clusions, the death of his own writing. He was following the weary funeral procession of his own thought. It was as if one of his limbs was rotting in the deaf indifference of the rest of his body. Gide was burying Gide, without witnesses and without prayer, in the sick mu-sic of a crumpled morning. Why insist on making these calligraphic marks in the notebook? The last dot, the last sentence of what pos-terity would consider his Œuvre, were already far, far behind, so terri-bly far that the decrepit old adolescent was prodding himself for nothing, his thin hands fumbling over a prose that was mortally wounded, his stubborn, obstinate hands, curved as though with gan-grene or tumors, like a paralyzed flourish of one final cramp. Old Gide was writing in death, writing to death itself, among the granite and the marble, the crowns and eternity, under the gray and sunken clarity, bruised by the end of the waves of dawn. Old Gide was writ-ing under the misty and steady rain, his fingers stiff in the morning chill, frozen like the mast of a ship caught in the polar ice. Old Gide was running on empty, his gaze contorted by age, his pace wobbly. And the endless rain pummeled the roofs, crackling like the keys of a typewriter full of inspiration and promises.

Goldman, Pierre

Pierre Goldman is my yellow star. I wear it in my heart, folded shut like a mouth that does not denounce. He made me a Jew. A Jew to the point of having courage before the fallibility of justice, and a Jew to the point of a phobia of posthumous Fascisms. He was a war-rior of the ideal, and now he is nothing but attenuated dust. Misun-derstandings pile up, like the heedless years, on his poor tomb.

Che Guevara became a legend, first in a specific location, then

everywhere; Goldman is just the embodiment of some vague miscar-
riage of justice faded by time, like the flash of a revolution that never
took place. So am I the only one, of those in our thirties, to survey
Pigalle, evenings, in his memory? How many of us spend our evenings
at home, reading and rereading, since adolescence, the *Obscure Memoirs
of a Polish Jew Born in France*? I can still see the incredulous face of his
friend Yves Janin's muse, when she heard me answer him six years
ago that the one person in the world that I would most like to meet
was named Pierre Goldman. I never made him an icon, which he
would not have tolerated, but the wild claws of insubordination incarnate. Not an insubordination of principle, theoretical, intellectual-
ized, but a physical insubordination, a little bit swaggering, something like the *guérillero* hugging his bazooka in the night. On the contrary, what is attractive about Goldman is the contradiction between
the appeal of the group and the desire to be alone. To be Jewish, for
him, is to be heir to a loneliness that carries along all its sufferings,
and the memory of the Shoah. To follow Goldman would not make
sense: his life remains forever inimitable, for Goldman did not live.
Pierre Goldman's obsession was to transform his life into destiny. In
other words: to make his death a masterpiece. His entire existence
led up to a magnificent end that, like a bolt of lightning, would justify
the years of wandering and everything else. Dying is a rite of passage
by which life can finally, retrospectively, be given reality. Every one
of Goldman's actions, whether we are talking about an antifascist
demonstration at the Sorbonne accompanied by the "katangais" or
marching through the Venezuelan jungle to quote Lenin, carried
within it the obsessive *telos* that gnawed his daily existence: death
would make sense of that magma of errors and pathways that make
up life. Then, relentlessly, he would seek (sometimes to the point of
the ridiculous) an apotheosis whose fulguration, far from elevating
him to the mythical status of a hero for armed youths, would cleanse
him of the unbearable stain of having been. However, to live outside
of oneself, to scorn the rules of society, to refuse any other morals that

one's own impulses, is to increase one's chances of coming to a singular demise. A farewell proportional to one's excesses. Thus, Pierre Goldman did not live. Rather, he embodied being. A Heideggerian "being for death," seeking at all costs to extract himself from himself, to become pure freedom. He is not an intellectual, but a body. A body moving at full speed which seeks its legend throughout its time, and causes it the way one gives birth to an idea. Goldman is a writer who wrote himself, using himself. His fists were his pen and the days of his life were the blank page. Anguish is there, persistent and full of arrogance: time must be filled.

In those explosive years, there was no lack of causes: Goldman kept his body busy visiting communist cells, with the UEC, supporting Algerian independence and, during the Assas sorties, busting fascists' heads with a crowbar. His own philosophical background was meager and, fundamentally, he wasn't much interested in politics. What was he looking for? What did he want? Nobody knows, including him, himself. He quoted Kant at the drop of a hat; but he is Kant. He became everything that he touched, embodied himself in the concepts, and he who was obsessed with time ended up becoming his time. That is why the crime of which he is accused — the assassination of a pharmacist, on Richard-Lenoir boulevard, in 1969 — was only a pretext to allow one era (that of the Giscardian liberal democracy) to sit in judgment on another, and the bastard to which it had given birth: Lenin-Marxist anarchy. Society, via Goldman, was removing a blemish, that of the years of the radical Left and the years of protest. To allow the new skin to form, it had to wash away its own bad memories. When it comes to Vichy, France chooses amnesia, protects the miscreants, and takes forty years to bring its lawsuit. When it comes to May '68, it dispatches the case in a few weeks, and chooses made-to-measure scapegoats. Goldman seems the most luminous, the most natural, the most obvious of them. His paramilitary excursions to Venezuela, his equivocal friends, his nights of Cuban drumming, his life as a dropout and, especially, his contempt of positive law, made him a peerless outlaw. The powers that be would use him to heal the traumas of the explosive years, when they hesitated. Goldman the Jew, at heart, aspired with all his force to that and nothing more, to that culpability emanating from the source, that absurd judgment, whose arbitrariness and violence linked him to the destiny of his accursed People. He deserved to pay the price of another's crime, because the existence a being such as he cannot make sense. There is no sense, since the Shoah. The only thing to be done is to pay. For everything. For everyone. Justice, injustice, these have no meaning when all values, all justices were left in Auschwitz. Legal, illegal, these have no meaning when you know that once upon a time the law was marked with the seal of the swastika. Guilty? But what does that word mean? "I am innocent *because* I am innocent," was Goldman's defense at the time of the trial. He was Goldman because he was Goldman. The only way to understand him was to be him. To plagiarize Lacan (whom he hated), we might say of Pierre Goldman, whose short life was a slip: never will he be made a Master. Neither today nor tomorrow.

Gombrowicz, Witold

If Witold Gombrowicz and Marcel Proust are the two greatest novelists of the 20th century, they also appear to be the two greatest specialists in jealousy of all times. *Ferdydurke* is not, as has too often been written, an early *Nausea*, but a late *On the Side of Swann*. Marcel and Witold (what a great title for a comparative essay, which has yet to be written) both know how to play metaphysics on decency and emotions, but they approach it differently. Where Proust sweeps across the entire landscape, like a Breton lighthouse arcing across the open water, Gombrowicz focuses on just one side of reality, leaving the rest in the shade. Proust takes everything back to square one, and gives us the whole story, whereas Gombrowicz picks up the narration along the way; that is, his novels start well before Page 1, but we will have not access to this "beginning," quite simply because the author did not consider it necessary to write it. Witoldo, his friends from Buenos Aires called him (he spent 24 years there, in exile — and I'd like to take this occasion to offer a toast to the memory of Mariano Betelu) — Witoldo's books are already in motion, and you have to catch them the way you jump onto a train that is already leaving the platform. "Without us:" that is the key sentence of these two monsters, Gombrowicz and Proust. Admittedly, no one knew better than they how to describe the vagaries of the human heart, its perversions, its pains, its bizarrities, its impulses and its dramas (in short, we find ourselves perfectly represented, as human beings, in their respective universes). At the same time, for us readers, these are literatures from which we are pitilessly excluded. What does Proust care about those who are "hors-sujet" (a meaningless expression used only by academics); he isn't afraid of being annoying, the question never comes up in those terms: he says what he has to say, and that is all. What difference does it make to Gombrowicz if we find ourselves in a sun-filled plain in the middle of an imaginary Poland, with birds hanging from the trees or with arrows painted on the kitchen ceiling: if the reader doesn't like it, he can always use the door — this universe will go on without him. Not the least effort, therefore, from either one of the two geniuses, to take anyone by the hand, to lead the narrative "in the style of" anyone. Nope: they invent, they invent themselves with every line, it is "keep walking or drop dead," and, in extreme cases, they do it not to be read but to have written for another day. I realize that, in life, things are more complicated: Gombrowicz and Proust would have liked to be read by the greatest possible number of readers. What I want to say is that this statistic, however imposing it may have been, never altered their style. Ultra-sensitive beings are the last ones who would cheat themselves.

Hala

Charles de Cuffin, a Picardy monk and brother of Luc the Dreadful, was terribly ugly, loved a thousand women and did us the favor of recounting for us the tale of the crusades. His chronicle breathes of the sand stained by the cold blood of men. In particular, his narration of the Franks' capture of Jerusalem is even better than Guillaume de Tyr's. But it is as Godefroy de Bouillon's historian that the centuries have chosen to remember him. His is *Piété de messire Godefroy, duc de Basse-Lotharingie et serviteur de Dieu* (1099) begins as follows. "The humble soldier of Christ, paragon of all Christian virtues, the model of temerity, departed for the Holy City, fatherland of the clouds, when forty winters had registered themselves in the lines of his great and worthy face. He was born intrepid, like his father, the impetuous count Eustace of Boulogne, and as soon as he was able to answer the villain's affront, he achieved the glory that attaches to the Carolingian lineage that his ardor would continue to trace, like the signature of courage, toward the stars of heaven. His name was Godefroy de Bouillon, named for the country of Bouillon, and his good fortune was to lived to the age of ten in France, and his misfortune was to be orphaned in Belgium. But the death of the father also made the child heir to the county of Verdun and certain other rich lands of obstinate roots. The scene was prepared for the legend. His legend was his life, for Godefroy was a hero."

It wasn't until the end of the French mandate in Syria, in 1946, that the efforts of the Reverend Father Estrada, of the University of Buenos Aires (where he also tried, in vain, to publicize and then to translate Gombrowicz's works) were made public with the full accord of the Institute of Christian Studies in Damascus. Based on written documents found during the great excavations of 1929-1930 at the Krak des Chevaliers, which I was able to consult this summer, the study entitled *Sketch of a biography of Godefroi de Bouillon* confirms that upon the death of his uncle Godefroi the Lame, young Godefroi, sixteen years old, accepted the marquisat of Antwerp, the duchy of Basse-Lotharingie. Later, from the top of a tower that looked out over the tall grasses, Pope Urbain II had exclaimed:

"It is God's wish!"

Superb and mitered, he invoked the cruelty of the Turks and the impatience of Christ. His finger pointed toward Jerusalem.

"And I exhort you," he continued, "and I beg you" (at this moment three crows passed overhead) "to persuade everyone, whatever his position in society may be — knight or pedestrian, rich or poor — by your frequent preachings, to go and help the Christians and to repel these noxious people far from our territories" (applause).

At an international conference held in Clermont, in June 1978, on the very scene of that speech, the American historian Warren Bozzio (University of Seattle) created a scandal by reconsidering the origin of the crusades. Let's get it out on the table immediately: for him, Hala Basha was the sole cause. One of my lecturers at Sciences Po had studied under Bozzio. I questioned him about this West Coast troublemaker who, in just one summer, had overturned nearly 900 years of research. George Duby answered with a series of virulent articles in *Le Monde*, where he called for the "condemnation of the sacrilegious theses of an apprentice researcher who, to establish a reputation that his intellect alone would not have allowed, was quick to set himself up as the archpriest of any oddball theory, tossing together the foundations of a new revisionist school of medieval history." What, actually, was Bozzio's thesis? A January 1979 interview granted by the author of *The Hidden Causes of the Crusades* to the Belgian magazine *Thucydide* will allow reader to grasp it in its broad outline.

Thucydide: "Can you remind us, very briefly, in what context Pope Urbain II called for the crusade?"

Warren Bozzio: "Urbain II — who, as I recall, came from the nobility and became a monk in the abbey of Cluny before becoming archdeacon in Rheims — Urbain II launched his appeal, a kind of June 18 appeal before the fact, at a time when there was a harsh competition underway between the power of the princes and the papacy. I point out to my detractors, from the start, that such a context does not in any way impinge upon the cogency of my recent work. But, I will come back to that. . ."

Thucydide: "What measures were actually taken at Clermont?"

Warren Bozzio: "I believe that, on this point, most historians are in complete agreement. The first measure was the confirmation of the excommunication of Philippe I, who was reproached for having forsaken the magnificent Berthe of Holland in favor of the lower Bertrade de Montfort, whom he ended up marrying. But, what do you want: that's how life goes, and the history of man is full of this kind of oddity. But it should be known that it was to find young Hala Ibrahim Basha that all this circus was set up. I explain all that in my books."

Hemingway, Ernest

Hemingway should be read in the forest. His books let silence speak. His body of work stupidly has been seen as a virile universe saturated with machine-guns, deer, wounds, a life of isolation on a boat, and badges of honor. Nabokov summed it up as follows: "Bulls, bells, balls." True, he liked the trail, courage, sweat. There are at least two kinds of writers: those who exaggerate their existence, to re-transcribe it calmly; and those who exaggerate their writing, to live in peace. Hemingway belongs to neither one: he didn't exaggerate anything. His fears, his many deaths, his cancers and the holes in his flesh, he lived them without showing off, he described that calm voice that confers on his writing a poetic serenity that is too often mistaken for chauvinist arrogance. However, turning the pages of his masterpieces (he wrote almost exclusively masterpieces, but *Beyond the River and Under the Trees* is even greater than the others), one realizes that he was as interested in foliage as in wars, and that no one but he could have flushed out the metaphysical dimension of a squirrel crouching under a rock, or the salty taste of women's lips in the night, during a battle. Hemingway is sentimental, he's squeamish, a hypersensitive lily-liver who does himself violence by seeking out violence. No war could break out without his dashing off to take a hit, get a wound, take on some suffering. But he would be better symbolized by a fishing rod than by a rifle. His style slips by under the water, like the black bass or the swordfish. Translucent, rather than transparent. You have to go and look for it, bring it out. It hides and wavers, it never bites immediately. This way of placing prose on paper shows a hint of the extreme patience of people of the open sea.

Houria

You don't love me anymore. I know. There's nothing to do about it. I am worn out, for you. All used up. There's no more flesh on my carcass, nothing more to tear off and chew. Bones. And you're not going to gnaw on bones. You've left me all alone. I'm so upset. Walking the streets, going to the movies, visiting a bookshop, getting a plane ticket for La Paz, nothing is fun when you're not there. And you're not there, anymore. You aren't there anymore, ever. Never. I don't see your body anymore moving from one room to another, getting into a taxi, stepping out through the front door. I am orphaned by all those gestures of yours. I cannot believe that it's really over. That I will never see these gestures again. I won't see your white teeth. I won't see you smile anymore. I know that we can see each other again. That's not a problem. All I have to do is dial your telephone number and be nice with you, a little bit funny, act like a man who is comfortable, detached, happy, a man who has another little friend; and I know, I know that it is okay, that you will agree to come to my empty apartment for breakfast. We've already done it. You brought croissants. Lots of croissants. I had a photographer come over, that day. I wanted him to take pictures of us. Of us as a couple that no longer existed. But, in my eyes, a photograph of the two of us was a way of still believing, of making me believe that your return was implicit, since it was officialized on film. The more so, since you were smiling in the photograph. You looked happy. Yes, happy. It was only afterward that I realized that something wasn't right, when you never asked how the pictures turned out; you weren't interested in the result at all. Moreover, the day you did see them, a few weeks later, you didn't think they were good. It's signs like that that show that love has died. I don't like it when you don't love me anymore, because you don't even remember having loved me. That feeling, experienced in the past, has become completely foreign to you. As if another had been with me during all that time and you, you had come to life again after she had finished her work. Hard work — for I know, Houria, that loving me was no picnic.

It's not that I'm sad every day. There are even entire weeks when everything seems fine. But it doesn't last. You always come back. Not to haunt me, but to live within me. Now I know that I would really like to have you at my side, for a long time, for life. And I bless the time that existed and that I cannot get over, when you wanted to go everywhere with me, and you even wanted me to hold your hand, whether we were going a long way or not far, no matter, you just adored being with me. Such a time existed. And because it did, of course, I did not love you. I took your love as my due. It seemed such a little thing. It was normal, perfectly normal, that a princess should hang on the arm of a novelist stinking with talent. Talent? Genius, you mean. For in that period of my existence, anybody who attributed only talent to me would have gotten my genius fist right in his mouth. I was a funny guy, a funny little shit. That was barely two years ago. I wanted them all, the princesses. One Houria, that was not enough for me. I was not about to restrict my pure genius to just one woman. The others should have the benefit of it, as well. Today, I don't brag anymore, my Houria. And look at my writing, which doesn't brag anymore, either. See these flat sentences, without sparkle, almost timid. Everything was set for things to go well for us. All we had to do was to meet. And we did meet. That was the hardest part, meeting (as proof: I've never met you again by chance, since then). The rest happened naturally. And it was the easiest part that we were unable to make succeed. And it's my fault, my fault alone. Because I am an intolerable jerk who destroys everything he is given. Because I am sick. I couldn't stop being mean to you, in the beginning. Pathetic little pranks, the kind that sick people like me can come up with, in their twisted little minds. It was enough for some hussy to leave an ambiguous message on my answering machine, and I would listen to it three, four, five times in front of you, going as far as to ask you to decipher the end of a supposedly inaudible sentence. I remember your dignity in those cases. You didn't carry on. You didn't say anything. But, in my bathroom mirror, your beautiful face, created to smile, would dissolve in offense. My neurosis damaged your beauty. Why I did do that, Houria? Because I am sick is not an answer. It is an explanation, but not an answer. I did that because I did that. A kind of monster, that I still have trouble controlling today, wanted to vomit out of me, to splash you. It lodges in my body. I know it is still there, running through my veins, giving me unbearable migraines. It is a creature with claws, it's malicious, and it doesn't feel good. It brings out its claws when I am happy. It dances when I sleep. And it destroys everything if I am happy. That is why you left. Because of this ménage à trois. It is because of its mouth full of thorns that I will never again hold you in my arms. Never.

After you left me, you tried, briefly, punctually, to conduct a test with me. You didn't say so, but I felt clearly that you had come to verify whether you had made a mistake in going away. I know that those who leave are unhappy too; and that, in both cases, mourning must take place. Being the one who leaves is hardly any more fun, any easier, any more comfortable, than being the one who is left. Even those tests, I blew them. Because it must have sensed, for a few seconds, that you would come back, the creature came to dance again.

When you came over, last year, it rained all the time. My apartment was empty and cold. November was lugubrious. Wednesday, we took your son to the movies to see Walt Disney. When we came out, it was dark and cold. We went down into the subway, at Clichy. We made the none too pleasant connection at Pigalle, then we arrived at Jules-Joffrin. Once we made it to rue Championnet, soaked, we only had to get upstairs for a hot chocolate. Then I deployed all the tricks of a Sioux to get you to agree to stay for dinner. It was like moving walls. Sometimes, you said yes and I had the impression that I might have won the day. And then, you set out again for Saint-Denis, behind the wheel of your big car. And you didn't think of me anymore.

I haven't changed: I only talk about myself. But I must go and get treatment. I promised you I would. By the time you receive this letter, I will already have been in treatment for a little while. I will be better, for sure. In any case, I have to get better to write real books. Real books are those that one does not feel obliged to dedicate to a woman. I dedicated my second book to you, *Cemeteries are Fields of Flowers*. I wrote that book only at night, after you would leave in your big car. At night, at home, I was cold, and I'd put on a sweater. I was hungry, and I didn't have anything to eat. I would chomp on a pickle. I would finish the leftovers that I didn't want.

Jackson, Michael

What is incredible about Michael Jackson is that he doesn't see his work as a totality, as the collection of all his recordings. No: for him, his work is always his latest album. It is there that he refines, that he extends, that he constantly updates what existed already — and he does the same thing with his physical appearance, through finishing touches, constant improvements. He accelerates the rhythms, and seasons them with techno. Jackson is like the weather report of music: he comes along every hour, on the hour.

Every one of his hits is a telegram, live. He doesn't follow fashion and he doesn't invent it. He is inside it, at the center of gravity. The old stuff, for him, is there only as the basis for endlessly making something new. Nothing is fixed. All of Jackson is always bound up in the last riff that embodies the three decades of his career since the Jackson Five — the rest is nothing but a draft, a throwaway, of what is yet to come, of "the authorized version." Jackson is considered to be the worst of megalomaniacs, but at the same time we have proof of his complete artistic humility, which makes the artist constantly say, "I can do better; next time will be the good one." And so, it is not surprising that his last album, *Bambi*, is primarily made up of "re-mixes" of the preceding album, *History*. And it is a masterpiece, like everything that Jackson has done or will do, Jackson, who will never be dethroned.

No pathetic scandal will ever damage him. He is unprofanable in perpetuity. Like *Bambi*, Jackson excites his fans because he never exhausts his dream. Twenty years ago, he was already there. Twenty years from now, he will still be there. His air pollution phobia is easily explained: his natural element is sound. He breathes only to sing. Anything that is not rhythm gives him asthma. It is lifelessness that he fears, the calm, the flat, silence, death. That is all explained in his albums, which are powerful and beautiful works, and which will testify, with those of Einstein and Picasso, over our century, which one day will be a century of ancestors. There is no Jackson "sound" or "style," no Jackson "era." There is a Jackson eternity. Until tomorrow.

Jarry, Alfred

The dawn is sowing its blue drops of liqueur, the air is frigid. The white frost is the ash left by the sleepless night as its embers die out. The sky grows hollow like cheeks: the day is hungry. A figure erases the street with drunken zigzags on its bicycle. A lock of dark hair whips the absent eyes of the bloated clown. He tears the fog into ribbons that wave above his shoulders, like standards flying on the prow of a drunken ship. The clouds smell of ether and absinth. Alfred Jarry is going home. In the light that accompanies him back to his own skin, sick winds whirl and are swallowed by the patched-together lining of his jacket. He pedals, and the pedals squeak. Sometimes the projectile skids, and he falls like a stone on the pavement: frost and blood mingle in a candy-pink lacquer with the chips of pearly ice. He trails behind him a locomotive vapor: it is his breath, swirling through the currents of air. A doped automaton, he pedals standing up, never touching the grungy leather seat. He is a thin, mechanical knife, cutting through the waves. His movements are like scattered theorems. He has parked the bicycle in the small courtyard. He is cold. He is naked under the bicycle jacket; his underpants, held up by an old piece of string because they slip down over his skinny torso, are in tatters. The left big toe, whose yellow nail is broken, cuts through an ash-gray slipper. It is five o'clock in the morning. In the lugubrious and icy room, skeletons and old dictionaries are piled up. Corpses of bottles lie about; it is a cemetery of glass. Next to the rumpled old bed, on the night table, sleeps a gun. It used to belong to a captain of the colonial troops. Grimacing puppets dance on the walls. Achras and Guignol, like figures of Christ. The floor is strewn with unfinished newspapers, and drawings. Flowers droop on the table and lichen fades on the ceiling. Everything is shimmering in a vague violet half-light, fluttered by chilly drafts. With a kind of haggard indifference, Ubu Père pours a bit of absinth into a cracked cup, mixes it with a little vinegar and brings it up to his moustache. He adds a drop of ink. And now, very gently, he will fade into a momentary death full of childhood, the sleep of harlequins.

His dreams are like a great sadness, like a giant tear drowning his entire being. His sleep encrusts him in Dürer's engravings. He roves from pillar to post, in his Gothic imagination. Where the dreams intersect, here is Caesar, the Antichrist, mute on the wind-blown pinnacles. Escaped from their stained glass, tall, pale angels with swords blow their ivory hunting horns. It is Cologne and Burgos, it is Rheims and Bamberg in ruffled robes. He feels his way across the enamels and bumps into the alabaster altar. Griffons howl, flapping the green wings of the dragon perched on a knob of rock. Saint Joan takes him in hand, lifting him through the vaulted nave all shot with pink and green reflections. Haldernablou deposits an arrow at the foot of the bed. Look! He grimaces and groans. A nightmare, of course: his dying voice cries out, but he is short of breath and wakes up. Hundreds of wraiths surround him, wailing, dancing. His mouth is a gargoyle's.

Mitterrand, François

The first time François Mitterrand died, it was for France, shot in the shoulder while picking wild strawberries, June 14, 1940. But youth has no memory of the wars: it sits on the scars and prefers the sensualist present to the mud pits of history. The splendid, recumbent body of Lieutenant Péguy, in the night at Villeroy? Forgotten by the rappers and the RM-ists, whose new St. Joan, teaser of all the butchers, goes by the name of Vanessa. Except at Saint-Cyr Military Academy, where they try to look older while trampling through the mud, youth no longer burnishes the anguish of the military with any sense of glory. To become eternal, François Mitterrand was going to have to take a different path, far from the trenches, far from the laced-up boots. Death has its whims: whereas, for James Dean and Jim Morrison, all it took was three films and two ditties to weave a legend, it required of Mitterrand fifty years of bruises, campaigns, speeches and dossiers. Apparently, posterity prefers longevity. But is the Mitterrand generation ready to punish Tonton on the altar of its admiration? For us, "the youth of France," as Malraux put it, Mitterrand was never anything *but* president. We were born into his Elyséen omnipotence. We never knew him as anything but moving, his gestures planned to the millimeter, in the fabulous tradition of gilt and marble. Shaped by the institutions. Draped in the standard of the Republic. Impossible, for our new skulls, to picture the poet in the stalag, in flannel waistcoat and greasy hair, enamored of Barrès and of lightning, deploying his rural prose to allure a blonde who did not like him. Impossible, in the mysterious gallery which is history, to associate the hussar and *l'Observatoire*, which launched his destiny while risking it at the same time. A phantom, still, that pit-bull candidate of 1965, who plucked the stars from the General's cap while biting France in the ankle. How distant, finally, is the rose-carrying figure from Épinay, putschist and greedy for the future.

For a long time, France had a certain idea of Mitterrand. Don Juan plus Machiavelli. But we, little jerks, never saw anyone but the Prince. A knight, François? Oh no, a short bald guy with crooked teeth and a round hat, speaking the word of God. Some guy who sat and said his prayers. A chief of the armed forces, who took planes. A monarch in all his State. He was our de Gaulle. Power obscures flashes of brilliance the same way that it dims the glories of youth. Still. . . still, you could still sense the *condottiere* in him. He was our de Gaulle, but less of a martinet. Our monarch, but only sort of. More at ease in the autumn morning addressing a Piney from the Landes as *tu* than, in the winter of his life, becoming an oak to be felled. He was happier with a cap pulled onto his head and tapping his way over the rocks with a walking stick than sniffing out, under a Louis-Philippe chandelier, the humors of an interest rate. More alive in front of the hearth, playing firebrand and resuscitating Chardonne, than supervising wars over the palace teleprompters. And that is basically why we, the youth of France, ended up liking him. There was a lot that we did not understand, in his socialist evolution: Stalinists in the government, Mauroy as copilot, the budget deficit, weapons in Iraq, colonial paternalism, Greenpeace, weapons in Iran, Pelat, wiretapping. . . the black rose also grows from panache, as the last gardeners of this contradiction-ridden Eden will say. You see all these crooked and crisscrossing furrows; in the final analysis, they don't delineate any certain path toward tomorrow.

New York City

Every time I get that annoying, persistent urge to give up on Paris and head for New York, I try to resist it by persuading myself that it is only a fad, a quasi-obligatory whim among the trendy crowd at Flore or the ridiculous writers at La Coupole, a fake desire, bordering on the pathetic, and that, actually, a week at Nevers would do me more good. And then, do you let go of the pediment and dash yourself to pieces on the sidewalk, do you give up possible bronchial pneumonia from the ambient pollution in exchange for the probability of aggravated pleurisy? Do you stop being a number in order to lose yourself in the multitude, extract yourself from the multitude to merge with the infinite? Upon reflection: no. Especially since New York, contrary to popular (and particularly snob) opinion, in spite of its Twin Towers, only comes up to the ankle of Chicago, world capital of live music.

However, just as a chess player or a neurotic lover can expect nothing from his passions but a flood of ever-increasing difficulties, what I seek in New York is a higher stage of the city, a more complete, more advanced avatar, a version that is unthinkable in Paris. I always have the impression, landing at JFK Airport, that I'm moving into a higher class. What I like about New York is that it is Paris under acceleration. A city is a speed. New York is an acceleration: it is the second derivative of the modern city. New York doesn't move, in the sense that a metropolis can be said to be dynamic or animated; its frame of reference is not repose, like Madrid's, London's or Berlin's: it is self-driven. New York has gone beyond the stage of movement, it is the movement of movement. Like the skyscrapers, time is elevated, but exponentially: while things advance, in Paris, in New York time progresses. Not in the uniform flow filled by the aggregation of human activities, but in a dynamic form, which self-sculpts by secreting its own intelligence, its intrinsic artistic, political and economic conscience: time becomes its own matter, it is always changing, always adapting to the space that it carries along in its heterogeneous course that is made up of a series of jolts and sudden starts, but it ignores or even erases its idiocies later on (or never), the detours and pauses that built Europe. It is a special time, a time that never sleeps; it doesn't expand but rather twists, coils up, bursts forth, makes its revolution, trips up, sometimes, slips and skids, a time that embodies itself in men and matter only to pull itself out again at once, a time-coitus that dies and revives, to reappear, to make a flashback cleansed of its stains (that is, freed from its restraints) and becomes again what it was, and is, only better. Currency? Time, data-interchange time and cellular time, electronic time and real time. It's no longer "Time is money," but "Money is time." If, for fun, we arbitrarily associated time as it flows in France with the color blue, in New York you would have to define the New York-ese equivalent, the language of cobalt, azure, and indigo; and to push the alphabet of nuances further, you would have currents of sea-green and jade, periwinkle and turquoise. New York is a city from another time. I mean "of a *different* time," which the artist might need, who knows, in order to move ahead with his intimate matter. They say that New York is the city of the future, but that's not quite right: it is the city of the total present, but of a present from which it rips itself away as a fox tears itself out of the iron jaws of a trap, even if he has to leave a bloody piece of his leg behind. Abolishing its own history, forgetting itself to some extent, certainly that is what gives time its upward speed, but who knows whether, in its arrogant and superior blaze, it will not smash into the stone of an ancient solar clock, which, breaking its ascent, will give its youth a little of the weight of the memory of older nations.

Pasolini, Pier Paolo

Pasolini's films are perfect. They are naked (desert, dust, rock). The bodies are very static, the faces pure or dreadful. It is a work of waiting; he creates waiting: that is the essence. Intellectuals, alas! grabbed onto Pasolini in an effort to make him into something or other: a martyr, a politician or, worse, a poet. Whereas Pasolini, quite simply, is the greatest scenario writer in the world.

Proust, Marcel

He is unbeatable and absolute. He is to literature what the speed of light is to physics. One may take after him, at best. *Remembrance of Things Past* is an asymptotic work. Everything that has been said and written about it (whether apt or idiotic) adds nothing, takes nothing away, and does not exist.

Coming Back

It is in autumn that the year begins, on the school calendar where our seasons are named for sweethearts sleeping in the depths of time. The scent of their auburn hair mingles with that of the falling leaves and new erasers. Their traces on the ground are like ink spots on a blotter. But the girls have disappeared; fickle, they don't play hopscotch or jump-rope anymore in the yard. They were young and knew us when we were still in shorts; now they're raising children of their own, who, in their turn, know the smell of pencils and the wet sound of the sponge on the blackboard when the arithmetic lesson is being erased. Autumn is the season for remembering girls whose skin is now creased by time. Women whose faces and knees we would no longer recognize, and who, before another summer is over, will perhaps become wives. We've grown up. But, all our life, we will come across phantoms of women we've loved, whose eyes will never again meet ours. I write my books with chalk, on a schoolboy's board whose texture and sounds my hands know so well. I draw all my loves from yesterday, the great ones, and the others, whom I also remember. That's it: dead leaves and dead loves. This is why I prefer the autumnal melancholy to the languor of summers that stretch, crushed by the sun and by boredom. Autumn, that is our history coming back. The laughter that is gone. It is the awakening of vocations, coming to claim their destiny, the violent arrival of the looked-for futures, the promise of possible loves. It is an incredibly white page, to be filled by fountain pen, with titles to be underlined, margins to be respected. Autumn is the real place for severe, final, unshakeable resolutions. The others have had two months to forget that we exist: we will multiply our existence by two, by ten, to show them who is the hero of the new year. Vacation was a vacation, for them; for us it was an epic, a saga, an adventure that transformed us. We are ready to face grimaces, lies, pains and winter. We are ready to read all the books, to see all the movies, to listen to all the records. And then we'll be back to the same old stories, and lassitude, and we'll be afraid that the year is going to turn out the same as the last one, with the same gallery of fools, the same standards and the procession of unfailing stars. Then, we will start dreaming of the same islands, we'll repeat the same sentences to the same friends, we'll make the same hypotheses about the same subjects, we'll walk with the same pace through the street, we'll hate the same films, we'll be heartbroken over the same love, we'll wear the same clothes, we'll make the same mistakes, and only our age will have changed a little. In the gusts of autumn wind, when the air has lost the scent of new notebooks and the caps of our pens will already be chewed, then we'll decide to write a book to say "I love you" to the woman in our life, who will probably be named Eve. With her, for her, we will remake the world, writing marital rhymes, evoking the yesteryear of desks and geography maps yellowed by the sun of days long since dead. We will return, hand in hand, to the playground. In the corridor, by the coat racks, we will kiss for the first time. We will draw the past with big colored markers. We will trace enormous and ridiculous hearts. We will make spectacular spelling mistakes. We will recite poems by René-Guy Cadou and Jean Moréas. We will collect beech leaves in the forest. We will have, in all our stupidity, the future before us.

Suarès, André

His failures did not ruin him. The abused child of the Republic of Letters, he lived out his glory in the broom cupboard of the NRF [the Nouvelle Revue Française]. They would take him out, from time to time (he was livid and thin, but his gaze remained straight and his eye, keen) and have him write the most intelligent article in the French press on Greco, Goethe or Shakespeare, then they would put him away again, among his friends, the mites, until the next article. Suarès was proud to be Suarès. And he tried to be just that, until the end: they prevented him from doing it, but it turns out that, removed from the context of his own blind epoch like a jack-in-the-box, he pops up to give us a lesson. We are still disciples of Suarès, and have been for a long time. His teaching is new: it has never been used. It is time we took a look at this fresh, virgin apparatus. A critical, philosophical, literary apparatus without the least equivalent in the 20th century, except perhaps for Proust. (The first works by Dédé Suarès that one should read are *Voyage du condottiere* and *Ecce homo*). Take a look, too, at the photographs of Suarès. With his felt hat embroidered with flowers, his cape and his pointed beard, and hair down to his shoulders, he was the very first hippie (but only in looks) of literature.

Truffaut, François

We are always being told to justify our choices, to comment on our tastes. I don't want to: I'll exercise my total freedom to affirm, absolutely gratuitously, that I am fanatical about Truffaut films. And about the man, as well. Truffaut never made a masterpiece and yet, with their amateurish aspect, a little old-fashioned, never realistic (especially his intimist films), his work, taken as a whole, forms an ensemble that is perfect in itself. It is an œuvre that should be kept in mind as a permanent frame of reference, as we speculate as to what, in *L'Enfant sauvage*, already presages *Adèle H.* and echoes *Quatre Cents*

Coups. You should see all of Truffaut before you see the first one.

Zappa, Frank

All his predecessors led up to him; all his successors are derived from him.

Yann Moix

William Styron

Position

An interview by Liliane Lazar

Have you lived in France, and for how long?

I came to Paris in 1952 and I had just written my first novel, *Lie Down in Darkness*. I was in my twenties. That time I stayed about nine months: from winter until fall.

Was that your only stay in France?

That was my longest, but I went many, many times after that.

Your four novels have been translated into French. You have been the subject of scholarly research. A great number of articles and book reviews have been written about your work in the major French journals and magazines. Your novel, Lie Down in Darkness, was on the "agrégation"* list of authors. How do you explain your great popularity in France?

* The *agrégation* is a competitive exam for French educators, roughly equivalent *to a PhD in education.*

I have often found it a mystery. I don't understand it myself. Certainly there are other American writers who might claim the attention of French readers, but why I seem to be so popular is a mystery. I think it might be due to a kind of *momentum* my work received at the beginning, with the translation of a book that was called *La Proie des Flammes (Set This House on Fire)*. It was translated by Maurice Edgar Coindreau, who was Faulkner's translator; and when the book appeared, in the early Sixties, well-translated by Coindreau, it was well-received. I think that that particular novel (which was not especially well-received in the U.S.) helped me gain recognition. It did extremely well in France and was a big bestseller for many weeks. I think my work gained a momentum at that point, and it has been going on from that time on. When *Lie Down in Darkness* was put on the *agrégation* list (because it was a very special list), it was read in English — back in the early Seventies. It was the only work in English by a living writer that was on the list. All the others I can remember were by Edgar Allen Poe, maybe Faulkner, and some plays by Shakespeare. I think that might have helped to give me recognition. I am still mystified as to why my work is so widely and popularly received. It is very pleasant, of course, but I don't have an explanation.

Do you think the writer in America is more isolated and less respected than the writer in Europe?

To some extent, yes. I would say this: in terms of the body politic, the mass of people, a writer has no recognition whatsoever. A writer is well below doctors and lawyers on the scale of importance in this country. On the other hand, we do have an intellectual society, subsociety, an intellectual grouping largely centered in the universities. Within that framework, writers are very highly regarded. The difference is that in Europe (except for England, which is very much like we are, in terms of attitudes towards writers), unlike in the United

States, the writer is accepted by the general public as a very important figure. This does not mean that a writer is not regarded highly in the framework of the intellectual community here.

You founded the Paris Review?

I was not really, technically, a founder. I was there when the *Paris Review* was begun in 1952. I was a friend of the various people involved in it. I was listed, if not as a founder, as one of the contributing editors.

What was the intent of this review at the beginning?

It was to be a literary review and it was intended mainly to publish creative works, as opposed to critical works. It has done very well. It flourished. I would suspect it is probably among the very few highly regarded purely literary reviews in this country.

Do you know why it is called the "Paris" Review?

Only because it was started in Paris. The initial impetus for the magazine was in Paris, because all the people involved in it were there: Peter Matthiessen, George Plimpton and several others.

Why and how did you start to write?

Well, that's one of those rather difficult questions. I was at Duke University in my late teens. I just had a passion for books and reading. I decided I wanted to become a writer, like most people do.

But not everyone succeeds like you.

It was a calling, a vocation.

> *Do you know what is the impulse that drives you to write: self dis-*
> *covery, self expression?*

Well, I suppose it is a desire to deal with life, using words.

> *Do you think any particular writer has influenced you, your style or*
> *your approach?*

I don't like to answer that question. If you are a writer and if you have been brought up in that culture, you read everything. As a student, early in my life, I began to read everything, French, Russian, American literature. I can't point to any particular writer at that early age. I have my favorite ones, of course, but I was such an avid reader that I can't point to any particular influence. Of course, Faulkner was an influence. Scott Fitzgerald was an influence. As I have always pointed out, especially to my French interviewers, Flaubert was an influence, but none of those could be pointed to specifically.

> *You have often been compared to Faulkner. What do you think of*
> *that comparison?*

I don't think it is a good comparison at all. I was *influenced* by Faulkner. Especially in France, I get very irritated by the hostility that has been expressed towards me by the professional French Faulkner scholars. There is a particularly vicious critic named André Bleinlasten who attacked me because, I think, he feels that I am some sort of rival to Faulkner. I don't know why, but the point is that it is gratuitous and stupid to attack me for not being as great as Faulkner, which of course I am not. It doesn't matter when people make lists like this. It is a stupid exercise. The point is, my work would not be valid, would not have its own power, if it were not the product of some originality. I would be the first to admit to being influenced by Faulkner. There is nothing wrong with that. Faulkner was influenced by Joyce and Proust. We are all influenced by someone. My work has achieved its own merit because it has my own voice in it, not anyone else's voice.

You are known for your wonderful prose and style. Have you tried to develop a style or did it come naturally?

Everyone tries to write as well as he can. I have done the best I can. I have struggled always to be a writer who places words with care and sensitivity. I hope I have succeeded. It does not come easily for me. That is why I honor Flaubert so much, because I see in him and his struggle a bit of my own struggle.

Do you write in drafts?

No, I don't. I try to perfect it as I go along.
Do you write every day, or under inspiration?

I try to write every day.

What is the difference for you between a short story and a novel?

I think a short story has it own set of rules and discipline. A novel is something else, which has its own rules also. I have written short stories as well as novels.

Did any of your novels originate as a short story?

To some extent, I would say that in some of my work I have had a small concept that developed into something larger. I remember, for instance, that my first novel *Lie Down in Darkness* was going to be something brief and then it just flowered, exfoliated and became a novel. I felt it was going to be a novel of 100 pages, and it became a long novel, 400 pages.

When you write a novel, what comes to you first, the characters or the story?

I don't think I can say. I think the two coexist. It is usually a theme. It varies from book to book.

Once a novel is finished, do you remain attached to your characters?

Once it is out of my system, I don't give any much thought any longer. That's why I find sort of annoying (and interesting at the same time) after I have finished a novel like *Sophie's Choice*, to get books about the Holocaust sent to me through the mail. I am still interested to some extent, but I feel I have delivered myself on that subject. I have said pretty much what I need to say. Therefore, I find that something like the Holocaust is behind me, not that I am not interested in it, but I don't want to deal with it anymore.

In Sophie's Choice, *was the character of Sophie purely fictional or is it based on a real character?*

It was both. Okay, the story that I told did not happen as I told it, but there was a Sophie in my life. There was a young woman whom I met in very much the circumstances I described in *Sophie's Choice* in a rooming house in Brooklyn after the war. I got to know her slightly, but I didn't get to know her terribly well. I was obviously very impressed with her. So the book *Sophie's Choice* is a fictional narrative based on what might have happened if I had stayed in that rooming house, got to know her better, got to know her lover Nathan better, and what might have happened had she told me this totally fictional description of going to Auschwitz and having to make this awful choice.

> *So you were really Stingo. To what extent is the character of Stingo autobiographical?*

Well, to some extent, but not really. I would say eighty percent of *Sophie's Choice* is an invention, a fabrication, a fiction. Twenty percent is perhaps autobiographical.

> *Did you get money, like Stingo, from your father, from the sales of slaves?*

I did actually get money from my father, but not that way.

> *Do you think Sophie's weak character is responsible for some of her misfortunes?*

I think she was certainly a victim of her own weaknesses, but she was also victimized in other ways not only by circumstances, but by people, by her father, by her husband, by the commandant of Auschwitz.

> *Concerning her father, Sophie said that, "Everything bad on earth, every evil that was ever invented, had to do with my father." The father figure who misguides his children is also portrayed in* Lie Down in Darkness *and* The Confession of Nat Turner. *Is this a theme that concerns you?*

I have conflicting views. If I may interpret my own work (and I don't know whether I can do that or not), I think there is a conflict between the good father and the bad father in *Sophie's Choice*. I am constantly referring to my own father as a man of great virtue and great quality, almost a model or an ideal father as opposed to the father of Sophie. The father in *Lie Down in Darkness* and in *The Confession of Nat Turner* are rather evil figures. They represent the weaknesses of human nature. The father in *The Confession of Nat Turner*, that is, the father figure, the owner of Nat, is well-meaning and basically a man of virtue, but he is also a man of enormous failings in the sense that he betrayed Nat Turner. So it is a conflicted, bifurcated, schizophrenic relationship.

> *One critic has stated that* Sophie's Choice *is more about Stingo and his choices than about Sophie and hers. Do you agree with this comment?*

No, I don't. I think that, as the narrator, Stingo carries the story along, but certainly I don't think that his choices are important to the work.

> *Several characters use Yiddish expressions. Do you know Yiddish?*

No. I don't know Yiddish, but if you live in a predominantly Jewish city like New York, you can't help learning some Yiddish almost by osmosis.

> *Did you speak with Auschwitz survivors to construct Sophie's character?*

No, I didn't.

> *How did you go about it, then?*

I went to Auschwitz. And I read a great deal of material, I read survivors' accounts and a great deal of survival literature; but I didn't feel it was necessary to talk with survivors. Sophie, herself, is a survivor. Of course I talked to her, but she did not tell me much. I sensed that she did not want to talk to me about it. So I gleaned most of my information from other sources, from reading.

Would you comment on the quotation from Malraux, used as an epigraph: "I seek that essential region of the soul where absolute evil confronts brotherhood."

I think that that is the essence of what the book. Absolute evil was represented by Auschwitz and its opposite, brotherhood, was represented by Sophie. Whatever her flaws and shortcomings she was, nevertheless, a person of decent instincts.

Besides the absolute evil of Auschwitz, isn't this novel also dealing with the theme of guilt?

Yes, I think it is. Guilt is an integral theme of the book. Certainly, Sophie's guilt is constant. Her guilt starts with her complicity with her father, and her distributing anti-Semitic pamphlets, even though she was trying by that means to save her children; still it was something she had to feel guilt about. And guilty over failing to join the Polish resistance, as she was asked to do. Memories like that haunted her, and then the final dilemma of having to choose one of her children, even though it was imposed upon her, in order to inflict the utmost punishment, was to make her feel for ever guilty for this dreadful decision.

Is it her revelations to Stingo that finally drive her to suicide?

I think, indeed, that she had to confess. Stingo was her confessor, the person to whom she unburdened her heart. After pouring everything out, she had no other place to go but into the arms of Nathan, to die there. He was on the verge of killing her anyway, and killing himself. So the two acts coincided.

I was surprised by the fact that Sophie was sent to Auschwitz for stealing a ham. Could such a thing really have happened?

Oh, this is absolutely real. I have a young friend — she was young during the war — she is younger than I am. She is now a middle-aged woman. She is one of my closest friends in the United States. When I was writing *Sophie's Choice*, she was a very important source of information. She is a Polish Catholic who lived in Warsaw during the Nazi occupation and she told me many of these things. One of the things she told me was that if you were caught smuggling ham or any meat or any significant food, the penalties were very severe, including being sent to Auschwitz.

Would you comment on the passage when Stingo draws a parallel between Sophie's Poland and the American South?

In the passage that I wrote, there is a clear resemblance between the American South and Poland. It is not so much anti-Semitism. The South, curiously enough, it is not a center for anti-Semitism, for very good reasons. Partially because the South has another racial animosity, namely the blacks. Partially because I don't think the South bred an anti-Semitic tradition to the same extent as the rest of the U.S.. Most Jews living in the South were rarely subjected to anti-Semitic violence or anything like that. There was always anti-Semitism, but it was almost never virulent. In Poland, of course the opposite applies. Poland was famous for anti-Semitism. One of the tragedies of Poland is the failure of the Poles to admit to their anti-Semitism. Many of them have, but it is still a nation that has not come to grips with the fact that it is anti-Semitic. I might add that the American South, although there is still an "anti-Negro" atmosphere, has done much better in terms of racial harmony than Poland. There is a lot of racism in America, but the Southerners have come to a sense of relative harmony with black people. On the other hand, I think the Poles remain very anti-Semitic even now.

Did you feel that the film Sophie's Choice *was successful in presenting your work?*

I thought it was reasonably successful. I would not have filmed it that way, myself. There are a lot of things I would have done differently. Certain ideas that were in the book are lost, but in balance, I think the film was quite successful and the interpretation was excellent.

Sophie's Choice *was published in 1979. Why haven't you written any novel since then?*

I have been writing short works instead. I have been working steadily on a novel, but it still isn't finished. Since then, I have published *A Tidewater Morning* and *Darkness Visible*.

A Tidewater Morning *is three short stories based on your youth, but I would like to talk about your first novel,* Lie Down in Darkness, *which was so highly acclaimed. The three main characters, Milton the father, Helen the mother, and Peyton the daughter, have a strong desire to return to adolescence and childhood, especially Peyton. Is this the cause of their inability to face responsibility?*

It may be.

I was struck by the simultaneity of Peyton's suicide and the dropping of the bomb on Hiroshima. Is this intended as a symbol?

I think it was a symbol of death and destruction covering the world.

What is the significance of the bird images that comes back so often in Peyton's dreams?

I don't know what that means. Critics have said that it is a flight from reality or various desires to escape one's self. It may be. I am not really sure. It is nothing that I, myself, had any conscious meaning to give.

Is the hatred between Helen and her daughter Peyton caused by the fact they are both victims of incestuous love for their respective fathers: Peyton for Milton and Helen for her God-like father?

It may be that. I think, in this case, Helen was a profoundly unhappy and neurotic woman who was extremely jealous of the attention being paid to Peyton by her husband. As a result she was unable to accept it. I don't think she was aware of any incestuous connection, but she felt that the affection being lavished upon Peyton by her husband cut her out of the picture. Whereas some women could be accepting it, she could not. She turned into a vile and vindictive person.

For the character of Peyton, were you inspired by Caddy Thompson in The Sound and the Fury? *Peyton and Caddy are both victims of their family?*

There is certainly a similarity there, but I didn't intend it to be a replica.

In The Long March, *a novel inspired by your experience as a marine, Captain Mannic protests against a thirty-six-mile forced march, but his revolt ends up as a defeat since he has to comply with it. Do you think rebellion is possible in the military system?*

I don't think that rebellion is ever successfully carried out, because the military is the personification of absolute power and you cannot rebel successfully against absolute power. You can rebel, but it is unlikely to be successful.

In your fiction, rebellion is associated with violence. Peyton uses violence against her body and commits suicide, Mannie tortures his men and himself, Nat Turner kills an innocent girl. Why do you associate violence with rebellion?

I think the two go hand in hand. Rebellion and violence are almost synonymous, but I suppose there such a thing as passive rebellion. Any time you react against power, you are likely to run into a violent situation, by the nature of the thing.

Rebellion is a major theme in your work. Why do you consider it so crucial?

I have always been, as a person, very strongly anti-authoritarian. I have resented authority, especially when authority has been unfair (which it so often is). I have had strong reactions against it, whether it is civil, personal, or ecclesiastic authority. It is part of my nature and this rebelliousness has found its way into my work.

Is that what attracted you to write about this black historical character Nat Turner?

Yes, certainly. If I was interested in rebellion, plainly, the idea of a black slave revolt would appeal to me. I come from that part of the country and it has never been written about it in any large sense. It seems inevitable that I should write about it.

While in prison, Nat achieves his full sense of identity like Camus'
Stranger. *Were you influenced by Camus' book when you wrote*
The Confession of Nat Turner?

I was very much influenced by *The Stranger*. Not to say that I drew on
it heavily as a contributing factor in my work. The very idea of a man
sitting in his jail, as Meursault was, waiting his execution, seemed to
me a key to the way I would approach Nat Turner, so *The Stranger* was
very influential to me in structuring *The Confession of Nat Turner.*

*Your other novels have existential themes of choice, freedom and
rebellion. Were you also influenced by Sartre?*

I read Sartre, but I felt, as interesting a philosopher as he was, he did-
n't have the artistic comprehension that Camus has.

*Would Nat Turner have been less violent and rebellious had he not
be so frustrated in his love-hate relationship with Margaret White-
head?*

That is an issue that has been brought up many times by people criti-
cizing my book. black writers in the book *Ten black Writers respond to
William Styron* were very critical about it. I wrote a long essay about
this, not too long ago. The historical evidence showed that the only
person in this rebellion that he killed was a young white girl. That's
all we know. As a novelist, it seemed inevitable for me to write about
their relationship. I tried to make it a complex relationship, love and
hate, but he probably hated as much as he loved and the black critics
totally misread that as being some kind of lust when in reality he was
far more complex. They also resented the idea that I would establish a
connection between a black man and a white woman, when in reality
it is the one theme that haunts the black man throughout American

history. It is their constant concern for white women. One after the other, black man have had relationships with white women. It has been their obsession. It does not mean that all black men are obsessed constantly by white women, but the fact remains, there seems to be a large attraction between black man and white women. Look at the O. J. Simpson case. I was merely drawing on that obvious fact, trying to describe the relationship between Nat Turner and Margaret White-head.

Were you surprised by the reactions of the black writers to The Confession of Nat Turner?

I was a bit surprised, because I felt I had written a book in which I had been very sympathetic to the hero Nat Turner and especially sympathetic to the plight of slaves and to the suffering of American Negro slavery. It came at a time when there was a great rift in the re-lations between blacks and whites. In retrospect, I realize that the book came at the wrong time; it came at a time when it was consid-ered *de trop* for me as a white person to try to describe black experi-ence of any sort and for me, in addition, to take on the persona of a black person. To have me describe this from a black man's point of view was more than they could handle.

Do you think they attacked you also because Nat Turner's revolt was a failure?

I don't think that was it at all. It could be said that the worst of it, the most distorted criticism against me, came from people who felt that I was trying to demonstrate the futility of black revolt. That was prepos-terous. I was not trying to demonstrate any such futility. I was trying to say that this was the wretched condition of black people under slavery. This man, Nat Turner, plainly, to my mind, was heroic in his attempt to try to commit this act of violence, as unsuccessful as it was.

*Do you see humans as "inhabitants of a fiery house"? I am referring
to your quotation from John Donne, as the epigraph for "Set this
House on Fire."*

I meant that as a sort of an existential statement. Although plainly
John Donne's statement had to do with God, I was trying myself to
make it appear as a lament or a cry.

So it is not a religious cry?

I felt that sense of abandonment by God that Donne expresses in that
statement that could have been made in our time. Donne had to use
the word God because, as you know, he was a preacher, but I felt it
was also an existential cry of anguish at the same time.

*Is there a symbolic meaning between North and South in the fact
that Mason Flagg, the corrupted playboy, comes from the North and
Peter, the narrator and his honest family, come from the South?*

I suppose I was trying to make a broad statement. I don't know how
valid it would be today, but I was trying to oppose the traditional values of the South to the more materialistic values of the North. Although that is an oversimplification, because certainly the North and
the South partake of both of these aspects of our culture. I was trying
to contrast the two.

*Do you think that the criticism that you wrote, in Set this House on
Fire, about America is still true today?*

Yes. I haven't reread the book in a long time, but I was trying to describe a certain emptiness of a totally materialistic society. I don't
think it is particularly American, I think it is Western. It could apply

to Europe too. I think in America we carry some of these things to an extreme, which I was trying to describe in the book. As an American I am often offended by the fact that we seem to be in the vanguard of cultural vulgarity and nihilism, but eventually it takes over the whole world. We are just doing it first. We got into this cultural wasteland before anyone else. For example, we invented television. It was here for a long time, and now it is all over the world. Russia is the worst place of all.

My point is that although Americans seem to carry this materialism to an extreme, eventually it is something that overtakes in the entire world. It is not purely American. We just do it bigger and better.

In your work, you have been concerned with the rapidly changing nature of American society. Twenty-five years later, what concerns you most about American society?

I don't think I can answer that. Society is much too complex. I could suggest a few things, but I can't pin down a specific thing, there are too many. Among them, one of the worst aspects of American society is the absolute lack of control about guns, the total proliferation of guns. It is destroying thousands of people, mainly young people, most of them black. It is because we have an almost insane view about guns and weapons. The sad thing is that it is much too late to exert any real control. Attempts are being made, but I don't think they are too successful. It is not getting any better. There are allowing more and more freedom to get guns. I think it is terrible.

Many of the characters in your novels show an inability to love. What do you think causes that incapacity?

Possibly, I am trying to make a statement about the failure of our society to provide the necessary support for sound connections between people who are fragmented by the kind of society we have created. It has caused a kind of explosion in the family. It is not that I believe in that "Republican" idea of "family values." I am not talking about that. I am talking about the cement that makes people hang together. It has been lost now, the sense of close connections.

Most of your novels start with a dramatic event and involve narrations within narrations, flashbacks within flashbacks, creating a view from a view. Is there a special purpose for this narrative technique?

I have always been fascinated by the mystery of time and the way we perceive it, the way we perceive memory and its connection with time. Our lives are really not linear. They are all kinds of short circuits, cuts and detours. That's what I try to convey. Existence is not a straight line. It's a zigzag.

Did writing Darkness Visible *bring you some personal relief?*

It certainly did. It was very important catharsis. A way to work the whole experience out of my system. I struggled for a long time to find my voice. I tried to write it as a novel. I wrote ten or twelve thousand words of the work as a novel and I abandoned that because I realized that is not suitable. Then, finally, after I experienced this for four years, I suddenly realized I had to tell it very much as it happened. So I did it that way. It was wonderful relief for me to get out of myself.

Did you do it also to help other people who suffer from depression?

I don't think I intentionally did it for that reason. I did it merely to render my own experience, the same as one goes about anything. Of course, I have been very pleased, in many ways, to discover that the book has been a great help to people suffering from depression. Plainly, it had a great impact that way. I receive letters all the time to that effect.

The depression had not recurred for you?

No. I think all my life I have been somewhat a depressed person. I have a depressed personality. This thing that happened to me and what I described in *Darkness Visible* was a kind of explosion of the illness in a magnified way. Although I am never totally free of depression, I have never experienced another major explosion, another storm.

And it left you suddenly — one morning, as you explained in the book, you realized you were not so depressed...

In the hospital, I began to sense that I was recovering. The thing that defines depression at its worst is that you can't tolerate it. You want to die because the pain is so severe. The daily pain.

Is it a physical pain?

It's like a physical pain. It's in the head. It's very hard to describe. As I said in the book, it is virtually impossible to describe, because it is not connected with any normal experience any of us understand.

What has been your most difficult problem as a writer?

To organize my thoughts and create works in the abundance I would have liked; but I can't do anything about that. Writing simply doesn't come easily to me. That's why I am happy to report that Flaubert had similar problems. He just managed to do what he had to do on his own terms. To some degree, I feel a kinship to Flaubert. I am not trying to compare myself to Flaubert. But our working habits and our struggle have been the some.

What is the future of literature in our electronic age?

I still think literature is the best way of understanding ourselves. I hope it won't disappear. There is a lot of talk recently about electronic publication replacing books.

Do you think this would be possible?

I think it is always possible, but there is something indispensable about reading words on paper. I will give you an example. I like to read in bed. Not too long ago, I was reading *Newsweek* magazine. In the magazine, they were describing the fact that a well-known magazine columnist named Michael Kinsley had been lured out to the West Coast to start an electronic magazine, that is, a magazine you would have on the Internet. I said to myself, here I am reading a magazine in this leisurely way and I am reading about something that, if it came to fruition, would require me to get out of bed and sit in front of a screen in order to get it, and not to turn pages. I am sure in many ways it would be convenient, but then I would still have to access, as they call it, and do all these things when, in fact, right in front of me I have all these pages. No way is that going to supplant the leisurely pleasure of reading a magazine in print. It can't be done. It is impossible, unless we go into some other state of existence that you and I know nothing about. The point is that it remains superior to read linear print on a page than to sit in front of a screen and absorb it that way. Simply it is easier on all human levels.

Even for the young people who deal more and more with computers?

Clearly, computers have their magnet. There is a great magnetic appeal. There is no doubt about that, but I submit that it cannot supplant the idea of holding a few ounces of paper in your hand and being able to absorb the information that way. Some things you can absorb very rapidly on the Internet. You can access any information. That's wonderful. I am not trying to minimize the advantage, but I still think there are things that can be gotten through a book that can never be supplanted. So I see it not being supplanted one way or another, but the two existing parallel to each other.

So you don't think literature is in danger?

I don't. I think it will take another form, possibly. I remember being told that when the movies came into existence, when they became more than just primitive, let's say in the early twenties, there was a lot of talk about movies supplanting literature. Then it became even more intense at the end of the twenties, when sound was added. Then no one was going to read a book. Everyone would be going to the movies. But look what happened, books have existed, and books have existed parallel to television. Magazines are more seductive. I think that these new electronic developments often siphon off some of the attention, but finally they end up existing in parallel with the written word.

Do you use the computer?

I don't. I have a secretary who types and puts it on her word processor. I am all for these things. I am not against it. I am not what they call a Luddite. I don't believe in destroying these things, but I have my own pace and rhythm. I use what is best for me.

In Sophie's Choice, you mentioned that Southern literary tradition would disappear and the Jewish writers would emerge. Is that something that you felt at that point?

No. It was a sort of a joke. There was a period when the Jewish writers were appearing, back thirty years ago. Actually, they were terrific writers and because America has had these ethnic strains, for example Faulkner and Saul Bellow, there was the idea that there would be no more Southern white protestant literature. It would all be Jewish. After that, black, or something like that. But of course, again, no one supplants any one else. There was a very big movement: American Jewish writing. It was very real and vital. It doesn't mean that it obscures or prevents any other writing from happening.

How do you feel about the situation of literature today in America?

I feel that today it is very vital — although I think it is considerably more difficult to produce a first novel. It is very tough for a beginning novelist.

Wasn't it always so?

It always was, but I think it is even more difficult. There is so much commercialism. There is so much desire to have a big blockbuster.

Do you think people read more now?

Oh, yes! As a culture, America is not a book-reading culture, but then few cultures have been book-reading cultures. In the famous period of the Russian novel, almost all Russians were illiterate. They could not read. Russians who could read were just a tiny minority. It has always been this way. Books have never been an object of mass culture. So it is a matter of relativism. You can go through a whole state in the U.S. and not find a bookstore. On the other hand, thousands and thousands of readers exist in New York and in Los Angeles. There are more and more books, and they are more plentiful because of the paperback. So I don't see the habit of reading disappearing at all.

Do you have any plans for future works?

Yes, but it is something I usually don't talk about.

Most writers don't, unless it is finished. Do you still lecture?

Sometimes, not much. I get a lot of invitations to talk about *Darkness Visible* and depression, from organizations having to do with mental health. I do it sometimes. I did an article for the newspaper, *Le Monde*, but it was translated. I am always pleased to have this reception in France. I don't feel ignored in the U.S., but I don't feel the same kind of affection here for my work. It is wonderful to have a country where one's work is widely read. It makes me feel very good. The French are very receptive to foreign works.

Interviewed by Liliane Lazar

The Survey:

What good are intellectuals?

*

David Albahari, Tahar Ben Jelloun,
Rachid Boudjedra, Breyten Breytenbach, André Brink,
Hans Christoph Buch, Guillermo Cabrera Infante,
Édouard El-Kharrât, Péter Esterházy, Nadine Gordimer,
Juan Goytisolo, David Grossman, Yoram Kaniuk,
Ivan Klíma, Aïcha Lemsine, Antonio Lobo Antunes, Claudio
Magris, Naguib Mahfouz, Eduardo Manet, Pierre Mertens,
Czeslaw Milosz, Arthur Miller, Joyce Carol Oates,
Cynthia Ozick, Orhan Pamuk, Octavio Paz, Victor Pelevine,
Salman Rushdie, Fernando Savater, Peter Schneider,
Philippe Sollers, Susan Sontag, Henrick Stangerup,
Mario Vargas Llosa, William Styron, A. B. Yehoshua.

The Survey

Intellectuals: their role, their influence. Have they lost their importance? Has the emergence of a Sartre, a Camus or a Zola suddenly become inconceivable? Has the role disappeared from our repertory, or is it simply constrained to redefine itself under the treble pressures of the philosophies of suspicion, the media invasion of Western societies, and the new relationship between writers and their readers? Have intellectuals failed to take on their responsibilities — or has it become harder (why?) for them to speak and make themselves heard?

These are the questions we had in mind when we decided to launch this survey. We sent a letter from Bernard-Henri Levy all around the world, to all the writers with whom we felt closest; their replies, sometimes elaborate, sometimes more laconic, were gathered over the course of many months. Here they are, in whatever form each writer chose, providing a status report on "the intellectual question" at the turn of the millennium.

Gabi Gleichmann

Six Questions:

1. What does the word "intellectual" mean to you, today? Are you an intellectual — or do you reject that term?

2. Have any intellectual figures influenced you in a decisive way? (which ones?) Any "examples" who have inspired you, shaped you, whom you can invoke even today to clarify your mind?

3. What role do intellectuals play at the turn of the 20th century? Do you, like some people, think their role is finished?

4. We have heard a great deal about the "errors" committed by intellectuals, their "blindness," and sometimes their "irresponsibility." What do you think of these charges? Do you agree with their severity? Or would you moderate, even contradict them?

5. In the country where you live and work, what do you think are the greatest obstacles to intellectuals: the indifference of the media; the confusion of opinions; police repression; soft repression and competition from public spectacles, with all the illusions and lures that go with them; or other obstacles?

6. What tasks do you see as most urgent, today or always; what is your task? What prejudices are the most threatening, what causes must be defended, what perils must be averted? In short, what, in your eyes, are today's greatest priorities for thought and action?

David Albahari

1.   I still think of an intellectual as somebody who is capable of making a new synthesis within his field of work, and coming up with a completely new understanding of the matters involved. I do not consider myself an intellectual, in that sense, only a writer, too emotional to be an intellectual. However, I do not reject that term. I have nothing against it, and I don't worry much about whether it's ever mentioned in connection with my name.

2.   I realize, now, that the ones who have influenced me most make up quite a diverse group: Søren Kierkegaard, Martin Buber, D.T. Suzuki, David Bohm. And also Danilo Kiš: he is clear proof that one can reconcile the intellect and hyper-sensibility (whatever I might think). I still have much to learn from him.

3.   As the 20th century came to an end, intellectuals (in the broadest sense of that word) had yet to determine the true meaning of the century. Historic revisionism, which seems to have grown stronger and stronger in the last decade, shows how much remains to be done. We still lack a kind of a final, all-inclusive explanation of the century's events, shaped as they were by different nationalist and political programs; and unless we get one I presume that the possibility of their repetition will be carried over into the next century. Yes, as long as the intellectual keeps an independent position, his presence will be important to our world.

4.   The only possible answer to these questions is that some of the accusations are fair, while others are wrong. In fact, the real question is whether intellectuals are allowed to make mistakes. Why not? After all, they are just as human as everybody else (although some of

them would not agree). In other words, it is appropriate to criticize intellectuals when they make mistakes, and to punish them just as other people are punished for similar mistakes, but also not to stigmatize them for errors that are pardoned in others.

5.   I believe that the major obstacle for intellectuals in every part of the former Yugoslavia, especially in Serbia, lies inside themselves. There are other obstacles, of course, like government control of the media in Croatia and Serbia, or the chaos of opinions wherever you go, but the most important one is the unwillingness of most intellectuals to move beyond the totalitarian way of thinking, the legacy of debating with your opponents the way communists did. This is perhaps normal for a country with no tradition of democracy, and maybe we should wait for a new generation of intellectuals there, the one that will grow up in a more open society, learning how to play according to "the rules of the game."

6.   Since I live in North America now, I am inclined to think that the development of the so-called "politically correct" represents the greatest danger to the world. It is one of the most effective forms of censorship, permeating all aspects of living and thinking. In combination with right-wing ideology (religious or secular, it does not matter which) it might effectively and quickly destroy democratic tradition in the West.

On the other hand, living on this continent (and in combination with the experience of the ethnic conflict in the former Yugoslavia) has made me more aware of the challenges of our multicultural and multiethnic world. If, as some thinkers predict, the next century really turns out to be the century of migrations, then intellectuals are faced with the serious challenge of redefining our whole tradition and culture. What a magnificent, and perilous, task! One false move could provoke a disaster of terrible proportions. I only hope that intellectuals will be strong enough to see it through, for I don't know anyone else who could.

Tahar Ben Jelloun

1.   I like knowing that Captain Dreyfus's adversaries frequently used the word "intellectual" to designate writers who had taken up his cause.

I come from a country where this word is synonymous with "well-read" and "engaged." In that sense, I define myself as an intellectual, more because of my commitment to the values of freedom, justice and truth than for my cultural baggage.

The word cannot remain neutral. As soon as it is used, its literal meaning is charged with political overtones. I remember the time, in the Sixties, when Sartre was regarded as a committed intellectual (inevitably for progressive values) and Aron was considered a philosophy professor who was not called "intellectual" because he was more inclined toward the Right. It was absurd, but what characterizes youth is the tendency toward intolerance and sometimes to diagrammatic thought. We in Morocco at that time were great readers of Frantz Fanon, Paul Nizan, André Malraux — the younger, not de Gaulle's minister — and of course Sartre and Camus, whose estrangement we followed with passion.

Today, things have changed. I try to eliminate Manicheism from my thought. I use the word "intellectual" to cover a broader and pluralist spectrum. But I have trouble considering ideologists of racism, negativism and fundamentalism as intellectuals. They are manipulators. I am not always able to be neutral. The word encompasses "intelligence," spirit, thought. It is difficult for me to consider the exercise of thought and reflection apart from the idea of progress and openness. Maybe I'm wrong, a Utopian, perhaps. I have always been intrigued by the expression that designates spying, "intelligence for the enemy." That seems to me to be a different matter. Intelligence has not always been used in the human sense.

2.   Poets of the resistance, whether the mystic Al-Halladj, who was condemned to death and executed on the cross in 922 AD in Baghdad and who maintained, to his last breath, the assertion that brought him death: "I am the Truth," thus merging with Allah (union, or more precisely, fusion with God is intolerable in Islam), or Ibn Al-Mouqaffaa, who introduced into the Arab world the Indian fables *Kalila wa Dimna* (which inspired La Fontaine) and who was executed because of his freedom of thought, in the year 757, by the governor of Bassora in Iraq.

Closer to us, in time, were the poets of the Resistance in France, René Char, Pierre Emmanuel, Paul Éluard and even Aragon, and then the Turk Nazim Hikmet, the Palestinian Mahmoud Darwish, and the Egyptian theorist Hamed Abou Zeïd who was condemned by his country's judicial system (under the pressure of the Islamists) to divorce his wife for apostasy.

I love rigorous intellectuals. In the Arab world, I have regard and admiration for the Moroccan historian Abdallah Laroui, who wrote a masterly essay, *Contemporary Arab Ideology* (Maspero, 1967); the Palestinian Edward Saïd; and screenwriter Youssef Chahine, for his talent and impertinence.

I could also cite a number of intellectuals whom I admire for their courage, for the passion with which they live out their ideas in the coherence and significant intelligence of artists, and writers who are engaged in fighting for the respect of man's dignity.

3.   Their role will never be completed, for it is a gigantic enterprise. There are plenty of wounds, and injustices. More and more people

need to have their words reported, brought out of the silence. The role of the intellectual starts by reflecting the breadth of these voices that come from the night and from loneliness. This role merges with the emergency in the countries where freedom, the democracy and the State of law are lacking. In Europe, that is no longer the case. That is why the roles are not the same and the risks incurred are not of the same gravity. In Nigeria, the regime could condemn a writer, Ken Saro-Wiwa, to death (November 1995) because he upset the interests of Shell and the reigning junta. In certain Arab states, intellectuals who express themselves are always on the lookout because they live under a close monitoring from two sides: the traditional State censors and the fanatics who act on impulse and are quick to assassinate, especially in Egypt and Algeria.

More than ever, the intellectuals have a role to play. In the non-democratic countries, they are taken seriously by the public, which asks them to be lawyers, trade unionists, and artists at the same time. They are invested with confidence, respect, admiration and also with a great demand. Disappointment, breach of word, lack of commitment or, worse, treason (collaborating with the powers) are inadmissible. Moreover, in a country with a high rate of illiteracy, the intellectual seems like a privileged person who has responsibilities towards his society.

4.   As Cioran wrote, "A writer's 'sources' are his shames; anyone who does not discover any of them in himself, or who conceals them, is dedicated to plagiarism or to criticism." It's possible to make a mistake. To not admit it, to stubbornly fail to see it, is worse than the fact of having made it. Our "shames" are sometimes our terrain, i.e. our doubts, our weaknesses and our humanity. An intellectual who never makes mistakes, that is, who does not doubt, would frighten me. Only dictators, fanatics, have a monopoly on certainty.

French intellectuals have been mistaken about Marxism applied with authority in various countries, about revolutions that were quickly reversed, about men and hopes. The list is long. To consider only the post-war period, we must mention one after the other: the Eastern European countries, Cuba, Algeria (the silence and the complacency of the media and the leftist intellectuals with regard to the Algerian policy of independence in 1990 are very grave; due to guilty feelings and the neurotic relationship between France and Algeria, they had dramatic consequences which we know today), Kampuchea, Vietnam, Afghanistan, Iran (the blindness was brutal, to the point of sweeping up Michel Foucault in an unfortunate delusion. Jean Genet, more malignant, said he sympathized with old Khomeyni because he was "screwing" the West!), and so forth.

What is missing with most of these intellectuals who make mistakes is the practice of self-criticism, of questioning their own decisions, and a little more humility. It is better to be mistaken and admit it than to remain inactive, passive and apart from the world.

5.   The intellectuals in Europe have begun to have a bad reputation. This is good sign.   Putting on a show, being pleasing at all costs, these attitudes are a complete contradiction of their role and their status. The obstacles come from their own conduct. The intellectual is a person who disturbs, he speaks with sincerity, not with clichés, without complacency. If he makes concessions, if he sacrifices certain truths to satisfy his desire to be part of the show, then he himself sows the obstacles that will dilute his word or will make his actions into nothing but sweet images that dissolve in water.

In the Maghreb, the obstacles are political in nature. In Algeria, any free speech is rendered impossible by terror and counter-terror. In Tunisia and Morocco, there is a semi-freedom. One can speak about a certain number of subjects, but there are taboos: the Head of State, the army, Islam. Windows are opening; one can breathe a little. Democracy is being established in homeopathic doses. We must believe in the virtues of homeopathy . . .

The gravest issue is the word of the intellectual who no longer has a good grasp of reality. That is currently the case in Europe.

There is no more leader, no more master of thinking. The last time the intellectuals of France mobilized, against the Debré law (on foreigners' rights of entry and sojourn), they were, in fact, led by various categories of artists.

6.   In France, the most urgent need is to find the most effective method of countering the National Front. That will take imagination. It is an increasingly real and serious threat to freedom in this country.

Racism must be fought differently. We have to start in primary school, the only territory where prejudices have not yet entered. Artists, writers should agree to meet with children at school, to speak with them, to tell them simple things about human diversity, to explain the nonsense of racist ideas.

On another, theoretical, level, we have to start a thorough and new reflection on the mechanisms of racism, fanaticism and the dismissal of historical truth.

On a more general level, we must lend assistance to intellectuals who are threatened in countries where freedom of thought, of writing and of creation is severely controlled. To maintain a lively solidarity, for example, around Salman Rushdie, who has become the symbol of freedom confiscated and a life taken hostage by a totalitarian State.

We must act daily; we must reconsider the mechanisms of the deterioration of the human condition; we need to establish solidarity with intellectuals whose life is in danger.

Rachid Boudjedra

1.   The word "intellectual" does not have any precise meaning. It is only a synonym for various words: probity, integrity and generosity to the world. Given that I cannot define the word "intellectual," that gives us a way of challenging it without completely throwing it out.

The meaning of this word has been so much perverted in the course of history that any dogmatic assertion would make pervert it, "disfigure" it, further still.

2.   There have been some. From Averroès, Galileo, and Giordano Bruno to, paradoxically, Sartre and Malraux, to mention only the French. To me, these models have something in common: they all went as far as they could to develop their principles, their vision of the world.

3.   Let's not affirm the end of philosophy, of ideology and thus of their producers, i.e. the intellectuals. Their role is weakened but their mission has not been completed, because they are in crisis themselves, because the world is in crisis, we've all lost our bearings. The concepts of evil and good, for example, have become so fuzzy that we've invented an intermediate concept, the "good-and-bad." Thus the provisional distress of the intellectuals. But they always have something to contribute to the discussion. Their influence may be more discreet, but more effective.

4.   An intellectual is someone who flirts with error and constantly plays on the brink of irresponsibility. The judgment that people are visiting upon intellectuals is a judgment on ideology, by the financial power that relentlessly dominates, manages and rules the world. They have been able to co-opt some intellectuals by seducing them and by locking into the stock market or the media carnival. They are, in fact, very few because they've lost their "concern" for mankind and the world, which — the concern — could be the true definition of intellect.

5.   I have the feeling that in my country, and in every other country without exception, intellectuals are confronted by the same obstacles

that you cite here. The difference lies in the fact that in the so-called developed countries, the obstacles are more subtle, more perverse and Machiavellian, while in the so-called underdeveloped countries, they are honest, clear and brutal.

6.   The most urgent task is clarification.   Indeed, the boundaries have been purposely erased and the intellectual has often been deceived. He has found himself playing his most underhanded and most cynical adversaries' game, and that is why we need to go for a kind of Manicheism where bad is bad and good is good. We have to break with the consensus and the vague compromise. In Algeria, one cannot oppose the Islamist cruelty that cuts women's and babies' throats, and at the same time call for negotiations with the killers.

Rather than denouncing others, the intellectual must first of all rebuild his deontology. Tired humanism and the well-worn democratism of Western intellectuals reinforce the slyness of the Islamist fundamentalists at home. Suddenly, these intellectuals are to some extent accomplices in the atrocities being perpetrated there, because they do not adopt a clear attitude and are swallowed up in fickleness. Dogmatism with regard to the concepts of democracy and humanism transforms them into fundamentalists of these two completely distorted worldviews.

For example, it is accepted, among Western intellectuals, to denounce the crimes of Communism, but we don't hear much anymore about the crimes of imperialism and colonialism. The subject is taboo or, worse yet, a matter of derision.

What's at stake today in Algeria is the return to an implacable intellectual rigor in the field of thinking and to concerted engagement against the real enemies of freedom and humanity, in terms of action, not just words.

Breyten Breytenbach

I would have agreed entirely with the statements that are referenced in Question 4, and so all the other questions would have been obviated.

"Intellectual" is a shadow of the French ego, kept alive artificially only in Parisian salons (as vibrators for male masturbation, preferably in public). It is gone, like the Zeppelin. Halleluja!

André Brink

Ever since Julien Benda's *Le Trahison des Clercs*, intellectuals have been finding themselves in an increasingly precarious situation. But it is impossible to generalize, since the function of the intellectual, if any, is surely wholly determined by the situation in which he/she operates. South Africa, which has constituted my own context over several decades, presents an interesting illustration.

During the apartheid years, in which an all-dominating ideology, supported by the fearsome apparatus of the state, ensured its own survival through brutal repression, the function of the intellectual was defined with remarkable clarity as one of direct opposition. In those dire circumstances it always seemed to me that the writer, in his/her capacity as the archetypal intellectual, became almost by definition the Sisyphean rebel, the Antigone who never ceases to hurl her creative and affirmative "No!" in the face of the tyrant. Camus provided the model for this — and then, as now, he remains to my mind the greatest example of the intellectual in our much-troubled century. Much more than Sartre, in his commitment to specific causes in the evolving situation of his country, Camus managed constantly to relate a particular political stance to a larger intellectual debate and to a fundamental moral stance. Even when he faltered, as in his notorious expression of allegiance to his mother, which took precedence over profoundly serious political divisions, the integrity of his moral conviction could not be faulted. His cards were always on the table: there was no hidden agenda, no posing or posturing, no play for the popular position, and no arrogance. In all these respects, in which he was often the diametrically opposite to Sartre, Camus provided a model for an intellectual stance — not merely for what he *said* but for what he *was*, and not merely (briefly to slip into Sartrean terminology) for the 'gestures' he made but for the 'actions' he performed. More than most others, it seems to me, Camus demonstrated the way in which the word of the intellectual acquired the weight of action.

This certainly happened during the state-controlled terrorism of apartheid, which spanned not only the regimes of Verwoerd, Vorster and P. W. Botha but also, as is increasingly demonstrated by the workings of the Truth and Reconciliation Commission, the rule of F. W. de Klerk. Precisely because in those years of darkness intellectuals (read, more specifically, "writers") were branded enemies of the regime, their words of opposition, resistance and revolt became rallying points for action against the system. It is never easy to quantify such matters: exactly what share of the success in the struggle against apartheid can be apportioned to intellectual action, specifically to literature, is impossible to say. But from the testimonies of many of those who bore the brunt of the liberation struggle, including President Mandela himself, it is quite obvious that the impact of intellectual activity cannot be underestimated. We know that the inmates of the grim prison on Robben Island sustained themselves by establishing an informal and unofficial "university" in which each prisoner with a fair amount of expertise in a given discipline (history, economics, law, letters) offered courses to the others. At the same time they, and the many anonymous others outside the prison walls and beyond the angry blue stretch of sea that separated the island from the mainland, were sustained by the writings of a wide array of intellectuals: sociologists, historians, economists, poets, novelists.

By and large, such writings may be said to have fulfilled two quite different kinds of functions, operating along the racial divide that marked the country: on the one hand, the victims of the system were encouraged by the constant reaffirmation of the fact that they were not alone in the struggle; on the other, members of one racial group were encouraged to learn that they could count on the understanding, and the solidarity, of at least *some* of those on the "other" side of the divide.

Especially since the wave of resistance that broke over the country with the youth revolt of 1976, the struggle for liberation was to an important extent reinforced by the massive gatherings of people at concerts, demonstrations or even funerals, at which poetry was recited or plays performed to encourage the disconsolate and galvanize them into continuing active resistance. I have had occasion before to repeat an anecdote told to me by the young 'struggle' poet Sandile Dikeni. While he was in detention, he would compose a new poem every day to focus his mind; and at lights-out at night he would recite this poem through the bars of his window, when all the other prisoners and detainees would cluster to their windows to listen. Attempts by the authorities to stop these recitals were met by such fierce protest that the warders had to back down. One morning, Sandile Dikeni says, he was accosted by one of the other inmates who asked him about a word from the previous night's poem which the other man couldn't understand with his own limited vocabulary. The word was 'soliloquy'. When Sandile heard this, he said, 'I'm sorry. I promise you I won't use difficult words again.' But his fellow prisoner responded excitedly, 'Oh no, you must, you must! Because now I have learned a new word.'

The intellectual does not need dramatic action to make an impression; often the most subtle insinuations of new meaning can bring about the slight shift in the perceptions of an individual mind which, multiplied a thousand or a million times, results in social change. We have seen this, we have lived this, in South Africa.

Many, many different actions have contributed to the fall of apartheid: international pressure through sanctions and boycotts, internal opposition on the factory floors, in educational institutions, in the churches, increasing resentment in an army of young conscripts, staggering corruption within the establishment, escalating violence — plus the basic logistics of a situation in which a handful of the privileged were trying to contain the resistance of a vast oppressed majority. But arching over all these various pressures there was the action of committed intellectuals who helped to fuse the different streams and elements to formulate and establish bases for concerted action, to define goals, to inspire the weak and the doubtful. And this action was not just vague and idealistic. There were very specific programs structured and directed by organizations like the Institute for a Democratic Alternative in South Africa (IDASA) run at the time by Van Zyl Slabbert and Alex Boraine: when they arranged in 1987 the first-ever encounter between representatives of the exiled ANC and a group of Afrikaner intellectuals in Dakar, Senegal, the internal group were branded traitors to the nation by the Botha government (in which De Klerk played a dominant role) and state reaction went to within a hair's breadth of the mass arrest of all the delegates upon their return. This event (followed by similar encounters with the ANC in Zambia, 1988 and Paris, 1989) had an amazing ripple-effect throughout the South African society, because most of the delegates convened mass meetings upon their return to report back to the nation: and for the first time, from within the ranks of the power establishment itself (that is, of Afrikanerdom), attempts were made to disseminate the real attitudes, opinions and doctrines of the ANC to a home audience. It was the end of the demonization of the ANC. At the same time it became possible to inform the exiled ANC of a much wider spectrum of opinions and attitudes within the ruling establishment. On *both sides* the misperceptions created by decades of separation began to be countered. From there, it was a relatively small step to the negotiations that brought the ANC to power. And this whole crucial last act in the movement that led to liberation was performed by intellectuals.

In the new South Africa which has come into being since the free elections of 1994 this entire situation has changed, and the change reveals distressingly much about the precarious situation of intellectuals everywhere in the 'free' world. Mandela's regime has brought about a radical shift in the position of intellectuals who now, for the first time in South Africa, find themselves no longer in opposition, but on the side of the new power establishment. At Mandela's inauguration, writers were invited to take the stage and read from their work to the hundreds of thousands of people gathered for that tremendous occasion. It was an acknowledgement of the power of the word, which would have been unthinkable under the previous regime. But in the long run this may be as disconcerting as it was for French socialists after Mitterrand's first triumph at the polls. It is indicative of the precariousness of the intellectual's position that this very acknowledgement may be the first step towards co-option. Because the functioning of the intellectual is optimal in a situation of opposition — even if such a situation does carry its own dangers, above all the danger of Manichean oppositionality and a process of dangerous over-simplification ('us' — 'them', 'good' — 'bad', 'right' — 'wrong'. . .)

This in itself illustrates a crucial problem for intellectuals. It would seem that in a repressive situation the efficacy of their situation is enhanced by being committed to a specific, opposition cause — like identifying with the ANC against the apartheid regime. Because in such a situation this choice is also a choice that goes beyond a mere party, to embrace the cause of *freedom*: freedom of speech, freedom to pursue the possibility of truth in the face of the lie, freedom to seek justice in the face of injustice. But once democracy has been established, the positioning of the intellectual within the ambit of a specific ideology or faction implies a *narrowing down* of the scope of free thought.

Which is why I could support the cause of the ANC while it was banned and in exile; but although I am naturally sympathetic towards the movement, even now that it finds itself in power, I cannot join the party as a member. I have no illusions about any individual's scope of being, truly, a 'free agent' in our world; *all* the choices we make have ideological implications. But in a free society, the only meaningful role for the intellectual would be to function as freely *as possible.*

In these circumstances, in the present South Africa, where many things are going alarmingly wrong (even though the essential idealism and direction of public affairs are still fairly intact), there has been an alarming *abdication* of responsibility by intellectuals. It may be understandable — there seems to be a general feeling that "we should give them a chance," or that, in view of the noble struggle they waged, "we shouldn't be too hard on those new to power." But the result is that the essential *vigilance* of intellectuals, which is the condition of their integrity, has been sacrificed to expediency and indulgence. And for any intellectual, these are cardinal sins. To give anyone in power the benefit of the doubt erodes the responsibility of the intellectual. Doubt is the *starting point* of intellectual activity. That is where Erasmus found his strength, that determines the greatness of Cervantes. Mandela embodies all the qualities the true intellectual has always, and against all odds, championed in society. But to tolerate lapses, or even sustained demonstrations of corruption, ineptitude, favoritism, lying and prevaricating, or the play of power for its own sake, which characterize far too many key figures in his administration, means to insult the very principles personified by Mandela.

If one drives along a narrow one-way street, as has happened to me, to find a car approaching in the wrong direction, with five oversized bullies in it who challenge you to clear the way for them, "because we are members of parliament, we have right of way," cannot be tolerated. This suggests that a whole dispensation has begun to move in the wrong direction. And in such circumstances, precisely because one is challenged, it is imperative for the intellectual to keep the voice of reason alive. It is the ultimate guarantee of humanity and of dignity in a world that has precious little of it left.

Hans Christoph Buch

1. "And there is nothing that I admire so much, in the USSR, as the great concern to protect and respect the characteristics of each people, of each little State included in the great Soviet Union. . . . A respect that flies in the face of the contemporary reproach against Communism and the USSR of trying to equalize, to level and standardize all the people of the immense Russia, in anticipation of being able to extend this ability over the entire world,"[1] André Gide proclaimed, to the applause of the deputies to the first international Congress of Writers for the Defense of Culture, in Paris, June 1935. And Peter Handke wrote in his 1977 journal, *The Weight of the World*, "Writers should definitely wear a characteristic uniform, like a police officer, so that people would pay a little attention to them!"[2]

Both of them soon made an about-face. In his *Back from the USSR*, published in 1936, André Gide proved exactly what he had previously denied so vehemently: the Soviet Union standardizes thinking. And Peter Handke himself endorsed a kind of uniform, at the end of 1995; during his winter trip to the former Yugoslavia, he transmuted into a Serbian Chetnik and sought to justify ethnic cleansing, with great effort of artistico-literary pathos.[3]

Handke and Gide are worlds apart, in history as in literature;

but they are examples that lend credence to the widespread fear that the process of European unification could lead to political uniformity and cultural monotony. More than ten years ago, in his historical essay *The Tragedy of Central Europe*,[4] Milan Kundera showed that the heart of the Old Continent, inscribed within the "Habsbourgeois" empire, was more than an ethnic patchwork, it was a rich multicultural biosphere with as many different species as a tropical rainy forest. Neither the emperors of the Germanic Roman Holy Empire nor the popes of Rome succeeded in unifying this vital space; neither Napoleon, Hitler, nor Stalin succeeded in breaking the passive resistance of the Europeans, and the principles of the French Revolution failed before their particularism just the same as the Cold War ideologies, and the Brezhnev and Hallstein doctrines. And there is no reason to think that the Treaty of Maastricht and the Brussels Eurocrats will enjoy any different fate. The only thing that persists in contemporary Europe, the lowest common denominator, is its diversity, confirmed in 1648 by the motto *Cujus regio, ejus religio*, which put an end to the era of the Wars of Religion. It was a small step from there to the Edict of Tolerance signed by enlightened absolutism: "Let each one go to heaven his own way."

The diversity of Europe, which has increased throughout history, is not an argument against but rather for unification (to which there is no serious alternative, in spite of all the setbacks and disappointments); the populist internationale of Europe's adversaries, from the Austrian Jörg Haider[5] and Le Pen to the French and German ex-Communist parties, reveals an alarming convergence of the right- and left-extremists. Nevertheless, we have to take seriously the fact that so many intellectuals seem to be tired of Europe, including, now, Pierre Bourdieu: after all, it is neither the Brussels economic union nor the Maastricht Treaty that caused unemployment in France and Germany. The causes are far deeper. The question is whether, behind the intellectuals' eloquent complaints about the globalization of the markets and the modernization of the economy, there is anything more than a simple anti-civilizing affect (that amalgam of Marxism, anti-Americanism and conservative cultural criticism, which is recycled every ten years under a new name)? To answer that, we would have to define the change that has occurred in the function that European intellectuals ascribe to themselves, and how their public role has changed since the fall of the Berlin Wall.

2.   They aren't experts in anything, not even in the language that is their most important instrument, and they presume to give everyone lessons although nobody asked them to do so. Although the majority of them have never studied political science, economics or law, they think they are better qualified than most politicians, economists and lawyers, although they neither wish to nor are able to replace them. On the contrary: their criticism is purely theoretical and does not contain any practical indication as to how to do things better. From this perspective, they are like a swimming instructor who never goes into the water, or the aerodynamics theorist described by Brecht, pointing to a bird and saying, "That bird doesn't fly the way it should."

The ancestor and model of all European intellectuals, unequaled to this day, is Socrates. He said that he didn't know anything, and he preferred to take the cup of poison rather than publicly refute his lack of knowledge. Plato, Socrates' disciple, chose a different approach. Irritated with the wealthy citizens of Athens who had condemned his master Socrates to death, he offered his services to the tyrant of Syracuse, Denys the Younger. Denys listened to Plato, when he advised him to remove from the State those intellectuals with a critical mind: he sold him into slavery to the Athenians' mortal enemies, in Sparta, and it was the wealthy citizens of Athens, scorned by Plato, who paid to release him from slavery. Even if it is not true, this story is well-conceived: it anticipates in a paradigmatic way what happened to the European intellectuals of the 20th century, who had to sail without compass between the Scylla of Fascism and the Charybdis of Stalinism. Their shipwrecks are well-known. The intellectuals provided the instruments of torture and the chains used by the totalitarian dictatorships to muzzle contrary voices. The so often quoted sentence, "When I hear the word 'culture,' I draw my pistol," does not come from Hitler or Goebbels, but from the writer Hanns Johst; it is less a reflection of Nazi ideology than of the antibourgeois revolt of expressionist literature. Conversely, the modern Edict of Tolerance, "You don't arrest Voltaire," did not come from a man of letters, but from a general.

"In terms of depravity and baseness, the writer is worse than other men," said Nadezhda Mandelstam, writing about the persecution and assassination of her husband, the poet Osip Mandelstam. A literary man from the Party, by the name of Pavlenko, listened in on Mandelstam's interrogation. He hid in a cupboard. He was not elected by the NKVD to do this; he wanted to satisfy his personal curiosity. Unlike the average Soviet, Pavlenko did not believe a word of the absurd charges levied against the poet. His pleasure in eavesdropping consisted in watching Mandelstam breaking down under torture.

Louis-Ferdinand Céline and Ezra Pound encouraged Hitler and Mussolini to intensify the persecution of the Jews. Curzio Malaparte,[6] had lunch with Hans Frank (the Nazi governor general of Poland) at the very moment when he was liquidating the Warsaw ghetto; Malaparte praised the intellectual brilliance of his Jewish friends and Frank did not contradict him. As we just mentioned, "In terms of depravity and baseness, the writer is worse than other men."

3.   Today too, the assessment is depressing. The intellectuals of Europe did not prevent the division of the continent, and they envisaged neither the construction nor the fall of the Berlin Wall. Their protests did not put an end to the murder in Bosnia and Chechnya; and as for prescriptions for abolishing unemployment or allowing the introduction of the euro, they are as divided in their opinions as the

politicians and the rest of the population.

But in spite of all that, there is no reason to dismiss intellectuals out of hand. Europe needs them more than ever: not only to sort out the illusions and the political crimes of the 20th century, religious fundamentalism included, but to defend the values that, without the criticism from the intellectuals, would be left to the mercy of the market or the ruling power. It is not as simple as favoring the book over the computer, film over television or the "new cuisine" over the hamburger. It is more a question of disseminating moral principles and aesthetic values via the media, and even with their assistance, values that, unlike plant and animal species that are threatened with extinction, are not recorded on any 'endangered' list. It is normal for each intellectual to work at the same time on his own self-promotion; without personal vanity and literary rivalry, there would have been no German romanticism, no French Enlightenment and no Italian Renaissance. Moreover, the era of the Enlightenment is not over, as a popular prejudice would have us believe — it has just begun. "Believing in progress doesn't mean that there has already been progress," wrote one of the great minds of the 20th century, Franz Kafka, who corresponds the least to the stereotype of the European intellectual.

Postscript for French readers

Isn't this assessment too negative in terms of the historical failure of intellectuals, and too optimistic as to their future role? This contradiction is resolved if one distinguishes two traditions that have moved in opposite directions: the Master-Philosophers such as Plato, Hegel and Marx, who served as godfathers for the birth of totalitarianism, and the moralists (often accused of naivety) who, without worrying about whether they would be blamed or applauded, openly denounced political lies, like André Gide and Albert Camus. In Germany, the dominant tradition is the first of these two, and thus one arrives at the grotesque result that Bertolt Brecht, an enlightened antifascist, was at the same time an enthusiastic partisan of Stalin, with certain reservations that made his commitment even more valuable in the eyes of the Party. In respect to Brecht's famous "ruse," which was often only a kind of accommodation, critical writers in the GDR were constrained to keep quiet. That explains why we never had, here, except for some isolated opponents, any real dissidence — no Charter 77 and no Solidarity. It is only after the Wall came down that it was revealed how profoundly the literature of the GDR had been infiltrated by informants and had been manipulated by the Stasi; and, since then, more than one eminent author has been knocked off his pedestal. Perhaps that explains why the role of the intellectual is debated with such violence today, in Germany. In the final analysis, it is not surprising in a nation that is struggling under the weight not only of the crimes of Nazism but a 40-year legacy from the dictatorship in the name of "real socialism."

Translated from German and annotated by Nicole Casanova

Notes

1. Andre Gide, *Littérature engagée*, texts collected and presented by Yvonne Davet, p. 83 and following; Gallimard, Paris, 1950.
2. A few passages were cut from the German original text, at the request of the author, and these lines are missing in the French translation by George Arthur Goldschmidt (Gallimard, Paris, 1980).
3. Peter Handke, *Un voyage hivernal vers le Danube, la Save, la Morava et la Drina*, translated from German by George Lorfèvre, Gallimard, Paris, 1996.
4. An essay by Milan Kundera, published in *La Lettre internationale* in 1983.
5. Jörg Haider, leader of the Austrian Freiheitliche Partei, a liberal party, spokesman of the extreme Right, is the Le Pen of Austria.
6. See Curzio Malaparte, *Kaputt*, 1944, an autobiographical novel.

Guillermo Cabrera Infante

1.   Somebody who remains committed even when commitment is out of style, but not the idea of commitment — and I don't particularly mean the idea of engagement as disseminated by the Communists, fellow travelers and ingenuous souls. I regarded myself as intellectual even before I started writing. Even when I was a professional journalist, I held intellectual positions: a) on popular culture, b) against the Batista regime and finally against Castro; in other words, against all flags. The epithet "intellectual" should be an *appellation contrôlée*.

2.   Trotsky, Orwell, Borges. The political man as an intellectual, the creative intellectual, the intellectual as artist. Trotsky was one political leader whom I followed at one time. Orwell, besides the obvious examples of *Animal Farm* and *1984*, influenced me through his articles on life at the bottom of the heap in the Indies and in Paris and London. His political essays are still admirable. But they don't influence me anymore. Borges is a kind of vice in reading: how one can be a reactionary and advanced, at the same time? And of course we'd have to include Camus, although that is such a commonplace.

3.   The intellectual will have always his bit to say. Unless, as General Queipo de Llano suggested, intelligence itself dies out. Of course, they have to have ethical values. With many intellectuals (there's no point in naming them), the only passion is fear. Oddly enough, that sentence comes from Sartre.

4.   When an intellectual makes a mistake, he has to denounce his error as vehemently as he asserted his view in the first place. The best-known example of the 20th century is Trotsky, fighting against

Stalinist terror. But there are other intellectuals who, benefiting from democracy, helped to destroy democracy; and when they realized their criminal error, they kept silent, covering up one crime with another.

One of them tried to justify Castro's crimes (public self-criticism, executions, banishment) by calling them chance mishaps; and he spoke French with an Argentine accent.

5.   I am exiled, from an English language that is either native or adopted. But I realize that England has never had intellectuals. The exceptions (Dr. Johnson, Oscar Wilde, George Bernard Shaw) were treated as criminals or eccentrics. Wilde has an extraordinary sentence in *Man and His Soul before Society*: "Any map of the world that doesn't include Utopia isn't even worth looking at." He did not see the possibility of "dystopia," and proposed that "Socialism will relieve us of the sordid necessity of living for other people." For Wilde, socialism (which he always wrote with a capital letter) would "lead us to individualism"! His contemporary, George Bernard Shaw, should have known more about it; he lived long enough to interview Stalin! During their interview, which lasted three hours, Shaw tried to convince Stalin . . . to become a vegetarian! Orwell's attitude before, during and after Stalinism, was always one of valor, valorous. Even after the Stalinist crimes were revealed, Orwell was hounded, badgered; and the publication of his book *Animal Farm* ran into opposition, including from (what a surprise!) T.S. Eliot. The misadventures of *1984* are well-known, but Orwell's reputation as a reactionary persisted even after his death. How can an intellectual thrive in such a climate?

6.   We must stand up to every form of blackmail: historical, moral, political. Let's not forget that Nazism, Stalinism and their proselytes lost their prestige not because the Berlin Wall came down, but because of the death of the totalitarian ideologies. But there is a trail of debris that transmits other known forms of cancer.

The concept of left and right, the way they arranged the chairs around the king at the National Constituent Assembly in 1789, is as obsolete as the absolutist Soviet Union. The design of the Assembly was replaced by a concept of reaction and progressivism with the same intention of historical blackmail. A few years ago a charming TV commentator, offering me a trap more than a seat, asked me, "And where do you prefer to be?" I told her, with a hint of truth, that I was a reactionary on the left.

Translated from Spanish by Albert Bensoussan

Édouard El-Kharrât

1.   To me, the word *intellectual* refers to a person who concerns himself with matters of the mind. The Arab word, *mouthaqqaf*, literally designates the cultivated person, whose field is, in my view, far broader. The cultivated man was experienced, he knew every facet of the human spirit in action, and that includes the activity of the senses, as well, the creative élan of the artist, the spiritual élan of the man. If I am not mistaken, that goes beyond the field of philosophical reflection, ethics, the strict field of reason and thought, and encompasses the affairs of the heart as well as those of the senses and the soul.

It is in this broader capacity that the intellectual has to play his part today. In this sense, in my capacity as a poet, novelist and critic, I do not reject the term at all.

What's more — and more important — this concern for completeness is exercised in a larger totality; the intellectual — and this is not a dead letter — is someone who is dedicated to the affairs of his people, of his fatherland — his city, to the great questions that confront humanity. His activity embraces and exceeds any specific competence. He does not act as a professional thinker who seeks to take the questions of his profession to more profound depths, but as a humanist who, through a broader vision, will break the vicious circle of determinisms, of sociology, of nationalities, of identities. In this sense, I consider myself an intellectual, a *mouthaqqaf*: a rationalist who reasons by the emotions of art and of the heart. Is this definition different from the "Western" definition of the term?

2.   I could not really say whether any great intellectual figures have marked me decisively . . . They certainly must have done so, since it is the emotions inspired by music, painting, works of art, and texts, that nourished me intimately since my earliest youth. But the fabric of my education is now too tight for me to disentangle the individual strands. Rather than individual influences, I believe, it is the direct experience of the activity of the mind that has left deep impressions in my memory; impressions which I could not summarize by naming one or several individuals, whose traces no longer bear any indication of their origins, for me. Structural orientations, on the other hand (and this may seem simplistic), remain well-defined, they still have a decisive influence on me: which thought is a departure from the core tenets of the classical models? How far can art, the adventure of creation, take us? And how far can knowledge, the search for *one* truth — the absolute truth, which reveals itself only by intermittent facets? And then, where shall we seek beauty, poetry? These are still determinant questions, for me. And reason, too, about which Abu Al-Ala Al-Maari, a great Arab poet of the 10th — 11th century, said: "Reason is the shepherd of a dumb flock." If reason is the master, the scout, the measuring instrument by which we probe our folly, our despair, then the man of reason within us must take his rightful place, that is, by sharing with the spiritual man, the poetic man, the creator, the one who is seeks beauty.

3.   I believe that the role of the intellectual is at least as important today. In the Third World, in our Arab world, their day is just beginning. Intellectuals in our part of the world have a heavier burden than ever, a weighty responsibility in the affairs of our city. They have a duty to speculate: to examine the present, to expand the range of what is possible, to sniff out the real questions that confront us — such as the disturbing question of our identity (spiritual, intellectual), our national identity, to seek out their deepest sources and to build from there, to avoid distractions by conducting the debate in terms of rationalism and the spiritual quest, in a spirit of adventure, too.

4.   No, this severity is not deserved in our countries. Of course, some intellectuals line up under the banner of the most powerful, of the prevailing powers, whatever forms they may take: the power of the holy texts or religious backwardness, the power of the standing governments or, more demagogically, the power of the man in the street. Those deserve the term, "betrayal of the intellectuals," but they must have been lacking from the very start that fundamental virtue that should have governed their action: probity. Intellectual, ethical, spiritual probity. Three components of the same honesty. But the others, the majority, have played their role among us and, for the most part, at a high price. Here, intellectuals still face real dangers, and continue to shoulder their responsibilities with courage, even if one would like to be able to go further today. Intellectuals are still being killed for their ideas, intellectuals have been imprisoned, most of them (of us) have spent long years in prisons and camps, the majority of them have been dispersed, exiled, deprived of the means of subsistence. Almost every intellectual, here, is still fighting today just to guarantee the liberty and the dignity of their people, of their country. And within their country, to guarantee their own liberty, their own dignity.

5.   The obstacles are very numerous, and they do not only come from the noise raised by the pseudo-intellectuals. Indifference from the media? More than indifference, the intentional, planned bias of the media, which operate under the guiding hand of the ruling power and conspire to blind, to waylay the people in the shifting sands of second-rate entertainments, to seduce and tame them, in order to make it easier to dissimulate and obscure reality. This is a way of justifying partiality in opinions, of vitiating the real debates. The natural consequence of all that is to marginalize culture and ethics as values; the great questions are not posed, despite all our efforts. Thus for us, the mixing, the meeting of ideas remains the essential thing, wearied as we are by the politically correct, the single acceptable thought, which prevailed for so long in our countries and which the newspapers, radio and television prolong, in their own way. More simply still, we are trying to arrive at a dialogue, a dialogue without interdicts and taboos. That would bring us happily back to the past, to the golden age of our history, our Arab culture. Everything — and I mean that quite literally — was put on the table in those days, for discussion and argument. Divinity, the absolute, and questions about the antiquity of the Koran (was the Koran created or no?), up to and including problems of metaphysics or scholastics, not excluding the domain of eroticism, everything was open to discussion. Anything could be accepted into the ranks of the joys of nature and the requirements of the spirit, including the famous debate over homosexuality.

However, while police repression is still noticeable in many Arab countries, it has, it should be said, recently declined in Egypt. But the religious powers still assume the right to legislate, to prohibit, to censure, to seize books. We very recently have made strong advances in obtaining a provision that nothing can be censured without the case being referred to a secular court, whose procedures guarantee the writer, the intellectual, an opportunity to defend his work. We will still have to be highly vigilant, however, to ensure that this achievement will be implemented effectively. But the "soft" repression of which you speak, the obliteration of the conscience through consumer pleasures, still has a rosy future ahead of it, and no doubt will further intensify, and become the major obstacle to our word.

6.   I mentioned above that the lucid analysis of the phenomena of society, of thought, of spirituality, urgently needs to be released from the subtle repressions imposed by the powers that be. We must discover new ways, find alternative solutions, appeal to reason over sectarianism, intolerance and narrow-mindedness, extremism and all forms of immobility and blind attachment to the established order. More than ever, we need to have the means of observing, of discussing, especially now that the West accuses us of obscurantism, accuses Islam itself of being a religion of violence, of fanaticism, of being the faith of assassins. This fundamentalism is revolting, but aren't the American fundamentalists, for example, the extremists, equally so? It's true that the road to power here is lined with meaningless religious slogans that are very far from the spirit of Islam. Although I am not a Muslim, enlightened Islam — that of tolerance, of reason — is my culture, and in my view it has a longer history than that of religious sectarianism.

This wave of obscurantism, of backwardness and intolerance clearly makes the role of the intellectual more essential than ever. The slogans are full of familiar resonances, of promises by which they conquer the man in the street. A thought that is hardly more than a pragmatic demand of the accession to power, of the will to dominate, is inevitably a threat to the mind, to justice, to freedom. The intellectual must reiterate his attachment today to the values of reason and dignity which are, for him — which appear to him — to be achievements, will perhaps seem old hat, even obsolete, to the Western reader. Viewed from here, their star has not faded, they seem so fragile, so easily threatened. Defending them is still vitally urgent.

Remarks recorded and translated from Arabic by C. Farhi

Péter Esterházy

1.   The writer lives in his room, the intellectual in society. Some-times I am an intellectual, or in any case, I should regard myself as one since other people consider me to be one. For me, the intellectual is someone who questions. Under that definition, the child who splits hairs, who thirsts for knowledge, and who spends his time asking questions is an intellectual; but the teacher who harps on the same answers in the name of education is not. Neither is the politician, who cannot question: he is condemned to give answers, he must al-ways behave as thought he knows what must be done.

2.   It would be pretentious of me to say that I have no thoughts on this matter; however, I do not like to make a point of naming any *one* source of inspiration, so I will close my eyes and answer: Danilo Kiš, Italo Calvino.

3.   For me, this question is too *vast*. My pretense of an answer is, by "intellectual" we unconsciously mean the traditional intellectual, the one who has studied the humanities. While perhaps his sphere of activity has not changed, his impact, clearly, has diminished palpably (which amounts to the same thing as saying that his sphere of activ-ity, too, has changed).

4.   Those who criticize intellectuals are obviously intellectuals themselves. In other words, every critic worthy of the name is a self-critic. In this sense, I fully agree with the criticism. The bankruptcy of the intelligentsia is so painful because it shows that even to be ra-tional, to be conscious, to maintain one's distance, is not enough to protect oneself from anything. That, for me, is the proof of the en-slavement of human thought, of human existence: we live under the

sign of Auschwitz.

5.   I learned how to play my role as an intellectual under a dictator-ship. That is not the best school. We believed that everyone thought like us, or exactly the reverse; that there were only these two ways of thinking. However, those two are not the only ways. Such an attitude, which passes for natural, obviously causes many errors in Hungary today. It may encourage the "chaotic multitude" and the concomitant terrors, then paralysis.

6.   But if I hear the word "fight," I am immediately overcome by fear and paralysis, so that I won't even answer this question. But, if I am told in absolute terms that it is forbidden, that it is prohibited, that it is impossible and that there is no valid reason for fighting, then I unsheathe my sword!

     There is a feeling that the guild of intellectuals has no grounds for rejoicing today, but obviously that will not be long in changing. It's always been that way, hasn't it?

Translated from Hungarian by Nicolas Cazelles

Nadine Gordimer

1.   One could hardly imagine a writer who, with any honesty, could deny being an intellectual! Although there are some who — in fear of the term being applied, as it is in some quarters, as one of abuse — nervously hasten to refute what they see as an accusation of elitism. And there is a political aspect to this rejection of the category of intellectual. I belong to the Left, I am an active member of the African National Congress, but I have never accepted the substitute of the term "cultural worker" for writer/intellectual. My argument has been: the

plumber calls himself a plumber, the veterinarian calls himself a veterinarian, the farmer calls himself a farmer — why should I be ashamed to call myself a writer? Doesn't that state precisely what nature of work I perform? Why should I be ashamed to be an intellectual? And hide under the generalization "cultural worker"? This is an absurdity of radical chic, an unacknowledged condescension, the yearning of those who happen to be blessed with talent to be as "humble" as they imagine the manual laborer to be!

Nevertheless, I believe the category of intellectual is too narrowly defined, certainly by Western culture. To be an intellectual is to be one who lives in the exploratory world of ideas as well as in the daily performance of subsistence and survival. Anyone who seeks to answer ontological self-questioning is an intellectual.

2.   Apart from novelists, poets and story-writers who influenced me in my youth as a writer, the intellectuals who come to mind, among others, are: Lukacs, Gandhi, Freud, Isaiah Berlin, Camus (*The Rebel*). I doubt if I can be influenced any longer, but the intellectual who interests me most at present is Edward Saïd.

3.   Even if God is dead. . .the intellectual's mission can never be complete. The human being is blessed or cursed by being the only animal capable of introspection. That is the basis of intellectualism. Without it we would turn evolution in reverse.

4.   I would hazard the opinion that the charges of irresponsibility and blindness (which imply indifference to the consequences of a particular position taken) can be leveled more justly at academia than at intellectuals in general. The exercise of the intellect is a debate, yes, but there is more to the world than university lecture halls and the published thesis; there is a restless, troubled, and aleatory world beyond the classroom.

5.   Intellectuals in South Africa, my country, are in the happy position of being free of political repression for the first time in the recorded history of South Africa, since for more than three centuries before apartheid there was colonial oppression. Freedom of expression is guaranteed in our Constitution, and, so far in our young democracy, is scrupulously maintained. The indifference of the press and television to intellectual ideas — literature and philosophy — and the concentration on the lowest forms of pop art in all its manifestations is the obstacle for intellectuals.

6.   The most dangerous prejudices: religious extremism and its expression as international terrorism.

The most important causes to defend: banning production of nuclear weapons. Banning production of land mines and defusing/removing them where they already exist. Promoting an international law to force each country to dispose of its own nuclear waste on its own territory; forbid dumping elsewhere.

The intellect can only function if we survive . . .

The principal challenge: to defend the written word against worldwide takeover by its transformation into image. For communication, the marvels of technology are lateral: less and less about more and more. In communication, literature (as expression of the intellect) is the height and depth.

Juan Goytisolo

1.   One cannot decide for oneself whether or not one is an "intellectual," just as one cannot ascribe to oneself the title of philosopher. It is for others to determine who it is who writes and conducts himself with rigor and with high ethical standards that are often contrary to the "national values" and who is simply merchant of his own

products or cheap national myths/fairytales.

2.   There are, in the sorry history of Spain, some examples of this commitment to truth and justice in patriotic opposition to the consensus and to the "essentialism" of the tribe. Y. M. Blanco White was exiled in first half of the 19th century, and the historian Americo Castro was exiled during Francoism. For me, they are models who have guided me throughout the last thirty years of my life. Their critical attitude toward their own values and their respect for the values of others, to the extent that they were respectable, kept them from falling into the trap of "us," from taking on the plural form as a united identity.

3.   With the end of the cold war and the collapse of the communist regimes, the intellectuals of both sides seem to have lost both their voice and their bearings. But, are we really living in a world that is so equitable and so perfect that we can justify such a silence in the face of the dizzying devaluation of the principles of the French Revolution, ratified by the United Nations Charter, in the face of the merciless fight for political, economic and cultural power, in the face of the lack of commitment to personal responsibilities and indifference to the sufferings and misery of the bulk of the world's population?

4.   The concept of the organic intellectual has resulted in many of them going along, initially, with mistakes and, finally, with horrors. As for me, I long ago came to this conclusion: it's better to be mistaken all alone and have reason as your watchword.

5.   The general commercialization of words, things, bodies and minds, nature and culture, denounced by the most lucid heads, leads to this mess where, because of the lack of true values, everything goes and crimes are permitted.

6.   In the context of the European Union, the most pressing threats are racism, xenophobia and ultra-nationalism. We must defend immigrants (with or without papers), Gypsies, and the minorities threatened with destruction. Today's intellectual must give up his habit of coming to a conclusion about subjects which he knows only by hearsay and stick with those that he knows about through proximity or direct knowledge: as for me, I think about Bosnia, Chechnya, the civil war in Algeria, the drama of the Palestinians. Not to mention, of course, support for writers who are persecuted because of a restrictive concept of society and religion.

David Grossman

I don't like the word "intellectual," (maybe because my religious and tough grandfather used to mock at those he suspected of being intellectuals.   He had a special deriding snort when he said, "*Inallectuals...*"). Spinoza would be "my" intellectual — i.e. an absolutely free soul, loyal only to his truth; and I would say that in my opinion, an intellectual is, first and foremost, a person who for one reason or another, takes the world and its phenomena very, very personally.

That being said, a couple of weeks ago I took part in the creation of a new protest movement in Israel, urging a renewed investigation of our Prime Minister [Benjamin Netanyahu], following an investigation that cleared him halfheartedly of some grave suspicions. In recent days we have collected almost 70,000 signatures of Israeli citizens, who, like us, demand to know the truth. In these days, I have had many thoughts about the role of the intellectual in my society: about the need to remain naive (in a very sober and decisive way), if one wants to be loyal to some basic moral values in the midst of so many contradictory political pressures and interests; and about the thick skin one has to develop in order to survive insults, hatred and aggression from people who think that words like "Democracy" or "Law" are only cunning western inventions of some "Elites" who try to eternalize their system.

Even if this initiative does not succeed, I will feel a little better; the air that I breathe will be a little clearer.

Yoram Kaniuk

I don't have the faintest idea what an intellectual is, exactly. If it means being wise or learned, then so were the greatest Nazis; if culture is a proof, then Hesse, the commandant of Auschwitz, loved classical music, avidly read poems and loved philosophy. An intellectual is someone who is not intellectual, who is not dead in spirit at the age of twenty-five, who is still capable of enthusiasm, who can cry or laugh because of a simple rainbow, who can feel guilt, who can feel shame for the guilt of others, who wants to change the world because he knows that a) it is immutable, and b) the world does not deserve to be changed for the better. If God exists and he created man, then this invention was not a success. Yet we have, at least, a mind capable of brilliance, a heart capable of tears, and enough courage or stupidity — take your pick — to stand alone, to believe that we are right even though everyone else thinks differently. To me, an intellectual is one who can stand alone, and remain ethical against even the morality of the herd, be lonely and, even if he's wrong, feel that at least he has tried.

All the ideas (almost!) that intellectuals (whatever they may be) have loved and cherished, absorbed and created, in the end became dogmas and brought about self-righteousness, bigotry and death. Over-simplicity is always a path toward tyranny. Almost all the great intellectual endeavors of the last five thousand years have brought about short-lived freedom, then brainwashing and then jailing. The human spirit that lived all by itself waiting to be touched, not grabbed, is not intellectual. Most governments encourage intellectuals, even if they put them in jail, because they know that they can change nothing while giving people the illusion that something better will emerge. It never does. However, we must believe in the endurance of the spirit, namely freedom — which will eventually turn into a dogma, yet is essential to human existence. You must believe, but also know that your belief might bring about disaster.

In the first Hebrew version of *Genesis*, God did not create but rather spoke, saying, "LET THERE BE," (and isn't that the hallmark of all real thought?), and thus became the creator. That's wonderful. Later on, the Hebrews had a dynasty of great kings: David, Solomon and so on. The intellectuals who edited the Bible didn't give any one of them a book in this collection of stories. David, the founder of ancient Israel, the most beloved king, appears in the Bible only in *Samuel I*. However, Jeremiah, a great and rebellious poet who encouraged his people to surrender, who betrayed his people and was put into the dungeon, he got a whole book! The intellectuals, whoever they are, are the people who represent — and thank God for that — the greatest avengers against heroes, who are always poetic, cruel, and unjust, yet they create nations, and revolutions. So it is a pure revenge, and a good one, at that. Or a bad one. All that was thought to be good later becomes bad, and vice versa. We live in a cage, trapped by the need to seek meaning; and the role of the intellectual is to struggle with meaning and, therefore, to go against the core of human nature. So is the intellectual man's bitter enemy? Perhaps. And a good one, indeed. We need the rebellious nature of the untamed, and the intellectual, if he exists, is the untamed, the man of spite, the lonely person who think he knows better.

According to a Moroccan proverb, when the king is sick, his chief servant gets the enema. When a society is sick (which is most of the time), the intellectual is the one who either gets the enema or, more often, gives it. The spirit is boundless, and dogmatism is born out of intellectuals to be attacked by other intellectuals, in order for them to catch the wayward spirit (which we all do), and while doing so we miss the most important point — what is good to you, what is pure, simple, and just, is the opposite to the other. In the Second World War, intellectuals on both sides — intellectual fascists, intellectual communists, all brilliant, all intellectuals, some great, fought what seemed to them was a just battle. In Sweden and Swaziland, the Nazi gold flowed. Jewish refugees were turned back, and intellectuals sang the sweet song of peace, denouncing the war and congratulating themselves for remaining neutral. How many people died because of these choices? An intellectual is liable to maintain a position or its opposite; intellectuals are like religious leaders who advertise Paradise, a place where they have never been, and sell it to people who will never get there.

Yet without intellectuals, the world would be dull and meaningless. An intellectual might come up with a reason why it is that way, but in the end he will be wrong, like millions before him. Today, many intellectuals have become fundamentalists, while many simple people without much wisdom want the opposite, to live, make money, and be free to worship their cars and TV sets — and to abolish the intellectual right to be profound and fundamentalist.

An intellectual would not write what I have just written. Indeed, he would oppose it vigorously. And so do I. That, to me, is the humble sign of my poor intellectualism, which dismisses intellectualism because otherwise I would have no right to preach, to create, to be me. Perhaps an intellectual is the one who, in the end, manages to become himself. And that is the essence of anti-intellectualism.

Ivan Klíma

1.   I do not reject the term "intellectual," but I do not like it. Its meaning is too vague. And for another reason: to become a professor or a scientist, a man has to prove his abilities, publish works, pass exams. But to become an intellectual? Everybody can proclaim himself an intellectual, and commit spiritual crimes and cover them by his "grand" mission. I never use the term!

2.   Albert Camus, Karel Capek and his philosophy of relativism. Erich Fromm, Graham Green, Paul Johnson, Alexander King and Bertrand Schneider and their *Limits to Growth*. Solzhenitzyn and many others.

4.   Since I don't like the term, it is difficult to answer. But I agree that educated people have committed or allowed others to commit many crimes in our century.

5.   I do not see any significant obstacle to any intellectual effort in the Czech Republic. It is a problem, of course, at the end of the millennium, that most of the public is far more interested in the attainments of the soccer or ice hockey players than in the attainments of those who play on the intellectual turf.

6.   The most dangerous prejudice is the pride of man, who believes that his mission is to rule nature, who again and again believes that he has discovered the undoubted Truth. To me, the misuse of mass media represents a major peril; it is helping to create a uniform mankind, a mob of robots craving entertainment, blood and brutality. And my greatest intellectual joy? It is still writing.

Aïcha Lemsine

1.   Philosopher, novelist, poet or playwright, "intellectual" is, in my view, a kind of magic word. The notion, with all the strength of its intelligence and sensitivity, uses the language of reality to try to turn away the evil fate that hangs over the existence both beings and things in the world. Whether it designates a "master of thought" or someone who is "isolated in an ivory tower," it is in any case an incantatory word, an attempt to cast a spell to divert, even to overturn the course of human destiny.

It's other people, not me, who have called me an "intellectual"! My political critics and the intellectuals alike (the first use black ink to ban a book, the latter take it upon themselves to broadcast systematic suspicion, denunciation, humiliation and exclusion — all in a "literary" pseudo-criticism cleansed of any "politically incorrect" intellectual thought . . . That adds up to the "rule of attack" against any writer who makes waves in Algeria. That, plus the brutal surge of Islamic terrorism, has reinforced my "intellectual identity."

And so, at first I thought I was just a novelist, writing solely out of a passion animated by the desire to understand and to know. Neither a message nor an assertion, just an intention of dialogue in the sense of questioning, and rejecting fatalism. But you must understand that my books, since the publication of *La Chrysalide* in 1976 (published by Des Femmes, Paris), *Ciel de porphyre* (novel), *Ordalie des voix* (an essay on the Arab and Muslim world), *Au Coeur du Hezbollah* (essay on the other hidden face of Islamism), and my articles in my country's press carry within them a certain power to awaken consciences, and therefore are liable to be *silenced* (I find that word, more significant than the word *censured*) by fundamentalists from all sides. Then, today, I assume my "status" of intellectual with all the risk that it entails for an Arab and Moslem woman. That is, the destruction of my life at any moment . . . in the infamy of exile imposed by terror, the pain of family dislocation and the material insecurity that makes human dignity a "cause" that is manipulated even within the ranks of the same people who preach "solidarity and protection" for persecuted writers.

2. A collection of intellectual futures have contributed to quenching my thirst for knowledge in the sense of the "flavor" and the "knowledge" of the most beautiful ideas of human thought. They gave me the taste of internal beauty, qualities that go by names like: sharing, tolerance, justice, freedom, solidarity — in other words, the opposite of an empty heart, full only of itself. Moslem woman that I am — raised not as Barthes would say, in "a buzz of language," but in the possessive fury of my three languages-sisters-enemies: Arabic, Berber, and French — these intellectual figures taught me how "to be." They broke the circle of various taboos and prejudices within which I had been defined, in thought and in speech, without realizing it. My "mother" tongues finally pacified, with no more rupture or wrenching separatist impulses, have become my allies in an immense language of freedom. Finally, I can say that following the example of my own experiences in the school of life, I have educated myself unceasingly in the thought of these philosopher-companions of my progression in life. By bringing to me the difference of their dreams, the difference of their cultures, they integrated me into a universe without borders, with the concern to be as human as possible, as close as possible to the truth.

Thus it is not so much for their "authority" as for the value of their spirit, the spirit of these thinkers that I call upon . . . Montaigne, for example, who was always against literary authoritarianism, and those who judge. He's "given me" the following advice: "Expect of any mind, however famous, not that it will teach you, but that you will recognize it by the value of the spirit." Moreover, he taught me humility (the opposite of intellectual arrogance): the search for truth in literature is "a thought being tested," not a message nor an example.

I still think of Voltaire as the one who put all the genius of his talent to the service of tolerance versus fanaticism. His "Prayer to God," today, takes on new meaning in the context of the fratricidal war that is tearing apart my country, especially the sentence: "You did not give us hearts in order that we should hate each other and hands to cut each others' throats. . ." But still, I hold as treasures, to ponder, the fraternity, courage and honesty of Victor Hugo, Lamartine, Zola, Gide, Malraux, Pablo Neruda and the Spaniards Machado and Lorca. For me, they were all sources of inspiration and examples of visionary and humanistic genius. And it is because they stayed as close as possible to the truth that they remain unquestionable guideposts. Regardless of the beauty of a text or the intellectual power of an author, regardless of the epoch to which he belongs, it is the "consistency" between his thought and his action that incites my respect. When their work comes to grip with the problems of their times, when they are willing to stake their reputations without taking up the "wrong" battles. . . then they become really examples. In this respect, I would evoke the memory of one of the greatest Maghrebian thinkers from the beginning of this century, Abulkacem Chabbi (my father's first cousin). My childhood was filled with the family's pride with regard to this famous relative. His thought was suffused with action, and his saying is famous throughout the Arab world: "If, one day, a people wants freedom, destiny will have to respond." And I have transposed this maxim to suit my condition as a woman: "If, one day, a *woman* wants freedom . . ." (and, to become a writer?) Abulkacem Chabbi . . . his blood runs in my veins, I am told. But I recognize him only in the value of his spirit palpitating in mine, in equal shares with the other above-cited thinkers, whom I have chosen as "family". . .

In addition to these examples, I should add those who have literally "whipped" my rational and conscious mind, guiding me beyond the unthinkable . . . Kierkegaard, Dostoyevsky, Nietzsche and Kafka.

It may seem paradoxical for a Moslem woman, but I still find today, in each one of them, the echo of my doubts, my faith, and my intellectual loneliness vis-à-vis an international morality (political, economic, cultural) built on forgery. . . They are, in my view, the four mighty "magical spells" against human fragility and desperation. Fathers of modern thought, they surpassed the boundaries of theology, philosophy, poetry and psychology to defy with their thought the entire dimension of human existence. Their words are fresher than ever in this turn-of-century with all its social, political and existential anguish. In their works I discovered the meaning of the real questions, those still being addressed by today's philosophers, each in his own manner . . . Kierkegaard, the precursor of modern existentialism in all its human facets (esthetics, morality and faith) of the temporal and the eternal, offended his most powerful contemporaries: the clergy and his intellectual fellow-citizens. "Truth is a power of suffering," he said, but also, as for the metamorphoses from which the truth suffers, he observed that the same contemporaries who had acted with contempt would say the opposite of what they said yesterday, and thus everything would be confused. For me, that applies to the moral responsibility of certain Algerian intellectuals and their support for repression against any "dialogue of national reconciliation," which plunged Algeria into years of carnage.

Yes, to exist means above all to exist morally and to face new choices every day.

Dostoyevsky's genius transcends the borders of time. Prophetic and visionary like Kierkegaard, he saw that the moral, political and religious crises signaled the breakdown of society. The characters in his novels are never abstract. All his art lies in having thought up the man of the future with the brain of anonymous man. His books are an immense map of still-applicable human psychology. In the field of human "psychic archaeology," Nietzsche admitted that he had learned a great deal from Dostoyevsky. This Russian author's thought, as it applies to religion, still applies in full to today's questions of religious fundamentalism. Thus, for Kierkegaard, as for Dostoyevsky, religious faith is not a *diktat* of the powers, it is an effort at "becoming," not "being." Great sinners find their way to God through other sinners and not inevitably by the intermediary of the official representatives of religious faith! Nietzsche's attack against religion is closely related to the challenges of the Danish philosopher and the Russian novelist. He went beyond the religious hierarchy to tackle God, whom he called "The one who contradicts man."

From his impassioned thesis of the "super-man" ("the slave of his own freedom" according to Sartrian existentialism) and from Camus anxiously asking, "Can I become a saint without believing in God?" the "subman" was created, a basis of German Nazism and, by extension, an arbitrary humanism, created for its own sake, in complacency unfettered by instincts, and which is finally rejected by moral reality, as shown by Nietzsche's tragic end.

The thought, work and lives of these splendid authors were just different facets of one jewel: human passion. Kafka, unlike the German philosopher, did not disavow God in his dialectical "vociferation," but in the silence, the world that is pathetic in the absence of God.

I have a great sympathy for Kafka, who didn't affirm anything, neither his belief in the Jewish faith nor a call to atheism. Torturers and victims, in his novels, all live in a world without God. But isn't that endlessly-probed "absence" another form of faith?

Thus I find Kafka, in his person and in his work, not an assertion of a "super-man" but the interrogation of human suffering given God's silence . . . Without seeking to impose an intellectual dogma, his thought is the painful awareness of human rights proscribed. His portrait of the demon and of nothingness as the ultimate destiny is another fall of man without faith.

In fact, for me, Kafka's philosophy is a theology in camouflage. The bridge that cannot be crossed between the master and the visitor, in *Le Château*, suggests man's relation with God. The absence of hope is a response to the idea of salvation and resurrection. Eternity is replaced by infinite nothingness in which God is lost. Isn't Kafka's despair a response to those who never completed the experience of faith "as an end or a beginning"? This path of passion (outside of any religious identity or membership) is found in a book by David R. Blumenthal (Emory University), a theology of protest entitled *Facing the Abusing God*.

This rather lengthy answer is necessary to explain how much these authors were and continue to be important for me, in all their quests — always new, demanding and tireless — to understand the world. In their disparate and at the same time complementary thought, I grasp the plurality of an intellectual quest that surpasses all certainty. In addition, they were the prototypes of a fantastic intellectual honesty.

Their work is proportionate to their great human suffering. They did not seek to recruit disciples, time alone showed them to be right. Far from establishing a dogma of thought, they opened up to us new ways of reflection and intellectual investigation. It is in that that they are splendidly human and authentically universal.

3.   Those who claim that the intellectuals' role is over are, consciously or not, playing into the game of the political and economic systems of relentless globalization, which aims to control people's destiny without too much trouble from "critics" and "witnesses." Or, you could call it a new "philosophy" that is convenient for self-marketing in the new chains of intellectual supermarkets. An intellectual who avoids taking a moral stance on the problems of his society, claiming to belong to the "esthetics" of abstract ideas (that do not compromise or that in fact may agree with the ideology of the moment), is better able to "sell" himself.

I think that in this regressive period, at the turn of the century, the intellectual must demonstrate great attention and a powerful presence with regard to the problems of his society. Unemployment, racism, violence from wherever it may come, social or civil conflicts are a social responsibility, and thus the responsibility of the intellectual. For, as Kant said, "Peace is the virtue of the people and not the princes" (who govern us). And thus peace (i.e. justice and social cohesion) concerns the virtue of the intellectual, since he is the one who must help the people to establish human rights.

When one's society is facing difficulties, the intellectual must, in my view, assume his responsibility. In any case, the bloody drama of my country taught me mine.

4.   I think we should moderate this notion of "irresponsibility" or the "errors" that intellectuals may have committed. Céline, Aragon, Foucault, Barthes all come to mind; each defended a political cause, and each, in a certain sense, was proven wrong by history.

They clearly lacked perspective, that is, a long-range vision of the world, but they certainly did not lack sincerity nor intellectual generosity. And while their ideas undoubtedly "misled" a generation of idealists, it's also true that they did not divide their fellow-citizens against themselves nor contribute to a civil war in their countries.

What we have to contradict is the language of intellectual demagoguery that manipulates the concepts of justice, freedom, and equality in a purely political context. Like, for example, those who, in the name of the "republican" or "democratic" values (concepts that have been tragically "commercialized" in certain countries when it comes to Islamism, or immigration), reject the opinion or culture of those who do not "think" like them. In the name of freedom, they cancel the freedom of others, with the axiom: "No democracy for those who do not recognize it!" And thus is propagated a whole body of thought that makes a mockery of the freedom of expression.

In formulating these questions, I am not unaware of the reality of the danger of the emergence of racist and fascistic speech, like Le Pen, or Islamist violence . . . but one cannot use legal or armed repression against them. On the contrary, it is only by investing their fields of propaganda (religion, human, political values) with the intelligence of the mind and the heart that one can demolish their fanatical theses. This effort to awaken the awareness of public opinion requires a permanent and "visible" debate through all the means of communication, conducted by politically neutral, intellectually credible and morally convinced and convincing individuals!

In Algeria, political Islamism would have lost its virulence and its "religious myth" if, as in Jordan, for example, it had been incorporated into an intelligent and imaginative political pluralism. Instead, repression has conferred upon it the "legitimacy of violence" and the "conviction" that backs its ferocity.

That is the essence of the question: an honest analysis of the responsibility for the intellectual's word in his society. And this word is not only individual, but also collective. It must incline toward harmony and peace, against division, injustice and the language of hatred, as the French intellectuals and artists showed recently in their opposition to the law on immigration and the racist speeches of the leader of the National Front in France. I believe, and I hope, that I will always defend the role of the intellectual: as a link of intelligence and generosity with his fellow-citizens. For, in my opinion, he represents *par excellence* "lucidity" against bellicose instincts and "progress" against obscurantism and fanaticism. But, to be credible, the intellectual must be consistent in himself, he must embody all that sensitivity, generosity and immense human intelligence that one ascribes to him.

Thus, instead of conducting a "trial" against intellectuals "blinded" by political passions, we should address the real problem of explaining the ethical stakes that the intellectuals must assume at this turn of the century.

5.   As an Algerian intellectual, I have endured the censure of
thought, right up to the public death of words in my country. So that
I finally find myself subjected to the terrifying alternative of exile or
the final solution.

Also, while the obstacles in my country are obvious, those
which I face every day in exile are many. They may not have fatal consequences for my life, but for my human dignity they surely do. . .
When one has no material resources, getting through exile is like
crossing an interminable Kafka-esque bridge. You have to have
"papers" to work, and to get papers, you have to be able to demonstrate professional activity. That all becomes especially complicated
when one is a woman, alone, and repulsed by the customary treatment in the intello-media show that focuses more on the effects of our
miseries than on their causes. This "way of the cross" is guaranteed, if
one does not belong to a popular ideological "church" nor to a given
clan.

The following testimony of my own experience of the "other obstacles" confronted in the minefield that is life in exile relates in particular to the moral principle on which rests the "solidarity among
intellectuals." The threat is greatest among our own ranks.

I must say that nothing in my life prepared me to face the precariousness of such a situation. As a child, I lived through the terrible
years of the war of national liberation in my country. Algeria was
then a vast battlefield, with all that that supposes in terms of loss and
mourning, in every family, especially those (like mine) who stayed
put, living from day to day through all those difficult years. But in
spite of all the dangers, there was the solidarity of a whole people,
and generosity, and sharing and protection between the families.
Fear was overcome by the confidence we each had in the other.

Today, the circle of repression and terrorism "by and against the
Algerians" has divided a whole people against itself. What is unbearable is not knowing who is threatening or who is killing, but knowing that it is the Algerian who imprisons, tortures or cuts the throat

of another Algerian.   This inglorious civil war (far from being "incipient"!) has fractured the country into three "armies" as the proverb says: "An army of cripples, an army of whiners and an army of thieves."

Before and during this drama, I had been a wife for thirty years, living in a house that held the memory of a whole limpid life of financial and political chicaneries (so prevalent in our countries). With the strength of my good conscience (naivety, no doubt!), I wrote in my country's press and for some reviews abroad (in America, Egypt, England), publicly expressing my ideas on my country's political crisis; in other words, I rejected the "strategic" trap of the brutal annulment of the Islamists' electoral victory, which was about to throw the entire civil population into a fratricidal carnage unprecedented in our history. By talking of the "dialogue of national reconciliation," I ended up being banned from writing in the press and, a little later, in early 1994, my name appeared on the posters at a mosque in Bab el-Wadi.

Since I was a member of neither a political party nor of any of the various associations then flowering in the country, affiliated neither "tribally" nor "vassally" to any of the new Masters of the regime, nobody in my entourage understood from where this threat might have come. However, it was clear that assassinations could be financed by any faction engaged in the power struggle.

Consequently, I had to leave my husband, my home and all that had until then represented my strength and my human dignity, to take up a life of random wandering. Thanks to an association of American women writers, I was able to live for more than a year in the United States, giving conferences and writing for reviews that specialized in questions of the Arab and Muslim world. Pen Writers of New York, that of the Netherlands and, in particular, that of Sweden did what they could to help me. But this life, riven with financial instability and constant anxiety that my "visa is about to expire," prevented me from finishing a book I had started writing in Algeria. On top of being so far away from my country, I had to adapt to American culture, to the syntax of the language and the mind, which stifled the language in which I write . . .

Finally, thanks to the assistance of the former president of PEN in Sweden, I managed to get into the network of "refuge cities" of the Association of the International Parliament of Writers (PIE) based in Strasbourg. And I arrived at Valladolid (Spain) on January 14, 1996.

As I speak Spanish fluently and as I was "closer" to my own country, I was better able to adapt to the new cultural environment. I organized my life around conferences that I would give, here and there, and finally devoted myself to writing my book. In theory, the residence term is one year (although that is not specified in the first agreement signed between the authorities of the city and the association), but an additional year can be granted to the same writer in the event of not-fulfillment of certain clauses. All that depends, in fact, on the goodwill of the town hall and the university of the city, since it is they who cover the residential expenses of the writer.

But I would never have believed that requesting a year's extension was going to unleash so much polemic, and strangely enough coming from those who were in "supposed solidarity" with me — the association, by the vote of its General Secretary, denied me the right of refuge in this city, while the city, against the mercantile winds and tides of the association, defended its right to extend this "reprieve." From an intellectual threatened by a nebulous instance of terrorism in my own country I became, here in Europe, an "intellectual persecuted by another intellectual," and what's more by a Frenchman — when speaking French is an offense for which the Islamist extremists kill us!

Indeed, by driving us to flee, our torturers know that although they may not get our heads, they burn our books in our brains along with all intellectual creative energy, for the path is not easy . . . our skin, our names, our culture, and even our freedom of expression will always be marked by a certain "color," on which other fundamentalists will feed. Indeed, look how they donned the mask of "intellectual solidarity" within the mission of the French PIE Association; how true it is that the threat is always lurking where one least expects it!

Nevertheless, if this negative experience taught me a certain reserve towards "the solidarity-show," I refuse to generalize at the expense of all those who, all over the world, far from any publicity, are sincerely working for freedom of expression, without caring about public opinion or culture. I met this intellectual altruism in America, the Netherlands and today in Spain, in Valladolid.

Considering that the current publication does not exist to showcase an intellectual ego, however great it may be, but to provide equal space of expression for all, I owe it to myself to challenge the whole family of thought. For I am directly experiencing the illusions, the lures and all the risks of exile, solely for the "fault" of being an intellectual in the view of the "political dialogue" in my country. Now, for me, I have to fight for the right to life the whole time. Against the shadows of exclusion and arbitrary punishment, and the specters of political, religious and intellectual terrorism.

That said, as far as "my" perception of the intellectual's freedom of expression in the West, today, I'll adopt Gide's reflection, and say: "We don't know any more from which source to drink, we believe too much in salutary water, and some drink from here, others drink from there."

This image more or less characterizes how intellectuals in general speak and act. In the logic of what I noted in the above paragraphs, we should be looking for the obstacles within our own ranks: we split up into various clans of ideological thought (externally, the Berlin Wall fell very nicely, but on the interior it still remains!), or band together to meet the immediate interests of "stardom." There isn't even any logic in their public anger . . . So-and-so puts all his talent on the line against the Bosnian genocide (and that is perfectly legitimate, this action will always be the honor of the intellectuals, who were, after all, its makers).

In this widespread cultural confusion, thought is most often re-pressed not by the censor's black pen, nor by terrorists' bullets, but more commonly through subtle economic censure. In the new order of programmed culture, commercial editors, salesmen and readers condition the writer. Then self-censorship is likely to lead him to please the public, whose taste is decided in advance, or he will write to order.

But still, there is obvious reluctance to take an interest in other people's cultures except through the perverted face of their miseries. Such as, for example, Islam, which inspires interest only because of Islamist terrorism. One would never assimilate the fanatic cults of David Koresh (Waco), or the Solar Temple, or the bombing of Okla-homa City by white fanatics, with Christendom. Thus, among Arab and Moslem authors, we are witnessing an intellectual poverty that is rather confused. They have been locked, for once and for all, into the topics of the harem and of Islamic terrorism; and the more morbidly they depict Islam, the better "chance" they have of becoming market-able and reaching a certain celebrity, a very factitious celebrity, I might add. Are we to believe that the West needs to keep fanning the flames of fear against "the dangers of Islam?" The risks today are fun-damentalisms in all the religions; and the veil and the violence against Moslem women who have chosen to live in their time, in other words in and with progress, are merely the consequences of more serious causes, which it is high time we looked into and analyzed.

In short, I believe that the spread of culture, like the word of all intellectuals, helps correct inequalities. And as the Chinese proverb says, "It's not the weeds that choke the good grain, it is the negligence of the farmer," that is, you, them, me.

6.   For me, any comment on today's problems must begin with the fundamental fact of Islamism and its terrorist violence connected to the regime's repression in my country. There will be no peace, as long as there is no political solution. For me, everything is connected to

the drama that is playing out in Algeria. Those among the writers of my country who support the "dialogue with the Islamists" have a hard life wherever they go. Exile subjects us to other complications when it comes to expression. The "to-the-very-end" proponents of the eradication of Islamism come across better in the media and they are anointed with the label of "democrat". . . . Whereas the opposite is true; an intellectual cannot espouse hatred, he must defuse it, using his arguments to demystify the motives behind religious or political terrorism.

The most urgent task is to come together with our various ideas, but a common language of acceptance, comprehension and solidarity, for we have a communality of destiny. To do this, we must avoid intellectual ghettos, and encourage the promotion of an intellectual voice of peace, a voice that will wake up people's minds to intelligence and tolerance, instead of putting forward the perennial "intellectual hawks." The most threatening prejudices are, *inter alia*, the language of oppression, exclusion and division, which must be countered. Today, humanity is at a historical watershed. And this transitional period on the verge of the second millennium encourages urgency in the debates and dialogues between us.

The subjects to be addressed are as varied as what is at stake. The same questions challenge us all, intellectuals of the "North" as well as those of the "South," for all face the same adversaries. Those who exploit the distress of the unemployed or who incite xenophobia against foreigners are the same ones who support persecution, dictatorships and obscurantists in the Third World countries. Therefore, every time the intellectuals of the developed countries help their society to defend its own interests, that contributes to the liberation of the other people.

The dangers are well-known and are dramatically exposed in the world news every day. Religious, ethnic, nationalist conflicts, Europe waking up to the smell of the Inquisition that produces a system of outcasts, and racism, racism and racism again, under various

masks, strangling us everywhere. Everything encourages the intellectuals to rise up together against the intolerable; we must not leave the
politicians, the technocrats, the scientists, and the military with a
monopoly on the major choices for the future. Today, the general
concept of the world is in question. The press, with the intellectuals,
can contribute to this demand for solidarity and continual mobiliza-
tion of attention.

Therefore we must take advantage of every opportunity to speak
and to set up information networks. This book gives us such an opportunity. And why not create a kind of liaison between all the
intellectuals of the world, from various cultures, our "Intellectuals
Without Borders?"

All this remains subject to discussion (or so I hope — and not in
some dusty archive!). I am certainly not a mainstay of the visible
"clubs" of world intellectuals, but by having given so much and risked
so much for my passion for literature, and having won my freedom
with the sweat of my imagination, I believe I deserve to be heard.

Antonio Lobo Antunes

1.   I have never considered myself an intellectual. I have a very mod-
est aim: I want to change the art of the novel. I don't have time to be
an intellectual. In my experience, intellectuals are more preoccupied
with each other's work than their own. Other people's success is
more important for them than their own books. Perhaps this is just
the Latin mentality. I don't really have any friends in the intellectual
milieu.

But if you really love music, painting, books, you have good
friends all over the world who are intellectuals: translators, publishers, journalists, literary critics. There are so many women and men

who share a passion without any envy, people from whom I have learned a lot about art and life, who taught me so much through their example. This is what books have given me: friends all over the world.

Intellectual success and glory are of minor importance to me. Success is like a prostitute — it comes and goes. One day the public loves you, the next day it turns its back on you. Faulkner and Hemingway lost their faith in success.

2.   If you want to be a writer, you must reject other people, especially those who are important for you. If you want to invent language, you must reject other people's language. My books are always built like symphonies. The biggest source of inspiration has been Beethoven's and Mahler's symphonies. My last four novels were conceived under the influence of Beethoven, Mahler and Brahms. Every art turns to music — and music, to silence.

For me, Goethe was a great and probably the last intellectual. His curiosity and appetite were enormous, and he had greatness as a human being.

However, I have also had many influences from other Portuguese writers. At the age of 15, I discovered the difference between good and bad writers. Searching after and finding a personal voice has been of outmost importance for me. I started at the age of 20 and it took me two decades to find my very personal way of writing. Making a lot of mistakes was my way of learning. I thought I was a genius. Today I have no faith in talent, just in work. I work 15 hours a day. There is only one way you can reach a certain simplicity, and that is to write and write and rewrite.

3.   I don't think that I can talk about the role of intellectuals. It would be to give them too much importance. I have my doubts about intellectuals. You can't change the world by writing. I think that aspirin is much more important than intellectuals and good novels.

As for me, my role is to write better books in the future than I did in the past. Writing keeps me away from depression and suicide. I can stop publishing books, but not writing books. It gives me a sense of living. Therefore, it's kind of funny for me to receive money for an act which, in a way, is to treat myself.

The role of the intellectual, to me, is to write in an honest way, not for the critics but for the salvation of mankind.

4.   We live in a postindustrial society, where a good football-player will always be more important than an intellectual. Madonna is more important than Keats. We must accept that people prefer Claudia Schifferman to Heinrich Boll. A mediocre football-player will earn three times the Nobel Prize money. Therefore, I would rather have a good left foot. Even if I have 100,000 readers, that will always be less attention than Jurgen Klingsmann receives. Of course, you could say that Mozart is still alive. But posthumous glory is not something to look forward to.

5.   It is easy today to be a Portuguese writer. Even if you have to compete with your predecessors, all the great writers who lived before you.

I have always been a Leftish person. Once, they even wanted to make me a candidate for the Communist party. But I started to know and understand how Portuguese politicians really are. They hate people and only care about personal power. They would all like to be like Mitterrand. For our politicians, democracy exists only once every fourth year, when it is election time. Democracy is only an abstraction for them, just a word. I've seen people being killed for abstractions and principles. Like honesty and patriotism.

6.   My biggest fear is not to be able to write a new novel. Writing is becoming more and more difficult. For me, the most urgent task is to be solid and honest and do good work.

Claudio Magris

A few months ago, during a university debate entitled "Literature and Borders," in Warsaw, the observation was made that politicians strive to establish fixed borders in the diplomatic sphere, while intellectuals work to keep them open in the realm of the mind and the soul, so that they cannot be used under any circumstance to divide mankind spiritually and cannot be used as obsessional and sanguinary idols. But Eugeniusz Kabalc (a writer and translator) retorted, sadly, that during the savage war in the former Yugoslavia it was precisely the writers and intellectuals who incited people to the most exaggerated hatred, by exhibiting a narrow-mindedness and chauvinism that was at least equal to those displayed by the people who were politically responsible for the tragedy.

Naturally, in the midst of so many horrors, there were writers and men of culture who offered luminous testimonies of courage, humanity and the spirit of peace. But the example of those who exalted fanaticism and massacre (like so many of their counterparts in other countries and other historical situations) should dissuade us from the naive opinion that exercising certain activities (related to literature, philosophy and art) would guarantee civil and enlightened humanity, as the debates on the role of intellectuals too often seem to suggest.

Our imagination too frequently contrasts the intellectual (even when he is politically engaged) to the politician, as a representative of values, truth and freedom, of a moral system excluding all compromise. This concept is often true, as shown by many examples of dissidence and resistance vis-à-vis totalitarian tyrannies, corruption, complicity and lies. Society always needs individuals equipped with conceptual clarity and the courage to oppose Antigone's "unwritten laws of the gods," absolute moral commandments, and the logic of power and domination. But, at the very least, it is debatable to assimilate (and is often attempted) the quality of being an "intellectual" with the possession of certain competences rather than others, as though sociologists and men of letters were required to be, *a priori* — even before the quality of their work is recognized — "more intellectual" than a dentist or a student of commercial law.

We are in the habit of automatically preferring psychoanalysts over orthopedists or insurance men, and yet there is no diploma, no level of education that necessarily can confer on its possessor the critical awareness and self-criticism, the capacity to transcend the immediate and visceral, which is the very essence of intellectual quality. A man of letters who absorbs the rites of his cultural clan is no less alienated than a workman on the assembly line, and it does not matter that one machine produces books and conferences, and the other produces bolts. Moreover, during tragic moments of political crisis or collective blindness, it has not been the most cultivated milieux (or those that claim to be such) that have shown the capacity to mount the greatest resistance.

Similarly, great intellectuals and great writers have not always demonstrated autonomy of judgment and a sense of humanity that is more highly developed than the politicians'. Djilas is a great intellectual who had the indisputable merit of revealing ambiguities in the new pro-Tito clique (that he had helped to bring to power), and he courageously paid the consequences; but Djilas was already an intellectual when he wrote, in the heat of the revolutionary struggle, that in Stalin's absence the sun would not shine so brightly (a silly bit of rhetoric and fanaticism that Tito, in this case more intellectual than he, never uttered and never would have uttered). And when Djilas, while he was in power, demanded Krieza's head (the great Croatian leftist writer, suspected of heresy), Tito (who was perfectly willing to resort to violence when he considered it necessary) protected the writer, showing himself, in his pragmatism, to be more humane than Djilas.

In one of his best books, *Life is Elsewhere*, Milan Kundera described the perverse bonds that sometimes are established between a totalistic/synthetic lyricism and political totalitarianism. Accepting one's own limitations — which often collide with the need to redeem one's life, and which we tend to reject out of hand in the name of radical purity — can be, in this case, a proof of responsibility, a sacrifice that enables one to avoid more serious evils.

Naturally, it is up to each person (whether or not he explicitly practices the profession of intellectual) to denounce relentlessly the politicians' pragmatism, which often degenerates into vulgar cynicism, contemptible corruption, cheap opportunism, ridiculous conformity, and even vicious crime. One must also resist the flatteries of those in power and the pathetic temptation to march in step with History, under the illusion of leading it. But such a denunciation of politics (whether it is debased or not) is worthy only if it combines intransigence with charity, knowing that any man, if he lowers his guard, is likely to be carried away by the mechanism of evil and error. Certain authors, among the greatest of our century, sang the praises of the cruelest tyrannies, from Nazism to Stalinism. We continue to love Céline and Hamsun; their writings teach us about suffering, and we understand the blindness that distorted their vision of the world; but in their unfortunate stand in favor of Nazism, we certainly cannot judge them to have been more open and more enlightened than the million individuals who, without celebrity and poetic genius, nonetheless demonstrated in this instance more intelligence and more humanity than they did.

The spirit moves in whatever direction it wishes and nobody — even if he has just written a masterpiece — can be certain that it has not abandoned him, leaving him deaf and blind vis-à-vis life and history.

Translated from Italian by Nathalie Bauer

Naguib Mahfouz

1.   We are all intellectuals. Everyone in society is an intellectual. The ambiguous concept of *mouthaqqaf*, in Arabic, denotes a man of culture and thought.

What is culture? Let's say that it is everything that proceeds from man: everything that he produces in his own environment is culture. When a potter shapes a statuette, when a man creates a religious foundation or builds a partition, that is all part of culture, and it is in this sense that I mean the word. One might say that no man is uncultured, and no intellectual is without knowledge. To take the term in its primary sense, even the humblest of *fellahs* in the village practices certain habits and customs, through songs, weddings, dances, and even the recent enthusiasm for television . . . He is cultivated: "human being" means "cultivated." Culture does have its specific details, but I am talking here about the general meaning, the common background. What is the specific meaning? That of the individual consciousness seeking its bearings, in life, literature, the arts, and intellectual reflection, in order to give the human being a position in existence.

But I do not see that intellectuals have any specific responsibility, I don't conceive of there being any particular work reserved for people who are authorized to say, "I am an intellectual," the way one would say, "I am a plumber." What I describe can be found among engineers, doctors, peasants . . . even ministers. Everyone. Among them are people engaged in thought, reason, art, literature; why not call them intellectuals? Most of them share the feeling of responsibility for the affairs of the city, which is perhaps shared even more generally by the thinkers, by the men of letters and the arts, but are we so sure of that, these days? And on what grounds would one object to that feeling being present in the ordinary citizen? As for me, of course

I do not challenge the term "intellectual," I only share it the same as everyone else does.

2.   Individuals have influenced me, certainly. But let us pass, for the moment, on the question of the intellectual. Who has influenced me? Everyone. Philosophers, writers, political leaders. Saad Zaghloul, a great Egyptian politician of the 1920's and 1930's, the father of our independence, had a major influence on me. And writers: Taha Husseyn, and Mahmoud Abbas Al-Aqqad, through their concept of our patrimony and the way in which they presented universal thought to us.

They were not the only ones. There are all those inescapable influences, all the others, from the Indies, Europe, the Americas. In my youth I was very much influenced by George Bernard Shaw and H.G. Wells, and Anatole France, and, although I am not a communist, by the thought of Karl Marx, who gave me so much. And Gandhi, and Tagore, various mystics, and still others. We could go through the whole alphabet. Their ideas, their philosophies, even when I did not adopt them, always impressed me. With Marxism, I felt that a great change had occurred in the world and in our vision of it. Bernard Shaw impressed me with the irony of his theatre, his humanism, and his socialism; and for me Tagore remains the model of a man, of a beautiful spirituality. Malraux, to a lesser degree, influenced me with his novels on China. It is very difficult for me to give you more examples. I have been reading for a whole lifetime and everything that I have read is imprinted in me.

3.   What role? In the end, wasn't it always to express the life and the affairs of the city? Why would you want that to be finished? Since the beginning of the world these things have never finished finishing. How and why would the role of the intellectuals end just when knowledge is circulating freely throughout the world beyond the mind and the word?

4.   Which "errors" and which intellectuals? Did the intellectuals collectively make these errors about which you speak? Did they all take the same positions? Let us beware of totalitarian judgments, the roots of prejudice. Whether it is a matter of totalitarian regimes, of devastating revolutions or of any other cause, lost or won, they did not take the same positions; that is the very principle of freedom. You can read simultaneously the defenders and the detractors of a given ideology, even in our own press . . . don't forget that dictatorships have been attacked as much as defended.

It would be unjust to say that intellectuals here have not played their part and that they have neglected the affairs of the world; that is not so. The values that we defend came to us through the intermediary of people who think. Deviant situations are attacked by thinkers, and thinkers defend them, and it's good that way.

5.   In certain countries the intellectual enjoys favorable conditions, in others, less so. The obstacles are not always the ones that you enumerate. It is not necessarily the police force and the ruling power that create the obstacles; sometimes they come from the bottom up: it is the unequal stage of development — of culture — that makes the difference. Yes, while certain constraints come from the government, fanaticism and intolerance can come from the people; and that is why the intellectuals, torn between two forces, can really suffer. That is what they are fighting against, at the price of prison and exile, escape, and the terror of concerted or spontaneous assassination.

6.   Of course I call for freedom as a foundation, and democracy as a regime — and I am not alone. But, there too, there is no consensus. You will find intellectuals who are neither for freedom nor for democracy. They don't find those concepts inspiring at all. What are they afraid of? Why, freedom and democracy, you understand. Perhaps they think they will have no more role to play?

The role of the intellectual is to play his part against intolerance in all its forms. Through writing, if he is a writer; through words, if he is a radio or television man; and through the law if he is in power. That is why I am against those who speak of intellectuals as a category, as a social class. Who are they, then? Customs, costumes, heritages, traditions, philosophy, science and the arts: culture is everybody's business. What man could be said to have none? Everyone dips his ladle in, and I couldn't tell you that he fits within any specific institutional or social framework.

To me, the professional of thought is no hero; in my eyes he is not the embodied conscience of a society. He who is devoted to thought, we call a thinker, and that is all; he acts as well as the others, but through a particular set of skills. We have thinkers who are very reactionary . . . the intellectual, our *mouthaqqaf*, is simply a watchman, ever on the alert, surveying the affairs of his world, yes, and giving his opinions with courage, however awkward that may be.

Eduardo Manet

1.   I assume the intellectual "word" in all its force, if only out of concern. Neo-fascism and neo-nazism are re-emerging in France, Europe and elsewhere. Remember the anecdote of the pro-Franco general who wanted to draw his pistol every time he heard the word *intellectual*. Even if they are not (yet) armed, the neo-fascists think only of that: to fire on the "brains."

2.   An example of a great intellectual figure? Don Miguel de Unamuno. A writer, a "non-aligned" philosopher, he could have played far more malignantly with Franco, and would have received honors in exchange for his silence. But no! He preferred honor to honors, and he defended republican freedom and ideas unambigu-

ously. Another example: Fritz Lang. Hitler liked his Wagnerian films. The day Goebbels suggested he "take German cinema in hand," Lang packed his bags and crossed the border.

3.   I find even the question shocking. To question the importance and the influence of the intellectual in the affairs of the city seems to me to be a kind of teasing. It is not a serious question. The law [in France] obliges us to help any person in danger. And who is in danger, nowadays, in the city? Thousands of people find their freedoms threatened.

4.   Yes, intellectuals have made errors, they have been very often blind. So?

It would be amusing, someday, to make a list of categories of society and the errors they have committed, such as:
- the military
- doctors
- trade union leaders
- municipal organizations
- the President . . .

I believe that it is also time to fight the cliché that the enemies of intellectuals always harp on when speaking about Jean-Paul Sartre, enumerating his many errors, his temporary spells of obtuseness. His flirtation with Castro, for example, and his very foolish suggestion to "Be Cuban," at the very moment when the revolutionary Cubans who were there, on the ground, were starting to raise serious questions about the *Líder máximo*'s expressed thirst for absolute power. Of course, on top of the fact that he was misguided on occasion, that he could have his moments of blindness, Sartre was completely wrong about certain questions. But that should not make us forget what he contributed to political analysis and modern thought.

5.   I have lived in France since September 22, 1968. Here (but maybe I am mistaken?) challenge number one would be to make the word of the intellectuals heard over the tumult, the cacophony that is poured out upon us through television. No matter what we hear from those who are optimists by nature (or blind and obtuse): people are reading less and less, and watching more and more. Some thirty cable channels are now supplemented by "digital bouquets." And this has made channel-flipping, alas! already part of our daily life. "Tell-me-what-you-have-to-say-in-three-seconds-or-I'll-zap-you." What to do?

We should take our place, whenever possible, in the first row. Occupy the space that is sometimes offered us on TV. I know that the more often such and such game show host or news commentator appears on TV, the more he is applauded and the more he is paid. I know, too, that when an intellectual appears too often on TV, he gets spat upon. Unless he plays the clown, like the late Jean-Édern Hallier. That is the real "trouble with France" today. A kind of pox of the spirit. Again, what to do?

We should use (but again, maybe I am mistaken) television as a weapon. Le Pen knows how to do it. His understudy and rival Mégret, too, is learning the rules of that game.

If intellectuals were to scorn TV in the name of Kant or Spinoza, to play at being haughty Greta Garbo's, would be a suicidal gesture. Of course, I don't mean to just show up on TV and say "yes" and smile. It's time to use television as a platform for launching ideas.

6.   What are the priorities today, for thought and action? They are clear:

   – to defend the right to free thought

   – to fight so that no one can prevent us from taking action and putting our ideas into practice.

Let us take a quick glance at the world today. Everywhere on the planet they are trying to get us to believe that freedom of the markets is the sister of the freedom of thought.

But what are the Chinese comrades doing before they take over the government of Hong Kong? They are striving to prohibit the free circulation of ideas, while letting the dollar circulate like mad.

What is Laurent-Désiré Kabila doing, in ex-Zaire, the new Congo? He starts by limiting the freedom of expression and courting the dollar — the solution to every evil.

What is Fidel Castro doing in Cuba? He lets the dollar circulate freely and prevents independent journalists from expressing their views and from providing information as to what they observe day by day: a country that is plunging, to the sound of the cha-cha and the salsa (to the great joy of the tourists, who are loaded with dollars), which is plunging, I say, into ideological cynicism, moral impoverishment, and general shame. And here, closer to home. . . what is happening in Toulon, Orange, Marignane? The machine is on the move. Let us act, speak, and think with complete freedom, from today onward, and keep the old demons from cropping up, keep tomorrow from being too late for free expression, too late for action.

Pierre Mertens

1.   An intellectual is someone who does not give in to the siren-song of culture and society and the populist demagogues, someone who isn't afraid of being unpopular and doesn't mind going against the grain.

2.   Proust, Kafka, Malraux, Bataille, Pasolini.

3.   More necessary than ever; and artists all the more so. Do they still have "their bit to say"? They'd better believe they do.

4.   Yes: we all have the right to make mistakes, but we must not abuse it. . . and we must get over our mistakes without taking refuge in convenient self-criticisms that are as indulgent as the error itself was! And we have, especially, the right (and sometimes the duty) to doubt.

5.   Conformity, a good conscience, cynicism, puritanism, vulgarity, the proselytism of ignorance, and militant amnesia.

6.   We have to fight against every form of terrorism, including certain fanatical types of moderation. . . , the press, the new misogyny. We need to rehabilitate the concept of nuance in all the spheres where it is being denounced and condemned as a provocation.

Arthur Miller

1.   I usually refer to myself as a writer-artist. There is too much I don't know and don't expect to ever know to call myself an intellectual.

2.   Marx was an early influence and still is — if only as a disappointment. Again, it was the artists rather than the thinkers — Beethoven, Mozart, Ibsen, Joyce, Hemingway for a time, Tolstoy, Dostoyevsky, Melville, Poe, Dickens and numerous other English and American

novelists and poets rather than thinkers, as such, who were important to my development.

3.   Intellectuals are needed more than ever because there is more reality to investigate, quantify, and analyze, from the high heaven to the sea bottom, the air we breathe, the water we drink. — Presuming that the intellectual's work is to put man in charge of reality.

4.   The biggest mistake, of course, was to allow a necessary alienation from bourgeois society to overwhelm the critical functions vis-à-vis the Soviets. However, very few, if any, on the right as well as the left, perceived the magnitude of the oncoming collapse of the East and the vastness of its failure as a civilization. In short, none of the prevailing ideologies helped very much in defining reality; the critical intelligence itself has been humiliated and hopefully will begin to confront this and learn from the experience. We must once again learn to see as well as to look, to listen as well as to hear.

5.   American business, often despite its own anti-intellectual prejudices, has an immense capacity to absorb intellectuals and utilize their minds. Brain power is more needed now than ever in history. Thus at least part, if not all, of the aim of many experimental scientists is to get rich from patents on their inventions, and the novelist likewise, and so on down the line. We have had far too many cases of scientists falsifying their reports in order to achieve instant recognition and money, and far too many writers who, often despite themselves, have moved inch by inch away from their own individuality in order to conform to the market's demands. The crucial contradiction for artist and/or intellectual: how to resolve the necessary impulse toward achievement with the pressure to make his product more palatable, popular or useable than its real complexities require. In a sense, the intellectual is the victim of his own success. The pre-

World War II physicist was like a monk; few knew what he was doing, his salary was very low; he had no fame or hope for it, usefulness had no part in his thinking. He did not expect to create ashes.

Then he blew up part of the world and could either threaten the planet or light it up. Until the present time, when at least the older generation of physicists cannot be certain that they haven't betrayed life itself by succeeding in making themselves useful. The net result of it all may be that, as once was true, the intellectual will be forced into a sharpened moral sense — the more so because his powers are so individual and far greater than those of other people. "The biggest perils to fight against," you ask?

Arrogance, greed, the sociopathic impulse — too many of the alienating qualities, in short, that helped make him an artist and/or intellectual in the first place. But when was the enemy anything else but man? And what victory ever mattered more than the victory over himself?

Czeslaw Milosz

What does the word "intellectual" mean to you today? Are you an intellectual? Or do you, on the contrary, contest that term?

You see, that is not actually a Polish word. And then, when speaking of intellectuals, one adapts to the accepted conventions. That emanates from where? From France, principally, because I do not believe that the word "intellectual" is very well-received in America (*a big laugh*). And then, in Poland, I think that it is a word that defines a very restricted circle of Polish society. As you know, in Poland we use the word *intelligentsia*.

That's a Russian word?

No, it is hard to say in which language this word first appeared, but I think it is of German origin. It appeared more or less at the same time in Russia and Poland, with a completely special connotation: people who have an education, but who are engaged in public affairs. First of all, I should say that because of the social structure, it was a group that originated in the nobility, the minor nobility. In Russia, they were generally sons of the clergy, of the orthodox priests, but it is difficult to say how this group is doing right now in Poland. In the last few years, you have probably read many complaints from old pessimists about this group, but I believe that if one judges by the publications, the number of books published in Poland, we are witnessing a very active intellectual life, in Krakow for example. There are so many invitations to various kinds of meetings, discussions, theater performances, recitals, concerts . . . Given all that, one can say that the *intelligentsia* is very much alive in Poland.

> *But you, are you an intellectual? In the French sense, you are an intellectual. For example, you got involved with Sarajevo; that would be a typical example of the writer who, in France, would be defined as an intellectual, because he gets involved in public life. So then, are you an intellectual, Mr. Milosz?*

I am a little bit allergic to that word. To a certain extent, because of the French intellectuals. If Sartre and Simone de Beauvoir embody, so to speak, the intellectuals, then I prefer not to be an intellectual. I am not so sure that Albert Camus regarded himself as an intellectual.

That brings me to the second question. Are there any intellectual figures who influenced you in a significant way, and if so, which ones? Any "examples" who inspire" you, shaped you, and whom you can still evoke today as authorities?

Yes. For example, Simone Weil. But can Simone Weil be limited to the concept of "intellectual"? She was insane. Too insane to be treated as an intellectual; insane in the positive sense of the word, in my opinion. But another figure was Chestov; Chestov was a Russian philosopher, he was part of the Russian intelligentsia; in his youth, he was a Marxist and then he lived in Paris. I am sure that, in Paris, he could be regarded as an intellectual. So then Chestov, he is an influence in my life.

Simone Weil, Chestov. Is that all?

No, no, certainly not (*laugh*). I must say that at one time in my life, it was Jacques Maritain who was influential. Certainly, there were others. . . I lived in America a long time. And certain Americans, like Dwight MacDonald, influenced me. And then Thomas Merton. Lately, the letters that we exchanged, he and I, were published in America. They were also published in Polish, but the letters were in English, with many French incursions, because Merton was bilingual.

Then my question is going to be difficult. What is the role of intellectuals at the end of the 20ᵗʰ century? Do you think, as some do, that their role is finished? Or do they, on the contrary, still have something to say in the affairs of the city?

Frankly, the question seems to me a little simplistic. I don't ask myself that question (*laugh*). I do not think in such general terms. I know that my responsibilities are defined by my position as a poet, a prose writer and all that. Primarily, I am responsible to the public for my language, i.e. the Polish language, though my books are translated into English and published in America. I am responsible as a poet to the American readers who like poetry, because my poetry also exists in English translations. I ask myself very personal and not general questions.

You feel yourself to be a citizen like the others, with an additional responsibility?

Perhaps.

We have heard a great deal about the "errors" committed by intel-lectuals, their "blindness," sometimes their "irresponsibility." What do you think of these charges? Do you agree with their severity? Or would you moderate, even contradict them?

I've read, for example, a book which you undoubtedly know, written by an American historian, Judt, on French intellectuals. It is a very interesting book that tries to find the roots of a certain blindness on the part of intellectuals in France. For me, you know, it was a very hard period because of that in France. Because it is not pleasant to be leprous (*laugh*). But it is a very European and very French discussion, and not necessarily closely connected to the past of intellectuals or the Polish intelligentsia. Because the French intellectuals had the freedom of choice. Polish intellectuals did not have this freedom, so they must be judged differently. I am not among those who condemn their colleagues who, at a given time, converted to Communism. I wonder how I would have behaved myself if I had remained in

Kraków, in my apartment, on Saint-Thomas St. (*laugh*).

> *What do you think are the obstacles, in the countries where you live
> and work, that stand in the way of the word of the intellectual: indif-
> ference from the media, the tumult of opinions, police repression,
> soft repression through the illusions and lures of public spectacles,
> or other obstacles?*

To answer honestly, in the United States, I was not interested in the
mass media. I do not aspire to that. I have my public; and then, perhaps America is an exceptional country, because there are often poetry readings where there may be a thousand people in the audience.
The bookshops are fantastic, they organize poetry readings in a small
room, and sometimes four hundred people show up. For example, I
read my poems at the Library of Congress; that is certainly enough for
me. It is a special public. But America is a pluralist country, so there
are many social groups, tastes, trends. That is enough for me.
In Poland, obviously, I do not have any trouble getting on television. I
speak fairly often on television, and I publish my books. And I am
somewhat optimistic, because the sector that must seemingly be disappearing is in fact very much alive, that is, difficult books very often
are subsidized by the local authorities, on many levels, the State, the
government, the municipalities, the universities. And it seems
strange because, when you go into a bookshop, it is atrocious to see
the kind of books translated from America, with their color covers;
you might think that there was nothing else, but it is misleading: the
number of solid books is surprising.

> *What tasks do you see as most urgent, today or always; what is
> your task? What prejudices are the most threatening, what causes
> must be defended, what perils must be averted? In short, what, in
> your eyes, are today's greatest priorities for thought and action?*

Obviously, it is the political game in my country, Poland, that interests me, that attracts my attention, not that I want to be a politician, but I have my preferences. Politics doesn't interest me in America, because it is reduced to the two political parties, the republicans and the democrats, and then the personalities involved are more or less unknown to me. I do not have any emotional ties.

In Poland, all that is very much alive for me, it's interesting. Obviously, in Poland, what matters most is, on the one hand, the post-Communists as a political party, and on the other hand the opposition from the Right — and in fact I don't much like these choices. I am all for the Democratic Union, i.e. I made a clear choice to vote; they say that the number of votes for Poland's Democratic Union matches the number of people with a higher education (*laugh*). It is a class vote. It is like the peasants who vote for the Rural Party, the PSL.

But, there is one crucial problem, and that is that the Church in Poland has a tendency — and maybe the Pope can have some influence to mitigate the tendencies of certain bishops in Poland; but it is a fact. I am in favor of *Tygodnik Powszechny*, i.e. the liberal Catholics who, more or less, are tied to the Democratic Union. I think my choice is fairly reasonable (*laugh*).

> But isn't the Democratic Union closer to the ex-Communists than
> to the Right?

No. And furthermore, while we use the term "Right," the Right is very much differentiated, and it is only at this particular moment that the Right is relatively unified. But no, I believe that a coalition between the Democratic Union and the ex-Communists, at this time, is far from probable and would be very difficult.

*What are the dangers that you see threatening Poland or even, in a
broader way, Central Europe and even Europe as a whole? Or are
you very optimistic on the future of Poland, Central Europe and
Europe in general?*

I attach great importance to a recent event, the visit of the presidents
of our part of Europe to Gniezno, at the Pope's invitation. It is a symbol of the unification of Europe. Since I was born in Lithuania, I am
always very interested in the problems of Eastern Central Europe,
and in good relations between Poland and the Ukraine and Lithuania.
Poor Byelorussia is in a mess: an abominable and stupid dictatorship.
But I find that the Polish president, Mr. Kwasniewski, is following a
firm policy now and he understands that that is how he will succeed.
He is following the advice of the editors of *Kultura*, in Paris, who already since the Forties have been prophesying a future cohabitation
and neighborly relations between Poland, the Ukraine and Lithuania.
From this standpoint, I am very optimistic as for the relations between our States.

Relations between Poland and the Ukraine, for example, must overcome a great deal of bitterness on both sides, because the past is
cruel, but what was done is done; and Poland was the first country to
recognize Ukraine's independence. The presence of Mr. Kuchma, the
Ukrainian president, at Gniezno during the presidential conference
was very important, in my view.

You asked me a question about the dangers. Russia is absolutely un-
predictable. Nobody knows what to expect from this country that is
in such a deplorable situation (internally, I mean). Thus, our part of
Europe is confronted with an unknown.

*The Poles want integration with Europe, etc. But I have the impression
that it is America that is in their dreams...*

That is understandable, after the European experiences. Obviously, Poland is Americanized, like other European countries. The films one sees are primarily American films. There has been a considerable change in morals, under the influence of the mass media, of course. And that is why, for me, one of the most interesting problems is the conflict between Catholicism and new the "lifestyle." For a writer, that is attractive. But when it comes to the fascination with America, I think that every year will bring a little more attention to what really America is, not the mythical but the real America, with its multitudes of problems.

I believe that this passion for America is temporary. Of course NATO is not directed solely against Russia, but the Poles understand that balance in Europe may be maintained only by the Americans' presence. At this time, Poland does not have any border disputes with anybody, but who knows?

I do not hide my ambiguous attitude with respect to France. I owe a lot to this country, especially to the literature: I was educated at a time when French was still the language of the educated classes of Europe. I can tell you the year in which the influence of French ended in Poland and that of English began: in 1938. I observed that everyone in Warsaw suddenly started to learn English.

Because of Munich?

No, that is too simple an explanation.

But there was nothing anyone could do...

In any case, I owe France a great deal.

Many Poles say to me: you, the French, dropped us in 1939. Poland entered the war with Germany on August 30, 1939. France and England declared war on Germany on September 2, 1939...

However, I must say that the fall of France in 1940 was seen in Poland as the end of Europe. The fall of France was felt deeply in Warsaw. And I must say here, in my defense (because I said that my attitude towards France is ambiguous) that in 1942 a book by Jacques Maritain, *À Travers le désastre*, was published by the Resistance in Warsaw, with my introduction, in which I defended the honor of France (*laugh*). And the book was published by Éditions Minuit in Paris, two years later .

Joyce Carol Oates

1.   The term "intellectual" is a very self-conscious one in the United States. To speak of oneself as an "intellectual" is equivalent to arrogance and egotism, for it suggests that there is a category of persons who are "not-intellectual."

2.   The philosophers who influenced my thinking are numerous, including Plato (though negatively — I am certainly not a "Platonist"), Nietzsche, William James, Henry David Thoreau and Ralph Waldo Emerson. I also consider writers like Melville, Dostoyevsky and, of course, Thomas Mann, "intellectuals" of the highest order.

3.   Intellectuals are individuals who hope to rise above emotion and superstition in assessing the world, and the world's problems, analytically. Our fundamental struggle continues to be the struggle to advance knowledge and "rationality" in the face of a continuous anti-

reason; the claims of "blood" and ethnic/religious identity. Such a mission is hardly completed.

5.   The major obstacles for intellectual discourse in the United States arise from shallow, rushed and bigoted discourse. A complex argument may be reduced to a 20-word statement by the media. One doesn't want to be drawn into such dialogues.

Cynthia Ozick

1.   I do reject it, because I think it's a term that belongs to scholars, historians, people who think in a serious, more to the point, a very consistent way about how society is structured. I think a writer who writes fiction and essays really lacks competence to comment on world structures, particularly on political matters.

2.   The founding fathers of the USA, the writers of the constitution, who in this backwater of the world, this no-place, showed so much insight and foresight and gave me the latitude to think freely.

3.   Their mission is just beginning, and it rests on the terrible lessons that should have been learned from the past century. The chief lesson would be to be wary of utopias.

4.   I absolutely agree. The intellectuals of the West were all sucked in by the Soviet lie for long time. The intellectual of the 20th century has had moral leaders on all sides of the political spectrum: Neville Chamberlain vis-à-vis *Mitteleuropa*, Neville Chamberlain vis-à-vis Eastern Europe, Neville Chamberlain vis-à-vis the Middle East. What

the intellectual has lacked is precisely that thing we call intellectual courage. Intellectual courage requires the bravery not to give in to the lies of convenience and self-gratification.

5.   Self-obfuscation. Fooling yourself.

6.   The greatest perils are obsessive fanaticism, religious and aggressive fanaticism, the fanaticism of hatred; and that is as old as Cain and Abel. The greatest joys is — and that, too, is as old as fratricide — is learning about what you don't know. Imagining what you don't know.

Orhan Pamuk

1.   The term intellectual has no particular significance for me. I am neither eager to see myself as one, nor do I reject it as elitist. The word has a widely used meaning and is useful. People such as artists, writers, journalists and academics who resist pressures that limit freedoms and erase differences, whether these pressures originate from the state, religion or the general public, are referred to as intellectuals. However, some people tend to call anyone involved in the arts, writing, journalism or scholarly research intellectuals. In Turkey, there are many journalists endeavoring to have freedoms restricted, books banned, and those holding different views declared traitors to their country. Perhaps these people who engage in mental activity, even if only to a limited extent, might be classified as intellectuals, but in my view they would more appropriately be called "technicians who support the state and government."

2.   Sartre has influenced me with his colorful personality, obstinacy, argumentativeness, and enmity towards bourgeois opinions. I am fond of him. He moved fast and creatively between general theories and philosophy and day-to-day politics and minutiae. But the way in which his ability as a novelist and creative writer evaporated with his increasing obsession with politics is a warning to all writers. Edward Saïd is a good example of an intellectual who transforms literary criticism and close perusal of texts into highly creative social criticism. But as a writer, I have been influenced by creative writers with little interest in politics, such as Proust and Borges.

3.   I do not believe that intellectuals have "roles" and "tasks." I do not view intellectuals as a separate species with a specific program of activities or goals. There will always be people who write, and who speak out against the government, the state, and oppressive ideas espoused by the majority. Intellectuals who talk of history and of missions bore me, and they are misguided. Intellectuals should see their tasks as more simple, and carry them out with more humility.

4.   Intellectuals may have many misconceptions, but it is largely second class intellectuals, those who support the state and nationalists, who bother with these. A widespread fault of intellectuals is to take themselves too seriously, to have an inflated idea of their own importance, and to speak of historic missions and such in an affected and pretentious manner. Another thing I have learnt in Turkey is that most intellectuals who believe that soon everything will improve, and that a better future is just around the corner — mainly thanks to their own sufferings and achievements — are usually disappointed and end up in despair.

5.   Being killed is a distinct possibility for Turkish intellectuals. Over the past twenty years, three prominent editorial writers from three leading newspapers in Turkey have been assassinated. Then

there is the likelihood of being imprisoned, having your writings banned, etc.. Being proclaimed a "traitor to the nation," pushed aside, and losing your newspaper column and your job at once, is another method. So is disinterest and impassiveness. Particularly in remote provincial towns, intellectuals and writers are killed, or arrested, tortured and sentenced to thirty years imprisonment and not even the Istanbul newspapers take any notice, never mind those in the West.

6.   I do not wish to use phrases like "the most urgent tasks" or "the most important causes," because I do not believe sufficiently in tasks and causes. I want to write the best novels. For me, things are simpler: there is a state that bans books and imprisons writers and some *baddies* who collaborate. I would like to do something about them. Since I am regarded as a famous writer and an intellectual, I sometimes think that what I do is of some use. The greatest intellectual joy of today is, of course, good literature. Good literature is rarer than good intellectuals.

Octavio Paz

1.   The word *intellectual* today has a variety of meanings. The old distinction is between manual labor and intellectual labor (and in many ways this is still valid). In modern times, the intellectuals are the imaginative writers, literary critics, philosophers. Of course, I see myself as an intellectual.

2.   There are so many figures who have inspired me, we would have to retrace the entire intellectual history of my life.

3.   The mission of the intellectuals, by definition, cannot be seen as completed. They live in a society, and societies are never perfect. A very important part of the intellectuals' role is a moral mission, to use their critical minds and to take a critical position in their societies. But the first and most important duty of intellectuals is, of course, to write the best they can. In other words, to be loyal, and loyal most of all to their writing.

4.   In the 20th century, a great number of intellectuals have abandoned their critical positions and become members of groups that participated in totalitarian ideologies. Ezra Pound, Céline and Knut Hamsun were attracted to fascism; meanwhile people like Neruda and Orwell sympathized with communism. For myself, I have never been a political person. But I have taken a stance on the most critical moral questions during my lifetime.

5.   I don't really want to talk about that now.

6.   Today there are many figures who express themselves through the electronic media, who have changed from the written word toward the spoken word. It is not the first time in history that such a shift has happened. But this is a very dangerous transition, because the written word invites to reflection, to be critical; the spoken word, on the other hand (for instance on TV), invites us only to oblivion, forgetfulness. However, nobody thinks of this. I am not against images, but I don't think they are enough.

In the past, I used to say that the most terrible word that exists in any language is the word "No." But now, I say that the intellectuals must resist, they must say no. Resist and say no to the commercial forces, to the advertising that tries to substitute images for literature and convert citizens to consumers. I think this is the biggest danger to our societies these days.

Victor Pelevine

1.   The noun "intellectual" is understood in an extraordinarily vague way today, and its meaning resides essentially in connotations. It's not customarily used to refer to real intellectuals, engineers and practitioners of the applied sciences, in other words the people who use their intellect so brilliantly as a useful instrument. An intellectual is someone who brings meaning and reveals the essence of things. But the meanings that are vomiting out of the intellect at the end of the 20th century are nauseatingly false and superfluous.   What gives meaning to the meanings is missing. I don't consider myself an intellectual, because for such a judgment to be passed, both a considerer and a consideree are required, and I have no desire to ascribe to myself the ability to play both roles. As far as denying the term, that would require a vain and superfluous intellectual effort.

2.   Buddha, who was the first to talk about the invalidity and insubstantiality of the intellect, the vanity of intellectual pursuits. Buddha showed that the intellect never discovers anything but itself under various guises. All the intellect can do is to put an end, to stop itself, in order to expose that which is generally obscured by the froth of its own constructs.

3.   The intellectual is a fashion model who trots out in the latest thoughts. There are all sorts of fashions in thinking, it has its own spring and fall collections. The mission of the intellectuals is similar to that of models, so that while one cannot say that they are completely obsolete, it is doubtful that any great tasks lie ahead for intellectuals in the future. There's no use dressing the intellect in ermine, the king is recognizable only because he is nude. But it's better to say

that *sotto voce*, as in the fable. Besides, the role of the intellectual is tragic because he functions as an "intellectual" only once or twice in his existence, when a new meaning comes along. All the rest of his days, he is condemned to serving as a decoration at cocktail and dinner parties, which can be torture.

4. Indeed, intellectuals' activities are often far from innocent. The most dangerous war criminals are the intellectuals who produce abstractions for which other people must perish. That is particularly clear in Russia. If we count up all who were killed for abstractions in the 20th century, we can understand many things about the guilt of intellectuals. Humanity has no more terrible enemy than abstract concepts. The only justification for these intellectuals is that they commit evil as if in a dream.

5. I see absolutely no obstacle to the intellect in Russia. And, therefore, no obstacle for intellectuals. Although they are disdained by those in power, who are too pragmatic and who content themselves with entertaining a few television clowns. What's more, the gross product of Russian intellectuals has always been fairly bizarre. At the beginning of the 20th century, it consisted in beating one's brow before the people; at the end of the century, they just reproach the people for preferring TV series from Mexico over those from America. In Russia as elsewhere, the intellectuals experience their responsibility for the events and their inability to provide any remedy. But the hard existential condition of writers would be palpably assuaged if they understood that they've never had any impact on reality, only on the movement of empty shapes in their minds. As for the illusions and make-believe, it's not the media or political repression that have imposed that on us. It's our natural environment. Nothing can force us into it; we're already there. There's nothing to be done but to get ourselves out of it, first through the intellect, that can de-

stroy them, and then by removing ourselves from the very sphere of the intellect, the principal generator of all these illusions, of all this make-believe (which flourishes only in the sphere of the intellect). In the final analysis, the intellect is destined for all eternity to be the serpent that bites its own tail and the intellectual, a fakir who exhibits that serpent to the man in the street.

6.   History shows that outside action on the part of the man who is enflamed with exalting ideas is most often destructive and dangerous for others. Thus it is essential to understand that these objectives and challenges are located not in the external world where we must combat adversaries in order to bring about "the triumph of the idea," but in the subjective space of the individual. They are only concepts forged by the mind. And that is just one step away from the realization that the distinction between "external reality" and "internal reality" is only verbal.

Salman Rushdie

1.   In countries that are not free, the existence and value of intellectuals is proved by their persecution. I accept that definition of the term on which all persecutors — Pol Pot, Stalin and the terrorists of Algeria, for example — would agree. An intellectual is a member of that class formed by education and defined by its ability — indeed, its need — to think and inquire for itself, if necessary outside the confines of received or imposed wisdom. Journalists, doctors, lawyers, scientists, philosophers, teachers, writers are all covered by this definition. Sometimes, in our century, the definition has been expanded to include anyone wearing spectacles, or reading a magazine. Some-

times it has included anyone with fillings in his teeth. When tyranny is born, people like these often die. And, yes, I see myself as a member of this class.

2.   In the modern age, I have been most moved by the courage of the Soviet dissidents, and the modernists seeking to reform the antiquated house of Islam.

3.   "To speak truth to power!" It's as important as ever. Even in Britain, even after the election of a Government in whose arrival, like most Britons, I rejoiced, it is already clear that without such rigorous and public truth-telling, the unchecked power of a Government with a large majority can be very alarming.

4.   Yes, many mistakes. Many Western intellectuals supported Communism, some supported Fascism. That is well known. The biggest mistake being made by intellectuals today is the idea of cultural relativism. It is blindness, indeed, to concede that universal values are merely culture-specific. People in all cultures fight for these values. Western intellectuals should not betray them.

5.   In Britain, the term "intellectual" is widely derided. It is used by public commentators to invalidate a person's ideas as elitist and self-important. I simply point out that in the Pol Pot definition (see above), all these public commentators would be classified as intellectuals, too, and would be dealt with accordingly.

6.   The most dangerous human prejudice is our fear of the Other, which expresses itself in many ways, including racism, religious bigotry, the practice of female circumcision, homophobia, etc.. The greatest intellectual joy is that the world is, as ever, inexhaustible, and filled with wonders.

Fernando Savater

1.   In my opinion, everyone who addresses others publicly as if they were intellectuals are intellectuals. That is, they do not try to intimidate them, to hypnotize them or to harangue them, but to foster rational comprehension and a critical spirit. In this sense, I try to be as "intellectual" as possible.

2.   Most of my fundamental heroes are intellectuals: Erasmus, Voltaire, Larra and, in our century, Bertrand Russell. But I admire them without adoring them, as Montaigne taught us.

3.   At a time like ours (and perhaps like all the others?), which is prone to scandal and to fanaticism, the still useful function of the intellectual is to wake up the intellectuality of those who read or listen to him. This is a necessary and fundamentally educational task. It is a question of informing people, and of not forcing anybody.

4.   The greatest danger to the intellectual is the desire to become a prophet or a necromancer: to always put forth the noisiest opinion in order to avoid being mistaken for a tepid or excessively "reasonable" (that is, tedious) person. But the errors made by intellectuals, their relative blindness, can also be useful for us. They teach us never to accept absolute Masters, to dissent even with those whom we admire most. Errors, even tragic errors, are a risk that cannot disqualify those who dare to have an opinion.

5.   The great obstacles are always vanity and pedantry: given the great din in the media, one may be tempted to take advantage of it by

making more noise than everyone else, and preferring to dazzle rather than to enlighten. One must always strive to remain above — morally speaking — the world in which one lives.

6.   We are going into a new century in which the number of living people may outstrip the total of all who have died in the entire history of humanity. It is not possible to address human problems at the level of the tribe when all the urgent solutions apparently require planetary measures. In my view, the intellectual should try to promote the practical reason that we share, and which makes us intractable enigmas for the others.

Translated from Spanish by Albert Bensoussan

Peter Schneider

1.   The term intellectual is rarely used in English, because it's supposed to be an overstatement: "I am more intelligent than you are." In European discourse, it has a certain function as an antidote to politics. In that sense, I am an intellectual.

2.   Quite a number. Lately Karl Popper. In earlier days, the classics: Socrates and Montaigne. When I was politically active in the 1960's, I was, of course influenced by Herbert Marcuse and the young Karl Marx.

3.   The mission of the intellectuals is not completed — and it will never be completed. The most important thing is to think without the protection of a party, an ideology or a camp. Belonging is not for free

thought. Every intellectual is, of course, a free citizen and has the right to belong somewhere. But as soon as he starts to write, he has to dis-integrate himself from the others,

In the German context, it's important for the intellectual to confess (not in the sense of the church). But you have to be honest about your position in the society. Today, we have no serious intellectual debate here, because after the unification of Germany the intellectuals started to defend themselves against history. I think it's completely wrong when thinking is limited to self-defense.

4.   Intellectuals are an endangered species. In the age of media, they are fading away. But they also belong to the most dangerous species. The biggest crimes have been linked to their ideas. I cannot understand why they were fascinated by the most vulgar and stupid fascism. By Hitler's fascism. They have enormous responsibility in the crimes of the 20th century. They must be wary of being abused. Of course they cannot control how politicians abuse their concepts, but they must speak up. (Nietzsche, of course, could not speak out against Hitler, but he was terribly abused.

5.   The major obstacle is intellectuals themselves, their inability to come to terms with their mistakes. Bernard-Henri Lévy is of one them; he has great talent with the media. The ability to work with the visual media gives a lot of power. But the visual media are not the realms of the intellectuals. We must live with this fact, and not be intimidated by the diminishing of our power and influence. We should never lower the concept of the philosophy of being an intellectual. But I am not very pessimistic, as I believe in non-linear development. The influence of the visual media will be reduced some day.

6.   The most fatal mistake of intellectuals is the belief in the idea that human beings are good, that it is bad conditions that cause cruelty and wars. We cannot talk, after 2000 years, about the goodness

of human nature. We should never seduce ourselves into believing that basic evil can be overcome. Evil is part of human nature. We are good and bad. It is only civilization that can balance the dark tenden-cies inside us, which is very unlikely to happen. We have to have a daily fight with ourselves, and civilization is a victory over the bad parts in us.

Philippe Sollers

1. Allow me to laugh a little at your question. What do you think the name "Sollers" means to intellectuals today, whatever their incli-nation? An abomination. Their response to me is supercilious, clerical, Pavlovian. In the long run, I will show what it means.

2. The history of my personal influence on the "great intellectuals" of my era remains to be written. I knew them all (and if you doubt it, read my books, particularly the one that is most intolerable for the clergy in question: *Femmes*).

3. The role of the intellectual these days is orchestrated, choreo-graphed, predictable. They are there especially not to speak about real matters (which far exceed their information and their compe-tence, in any case).

4. The pseudo-trial that is, from time to time, brought against in-tellectuals is just a wheel in a spectacular mechanical device. It re-freshes the illusion when that is convenient for the show that is being put on.

5.   What obstacles? Public demand (from the right as well as the left) has never been so strong. Watchdogs and denouncers of watch-dogs, here, always have full employment.

6.   Sorry, but no *task* is urgent, no prejudice is *threatening*, there is no cause to be *defended*, and no danger to be *averted*. Thought is never in jeopardy, and that is why, as time invariably shows, it is the only real action. "Thought is as clear as a crystal. A religion, whose lies depend upon it, can disturb it for a few minutes, if we wish to speak about effects that last a long time. When it comes to effects that last only briefly, the assassination of eight people at the gates of a capital, that will disturb it — certainly — until the end of all evil. And thought soon regains its limpidity."

Susan Sontag

What the word "intellectual" means to me today is, first of all, conferences and roundtable discussions, and symposia in magazines about the role of intellectuals, in which well-known intellectuals have agreed to pronounce on the inadequacy, credulity, disgrace, trea-son, irrelevance, obsolescence, and imminent or already perfected dis-appearance of the caste to which, as their participation in these events testifies, they belong.

Whether I see myself as one (I try to do as little seeing of myself as possible) is beside the point. I answer, if so called.

Being a citizen of a country whose political and ethical culture promotes and reinforces distrust, fear, and contempt for intellectuals (re-read Tocqueville), the country that has developed the most anti-intellectual tradition on the planet, I incline to a less-jaded view of the role of intellectuals than my colleagues in Europe. No, their "mission" (as your question has it) is not completed.

Of course, it's speaking far too well of intellectuals to expect the majority to have a taste for protesting against injustice, defending victims, challenging the reigning authoritarian pieties. Most intellectuals are as conformist — as willing, say, to support the prosecution of unjust wars — as most other people exercising educated professions. The number of people who have given intellectuals a good name, as troublemakers, voices of conscience, has always been small. Intellectuals responsibly taking sides, and putting themselves on the line for what they believe in (as opposed to signing petitions) is a good deal less common than intellectuals taking public positions either in conscious bad faith or in shameless ignorance of what they are pronouncing on: for every Gide or Orwell or Veil or Chomsky or Sakharov, we have ten of Romain Rolland or Ilya Ehrenburg or Jean Baudrillard or Peter Handke, etc. etc.

But could it be otherwise?

Although intellectuals come in all flavors, including the nationalist and the religious, I confess to being partial to the secular, cosmopolitan, anti-tribal variety. The "deracinated intellectual" seems to me an exemplary formula.

By "intellectual," I mean the "free" intellectual, someone who, beyond his or her professional or technical or artistic expertise, is committed to exercising (and thereby, implicitly, defending) the life of the mind as such.

A specialist may also be an intellectual. But an intellectual is never just a specialist. One is an intellectual because one has (or should have) certain standards of probity and responsibility in discourse. That is the one indispensable contribution of intellectuals: the notion of discourse that is not merely instrumental, i.e. conformist.

How many times has one heard, in the last decades, that intellectuals are obsolete, or that so-and-so is "the last intellectual"?

There are two tasks for intellectuals, today as yesterday. One task, educational, is to promote dialogue, support the right to be heard of a multiplicity of voices, promote skepticism about received opinion. This means standing up those whose idea of education and culture is the imprinting of ideas ("ideals") such as the love of the nation or tribe.

The other task is adversarial. There has been a vertiginous shift of moral attitudes in the last two decades in advanced capitalist countries. Its hallmark is the discrediting of all idealisms, of altruism itself; of high standards of all kinds, cultural as well as moral. Thatcherism is now the triumphant ideology everywhere on the planet, and the mass media, whose function is to promote consumption, disseminate the narratives and ideas of value and disvalue by which people everywhere understand themselves. Intellectuals have the Sisyphean task of continuing to embody (and defend) another standard of mental life, and of discourse, than the nihilistic one promoted by the mass media. By nihilism, I mean not only the relativism, the privatization of interest, which is ascendant among the educated classes everywhere, but also the more recent and more pernicious nihilism embodied in the ideology of so-called "cultural democracy"; the hatred of excellence and achievement as "elitist," exclusionary.

The moral duty of the intellectual will always be complex, because there is more than one "highest" value, and there are concrete circumstances in which not all that is unconditionally good can be honored — in which, indeed, two of these values may prove incompatible.

For instance, understanding the truth does not always facilitate the struggle for justice. And in order to bring about *justice*, it may seem right to suppress the truth.

One hopes not to have to choose. But when a choice (between truth and justice) is necessary — as, alas, it sometimes is — then it seems to me that an intellectual ought to decide for the truth.

This is not, by and large, what intellectuals, the best-intentioned intellectuals, have done. Invariably, when intellectuals subscribe to causes, it is the truth, in all its complexity, that gets short shrift.

A good rule before one goes marching or signing anything: Whatever your tug of sympathy, you have no right to a public opinion unless you've been there, experienced at first hand and on the ground and for some considerable time the country, the war, the injustice, etc. you are talking about.

In the absence of such first-hand knowledge and experience: silence.

On the subject of the presumption (it's worse than naivety) with which so many intellectuals subscribe to collective action when they know virtually nothing about what they are so pleased to have opinions on, nobody said it better than one of most compromised in-tellectuals of the 20th century, Bertolt Brecht (who surely knew whereof he spoke):

> When it comes to marching, many do not know
> That their enemy is marching at their head.
> The voice which gives them their orders
> Is the enemy's voice and
> The man who speaks of the enemy
> Is the enemy himself.

Henrick Stangerup

"Conservative," "liberal" or "socialist": either you are a Dreyfusard, or you are not.

I can only answer your question this way — thinking upon all those "intellectuals" who betrayed humanity all the way through the 20th century — nearly ever since Zola, in his generosity, considered it to be a true honor to be — an intellectual.

Mario Vargas Llosa

I am deeply sorry, but I won't be able to answer the questionnaire. I started to do it, and I discovered that each question requires a long and serious development of reasoning, if you don't want to fall in the stereotypes of banality.

In fact, the questions raise very serious issues about the relationship between literature and ethics, politics and the functioning of society, problems that have been following literature since the beginning of our civilization, without anyone having been able to reach definite and convincing answers.

I very much hope that my colleagues will be more apt than myself to participate in the inquiry, with more concise and specific ideas about these problems than myself.

William Styron

1. That's a difficult question. The term intellectual has a very different connotation in the USA and in other advanced countries. The USA has a strong tradition of anti-intellectualism. In America, people who would ordinarily consider themselves intellectuals tend to be defensive about the term. "Intellectual," in America, is not a badge of honor. Still, I suppose I consider myself an intellectual, meaning that I'm engaged in the literary pursuit, which in a way makes me different from the rest of the nation.

I just want to make myself clear: there has always been an extensive embarrassment in this country around the question of employment. Few people in Europe would feel that way. It has to do with the history of this nation. The masses who came to the USA were simple people. Intellectuals were considered to live in *irony towers*, and not to be part of building the country. They were not the makers and the shakers.

Plainly, this nation couldn't have become what it is without intellectuals. But the role of the intellectual has never been at the front and the center of this nation.

2. The most profound is Albert Camus. He still exercises great influence on me as an intellectual force. His writing happened to coincide with my life's aspiration. He has been broadening my horizon and has had enormous influence.

3. If anything, their task is more important today than every. There is a strong anti-intellectual force in this country: the popular culture in which we all interpenetrate. Therefore, there is a need for the intellectual, as never before, to make his voice felt in the world. Otherwise,

we absolutely would be drowned in this counter-culture.

4.   I don't take that criticism very seriously. Any group tends to make mistakes. Why focus on the intellectuals? Who doesn't make mistakes? Politicians? I am not free of mistakes. That's part of the human condition. We would not be intellectuals if we were faultless.

5.   I more or less answered this question above. The forces of mass-culture are the largest obstacle to work as an intellectual. We are all involved in mass-culture as the fabric of life — except if you are a hermit. Mass-culture is part of our bloodstream. Intellectuals must remove themselves from mass-culture and stand out individually. In Europe and the USA, we still live in democratic societies. Therefore, we not only can but also must oppose mass-culture's vulgarization. Also, we must oppose the destructive rise of fanaticism and religious bigotry.

6.   The biggest joy to me is the ability to express myself in a free way. I can without opposition write my work and reverberate it to other people.

A. B. Yehoshua

1.   No, I don't reject the term "intellectual." For me, it's a person who is capable of integrating ideas of life that generally are not combined together, like religion and culture, politics and literature. The more areas a person can combine, the more intellectual the person is. The Nobel Prize winner in physics can invent something very important for humanity, but he cannot be an intellectual if he doesn't

know how to integrate knowledge and life. I would define myself a person who tries to be an intellectual. As a writer, I have to combine differences.

2. I can cite Nietzsche as one example. Socrates is another, and probably the most famous intellectual of all. In the 20th century we had Sartre, a lousy writer, but a high-level intellectual, who integrated culture and politics. He pushed freedom to its extreme dimension for making true integration. Another person who meant very much to me is Yehosliua Leibowitz, a biologist and great thinker. He could speak about biology and Judaism, religion and politics. He is an example of a man who can speak courageously and address political questions with originality.

3. Their mission is greater today than before. Democracy tends to make everything pluralistic and relative. These are the two key-words of our age. The intellectual must speak on behalf of the absolute, the truth that stands and lasts. Today, everybody speaks about his specialization, but what we need is the philosopher who can integrate.

4. Many intellectuals have made lots of mistakes. Some said wrong things. But you can't think of the intellectuals as a group. I would say that 70 percent of intellectuals have always reacted correctly on the big questions of their time. In Israel, I see the majority of intellectuals as clear-sighted and courageous people. In a democracy we must have courageous people.

5. The biggest obstacle is that people are more and more dependent on the specialist. We have seen how specialists have been wrong in Vietnam and the Soviet Union. I would rather depend on the intuition of the intellectuals than the knowledge of the specialists.

6. The most important issue is the gap between the first and the

third world. This is increasing in the coming century and is a great threat, a much bigger threat than the consumer society or immigration. What can we do? We have to push these worlds closer to each other.

◆

so from **Algora Publishing**:

CLAUDIU A. SECARA
THE NEW COMMONWEALTH
From Bureaucratic Corporatism to Socialist Capitalism

The notion of an elite-driven worldwide perestroika has gained some credibility lately. The book examines in a historical perspective the most intriguing dialectic in the Soviet Union's "collapse" — from socialism to capitalism and back to socialist capitalism — and speculates on the global implications.

IGNACIO RAMONET
THE GEOPOLITICS OF CHAOS

The author, Director of *Le Monde Diplomatique*, presents an original, discriminating and lucid political matrix for understanding what he calls the "current disorder of the world" in terms of Internationalization, Cyberculture and Political Chaos.

TZVETAN TODOROV
A PASSION FOR DEMOCRACY –
Benjamin Constant

The French Revolution rang the death knell not only for a form of society, but also for a way of feeling and of living; and it is still not clear as yet what did we gain from the changes.

MICHEL PINÇON & MONIQUE PINÇON-CHARLOT
GRAND FORTUNES –
Dynasties of Wealth in France

Going back for generations, the fortunes of great families consist of far more than money— they are also symbols of culture and social interaction. In a nation known for democracy and meritocracy, piercing the secrets of the grand fortunes verges on a crime of lèse-majesté . . . *Grand Fortunes* succeeds at that.

CLAUDIU A. SECARA
TIME & EGO –
Judeo-Christian Egotheism and the Anglo-Saxon Industrial Revolution

The first question of abstract reflection that arouses controversy is the problem of Becoming. Being persists, beings constantly change; they are born and they pass away. How can Being change and yet be eternal? The quest for the logical and experimental answer has just taken off.

JEAN-MARIE ABGRALL
SOUL SNATCHERS: THE MECHANICS OF CULTS

Jean-Marie Abgrall, psychiatrist, criminologist, expert witness to the French Court of Appeals, and member of the Inter-Ministry Committee on Cults, is one of the experts most frequently consulted by the European judicial and legislative processes. The fruit of fifteen years of research, his book delivers the first methodical analysis of the sectarian phenomenon, decoding the mental manipulation on behalf of mystified observers as well as victims.

JEAN-CLAUDE GUILLEBAUD
THE TYRANNY OF PLEASURE

Guillebaud, a Sixties' radical, re-thinks liberation, taking a hard look at the question of sexual morals -- that is, the place of the forbidden -- in a modern society. For almost a whole generation, we have lived in the illusion that this question had ceased to exist. Today the illusion is faded, but a strange and tumultuous distress replaces it. No longer knowing very clearly where we stand, our societies painfully seek answers between unacceptable alternatives: bold-faced permissiveness or nostalgic moralism.

SOPHIE COIGNARD AND MARIE-THÉRÈSE GUICHARD
FRENCH CONNECTIONS –
The Secret History of Networks of Influence

They were born in the same region, went to the same schools, fought the same fights and made the same mistakes in youth. They share the same morals, the same fantasies of success and the same taste for money. They act behind the scenes to help each other, boosting careers, monopolizing business and information, making money, conspiring and, why not, becoming Presidents!

VLADIMIR PLOUGIN
RUSSIAN INTELLIGENCE SERVICES. Vol. I. Early Years

Mysterious episodes from Russia's past – alliances and betrayals, espionage and military feats – are unearthed and examined in this study, which is drawn from ancient chronicles and preserved documents from Russia, Greece, Byzantium and the Vatican Library. Scholarly analysis and narrative flair combine to give both the facts and the flavor of the battle scenes and the espionage milieu, including the establishment of secret services in Kievan rus, the heroes and the techniques of intelligence and counter-intelligence in the 10th-12th centuries, and the times of Vladimir.

JEAN-JACQUES ROSA
EURO ERROR

The European Superstate makes Jean-Jacques Rosa mad, for two reasons. First, actions taken to relieve unemployment have created inflation, but have not reduced unemployment. His second argument is even more intriguing: the 21st century will see the fragmentation of the U. S., not the unification of Europe.

ANDRÉ GAURON
EUROPEAN MISUNDERSTANDING

Few of the books decrying the European Monetary Union raise the level of the discussion to a higher plane. *European Misunderstanding* is one of these. Gauron gets it right, observing that the real problem facing Europe is its political future, not its economic future.

DOMINIQUE FERNANDEZ
PHOTOGRAPHER: FERRANTE FERRANTI
ROMANIAN RHAPSODY — An Overlooked Corner of Europe

"Romania doesn't get very good press." And so, renowned French travel writer Dominique Fernandez and top photographer Ferrante Ferranti head out to form their own images. In four long journeys over a 6-year span, they uncover a tantalizing blend of German efficiency and Latin nonchalance, French literature and Gypsy music, Western rationalism and Oriental mysteries. Fernandez reveals the rich Romanian essence. Attentive and precise, he digs beneath the somber heritage of communism to reach the deep roots of a European country that is so little-known.

PHILIPPE TRÉTIACK
ARE YOU AGITÉ? Treatise on Everyday Agitation

"A book filled with the exuberance of a new millennium, full of humor and relevance. Philippe Trétiack, a leading reporter for *Elle*, goes around the world and back, taking an interest in the futile as well as the essential. His flair for words, his undeniable culture, help us to catch on the fly what we really are: characters subject to the ballistic impulse of desires, fads and a click of the remote. His book invites us to take a healthy break from the breathless agitation in general." — *Aujourd'hui le Parisien*

"The 'Agité,' that human species that lives in international airports, jumps into taxis while dialing the cell phone, eats while clearing the table, reads the paper while watching TV and works during vacation – has just been given a new title." — *Le Monde des Livres*

PAUL LOMBARD
VICE & VIRTUE — Men of History, Great Crooks for the Greater Good

Personal passion has often guided powerful people more than the public interest. With what result? From the courtiers of Versailles to the back halls of Mitterand's government, from Danton — revealed to have been a paid agent for England — to the shady bankers of Mitterand's era, from the buddies of Mazarin to the builders of the Panama Canal, Paul Lombard unearths the secrets of the corridors of power. He reveals the vanity and the corruption, but also the grandeur and panache that characterize the great. This cavalcade over many centuries can be read as a subversive tract on how to lead.

RICHARD LABÉVIÈRE
DOLLARS FOR TERROR — The U.S. and Islam

"In this riveting, often shocking analysis, the U.S. is an accessory in the rise of Islam, because it manipulates and aids radical Moslem groups in its shortsighted pursuit of its economic interests, especially the energy resources of the Middle East and the oil- and mineral-rich former Soviet republics of Central Asia. Labévière shows how radical Islamic fundamentalism spreads its influence on two levels, above board, through investment firms, banks and shell companies, and clandestinely, though a network of drug dealing, weapons smuggling and money laundering. This important book sounds a wake-up call to U.S. policy-makers." — *Publishers Weekly*

JEANNINE VERDÈS-LEROUX
DECONSTRUCTING PIERRE BOURDIEU
Against Sociological Terrorism From the Left

Sociologist Pierre Bourdieu went from widely-criticized to widely-acclaimed, without adjusting his hastily constructed theories. Turning the guns of critical analysis on his own critics, he was happier jousting in the ring of (often quite undemocratic) political debate than reflecting and expanding upon his own propositions. Verdès-Leroux has spent 20 years researching the policy impact of intellectuals who play at the fringes of politics. She suggests that Bourdieu arrogated for himself the role of "total intellectual" and proved that a good offense is the best defense. A pessimistic Leninist bolstered by a ponderous scientific construct, Bourdieu stands out as the ultimate doctrinaire more concerned with self-promotion than with democratic intellectual engagements.

HENRI TROYAT
TERRIBLE TZARINAS

Who should succeed Peter the Great? Upon the death of this visionary and despotic reformer, the great families plotted to come up with a successor who would surpass everyone else — or at least, offend none. But there were only women — Catherine I, Anna Ivanovna, Anna Leopoldovna, Elizabeth I. These autocrats imposed their violent and dissolute natures upon the empire, along with their loves, their feuds, their cruelties. Born in 1911 in Moscow, Troyat is a member of the Académie française, recipient of Prix Goncourt.

JEAN-MARIE ABGRALL
HEALERS OR STEALERS — *Medical Charlatans in the New Age*

Jean-Marie Abgrall is Europe's foremost expert on cults and forensic medicine. He asks, are fear of illness and death the only reasons why people trust their fates to the wizards of the pseudo-revolutionary and the practitioners of pseudo-magic? We live in a bazaar of the bizarre, where everyday denial of rationality has turned many patients into ecstatic fools. While not all systems of nontraditional medicine are linked to cults, this is one of the surest avenues of recruitment, and the crisis of the modern world may be leading to a new mystique of medicine where patients check their powers of judgment at the door.

DR. DEBORAH SCHURMAN-KAUFLIN
THE NEW PREDATOR: WOMEN WHO ☐ ILL — *Profiles of Female Serial ☐ illers*
This is the *first book ever* based on face-to-face interviews with women serial killers.

VLADIMIR PLOUGIN
RUSSIAN INTELLIGENCE SERVICES — *I. The Early Years*

The most mysterious episodes from Russia's past are unearthed and examined in this study, which is drawn from ancient chronicles and preserved documents from Russia, Greece, Byzantium and the Vatican library. Scholarly analysis and narrative flair combine to give both the facts and the flavor of the battle scenes as well as of the espionage milieu: the establishment of the secret services in Kievan Rus, and the heroes and systems of intelligence and counter-intelligence in the 10th-11th centuries.